1

Outsider Notes:

Feminist Approaches to

Nation State Ideology,

Writers/Readers

and Publishing

Talonbooks · Vancouver · 1996

Acknowledgements

The work undertaken in this book occurred in the stimulating and supportive environment of the teaching and research on new writings in the English language, taking place at the University of Leeds, under the careful guidance of Shirley Chew. The arguments have continually interacted with the criticism of Margaret Beetham, Bryan Cheyette, Frank Davey, Peter Lichtenfels, and Hilary Rose, all of whom read parts of the script and offered new perspectives. The research would not have been possible without the support of the Canadian High Commission Academic Relations Office in London, the on-going discussions with members of the British Association of Canadian Studies' Literature Group, and the financial aid provided by the Canadian Studies Centre at the University of Leeds for preparing the typescript for publication. I would particularly like to thank Elizabeth Paget for tireless help with the preparation of the manuscript. To these and the virtual and actual communities of Canadians who have offered extraordinary intellectual generosity, and to *many* others, I am grateful.

TALONBOOKS
104 — 3100 Production Way
Burnaby, British Columbia V5A 4R4
Canada

Published with the assistance of the Canadian Studies Centre,
University of Leeds, and the Canada Council

Printed and bound in Canada by Hignell Printing Limited

CANADIAN CATALOGUING IN PUBLICATION DATA
Hunter, Lynette
Outsider Notes
(The New Canadian criticism series)
Includes bibliographical references and index.
ISBN 0-88922-363-7
1. Canadian Literature — 20th century — History and criticism. 2.
Feminism and literature — Canada. 3. Publishers and Publishing —
Canada. 4. Feminist literary criticism — Canada
I. Title. II. Series.
PS8071.4 H86 1996   C810.9'0054   C95-911218-9
PR9189.6H86 1996

Contents

Introduction

This collection of essays is written in an attempt to try out common grounds for reading across cultural, social and historical boundaries. It is structured throughout by approaches to knowledge informed by feminist practice, and a consciousness of women's lives and their relation to political activities in western nation states: specifically England where, although I am a Canadian, I live and work.

The essays are parted into three groups. The first consists of two commentaries on recent publishing history in Canada. In common with many other western capitalist states, Canadian nationalism is mediated largely by ideology and impinges directly on culture and education: for writing or reading, directly onto the ways that publication works through access to print, distribution, critical appraisal and response, patronage and grants, canonical acceptance and public recognition. On this common ground Canada plays out many different specific developments. Since the 1950s there have been extensive programs of federal, provincial and municipal financial subsidy for writing and publishing. In the face of much more powerful nation states such as the United States or England, it has been necessary to build a national ethos, to support a publically approved culture. Within this period of emphasis on Canadian Studies as the educational base for national ethos, the support that has been given to Canadian publishers and writers has enabled a number of texts to enter the English-language canon which has conventionally been fixed on British writers.

If the first essay engages with the formation of this canonical literature and the debates around it, the second addresses writing that has been marginal to some aspect of production or consumption of the publishing industry, because it has had dificulty gaining access to this aspect. While a variety of established methods of print publication for alternative voices have been used, a lot of writing from outside conventional and established canons has been able to find new means of print publication because of the availability of public financial support. And the effect of such public support has been not only to make publication of the literature possible but also to stamp the writing with a certain status, constructing for it a complicated set of relationships with the prevailing cultural canon.

Nation state ideology has been largely disseminated via print and publishing. The two are inextricably intertwined, and all printed writing is inexorably drawn into the complex relations that are in place to control the mediation. Yet printed writing, in popular literature, poetics, and the educational canon, has also always provided one site for response and even challenge to the apparent stability of ideology.

Within nation state ideologies of northern Europe, including Britain, and of many countries of the Americas, modernism has been a primary literary strategy for responding to ideology. The remarkably flexible and supportive structures for publication in Canada have opened out the modulations of this strategy to a wide range of writers and readers. Modernism and its extensions into postmodernism, which are broadly concerned with techniques and devices for foregrounding ideological artifice, take different forms. Postmodernism in particular is self-consciously nation- or region-specific. In the United States, postmodern theory has frequently emphasised the de-authorization of the 'master narratives,' the central stories that ideology puts forward as 'true.' In Europe, postmodern theory has focused on the creation of plural stories, at worst a set of parallel private worlds that mimic the rhetoric of ideology, and at best a dream of multicultural en-franchisement. But as recent postcolonial theory has increasingly indicated, pluralism simply perpetuates the club culture of the powerful: in effect the disempowered cannot create parallel private worlds of the same power. The multicultural dream simply commodifies cultures, cuts them to the cloth of the dominant ideology. Postcolonial theory suggests that we need instead cross-cultural strategies for constructing communities that are neither commodifying nor exclusive.

Yet none of these strategies are self-evident. The second section of the collection offers a set of readings on a number of non-canonical writings, or writings that have not straightforwardly gained canonical support or a public audience. The final section offers commentaries on writings that in one way or another, are increasingly accepted as canonical. Both of these groups of essays study how Canadian writings address prevailing ideology, especially in this period during which nation states are handing over effective power to multinational corporations and the net of private, personal, public, and community is loosening and giving way to the rather different emphases of a global economy. The nation state constructed the idea of a 'private' individual, and most people in western nation states are brought up or trained as such. We are used to isolation, and have more in common in our historical isolation from one another and in our subjection to the state, than many groups of individuals attempting common action that in its challenge to ideological stability impacts differently and less predictably on each personal life.

Current conventions about writing and reading are bound up into notions of private authorship and private reading, meeting in a kind of virtual public space categorized as the 'canon.' One effect has been to make it rather difficult for group-focused writings to enter this common literary ground for communities of readers. Many of the readings that follow are attending to writing from private individuals encouraged by conventional publishing procedures, including the royalty system. But the pattern of extensive government support for writers and publishers, has loosened some writing from the pressures of private production. Certainly, government subsidies have encouraged not only private individuals but also individuals who write from groups, groups writing collectively, and people writing to search for or to build communities.

The issues that are addressed in these readings range from authenticity, autobiography, popular culture and genre-writing, to the helpfulness of theory, the difficulty with language-focused writing, the reader's embarrassment with non-canonical texts, to the social immediacies of personal memory in public history, violence, racism, sexuality and community. There is no over-arching argument to this collection. Each of the readings given here works from the similarities to the differences and specificities offered by Canadian writing, perceived by an outside reader. The readings try to develop or elaborate upon elements in contemporary western cultural and social life that interact with words, writing and reader, through published print. They attempt to provide a brief background to some of the conditions for this very recent publishing history, and to engage with strategies that to an unusual extent move on past the ideology of the nation state.

Note: On several occasions the text addresses the reader with "you." It does this infrequently, but in order to avoid the illusion of the impersonal and the naturalized. Although it is mildly shocking, and often irritating, to be included within the sentence, the inclusion reinforces the need to position ourselves with respect to it.

Lynette Hunter
University of Leeds

Part One

CHAPTER ONE

Writing, Literature, and Ideology:

Institutions and the Making of Canadian Canons

Canada is a country similar to most in western Europe, where many of
the political, legal, and social structures are supported by what are still
predominantly print-based media. For an outside reader, this common
ground can provide a point of departure for reading since Canada is
also a 'print society' in the sense that writing, which for various socio-
historical and geographical reasons is the primary mode of communication, is transmitted via print even in the scripts read out during the
television news; testable knowledge leading to qualifications for work
is acquired through print from libraries, school manuals and in exams;
legal and political guidelines are integrated from the printed works of
jurisprudence and constitutional issues, and adequate day-to-day existence functions by printed means in shops, hospitals, insurance forms
and breakfast cereal packets. Print is not the only medium for communication or the most obviously persuasive and engaging medium of
culture, but its ubiquity renders it the necessary means for participating
fully in the society and raises the question of how the people who have
difficulty getting access to print can participate in their society.

Print society, as it appears to work in Canada, is part of a much
wider formation of political, economic, technological and cultural
pressures that gather around the post-Renaissance characterizations of
the nation state. In this, Canada which is of course one of the wealthy
G7 nations with a thoroughly capitalist economy, shares with many
European countries a common history of nation state politics and
capitalism, which are supported by the availability of print and its
distribution systems. One of the perceived common grounds for cross-
cultural readings between Europe, and in the case of the discussion
that follows, between Britain and Canada, is nation state political
practice and theory, particularly the conditions for the construction of
a stable and convincing nation state ethos by way of ideology. Yet the
print society of English-language Canada and its literary culture have

since the 1950s received an extraordinary amount of government
attention and aid that have produced conditions significantly different
to those in Britain. From the common ground for reading, this writing
will be trying to find a way of reading some of those differences.

This opening discussion is interested in a perceived splitting of
Canadian literary culture into formal or thematic and structural or
modal canons. The split is realized slightly differently both in the texts
chosen for teaching Canadian literature in Britain and in the texts on
the syllabuses of courses on Canadian literature offered by Canadian
universities. What follows here is an attempt to look at this split by
way of a contextualizing of it within print society as it works in
relation to the nation state—a nation state that is itself increasingly
turning into a cultural artefact in the face of multinational economic
organizations. These issues are part of an on-going discussion within
Canada,[1] and I offer this voice to that discussion in the spirit of engaging
in cross-cultural debate: in translation we may find helpful working
practices.

To begin then from a brief perspective of political and rhetorical
theory on ideology as it is constrained by recent trends in publishing:
Capitalism needs a broad power base and competitiveness between
players who have the possibility of achieving some equity or have
similar opportunities. Its ethical position is to allow for diverse voices
within a political system that can deal with, and diffuse, the potential
conflict between those competitive voices within the system. In a
sense capitalism in the early modern period is an extension of the
smaller court system into national politics: an attempt to deal with the
broader franchise of bourgeois empowerment, the commonwealth. It
benefits from nationalism not only because nationalism provides a
rationale for such a system, but specifically because the nation state
provides devices for protecting (opening up) certain markets, and
because the nation state provides structures to stabilize successfully
not only potential conflict among the powerful but also to stabilize
popular demand.

Nationalism and capitalism combined in this way have a number of
problems with rhetorical ethos and questions of legitimation.[2] The
traditional media for authoritative national statements in say the
Roman Empire, or in medieval city states, provide a rhetorical ethos
directly responsive to its audience.[3] But because nation state politics is
largely representative, the ethos cannot communicate directly with

an individual either in an oration or in writing, and the ethos becomes necessarily corporate. It counts on prior agreement for decision and action, and the various representative parliamentary systems in Europe and North America are there precisely to exercise corporate agreement. Given its needs, there has to be a way of stabilizing the reception of the group in power, and stabilizing the description or definition of the individual within the nation. These rhetorical implications for increasingly corporate nation state legitimation accurately replicate the needs of capitalism.

From the seventeenth century in Europe, we can note the urgency of the search for stable systems of representation. These have been most often discussed over the past 30 to 40 years in terms of the history of philosophy and of science, but they are found throughout the humanities, technology and medicine. What these recent histories indicate is that political and then increasingly the institutional structures of nations in Western Europe and North America move toward state systems because they promise a means of delivering stability. State systems construct a corporate ethos that is currently discussed under the word 'ideology.' And that ideology has quite specific rhetorical strategies: its stability of representation depends upon the public's willingness to forget that it is a representation.

Much of the theoretical background to the commentaries that follow takes documentation from cultural and social historians such as Foucault or McLuhan, writing on for example surveillance/punishment systems as a recognition of structures demanding stability and emphasizing norms. This is also part of the capitalist need for stable demand in order to make technology of long term use and hence profitable, and is notably clear in the growth of technology and industry in the nineteenth century. The way that markets represent an economic commodification of desire is obviously at the heart of Marx's critique of his own time.

At the same time the theoretical background also draws upon documentation from the psychoanalytical theory of the subject within the nation, either the country still subject to another nation state or the new nation itself, articulated both by Fanon from Freud into colonial critique, and by varieties of feminism often via Lacan into critiques of patriarchy. Both the post/neocolonial and the feminist are articulating problems arising from the nation state's need for a fixed, stable subject: the private individual defined as isolated, not immediately responsive, and without community.

These voices all comment upon the formal rhetoric of state institutional public discourse, which this discussion takes to define ideology. Ideology solves the legitimacy problem of the government of large spaces and diversified voices, simply by denying/ evading/ hiding/ ignoring the awareness of responsive ethos that can keep the potentially totalitarian dangers of corporate ethos in check. Ideology uses the medium of state institutions to imply that there is a norm, a convention, a natural state. There is no need to question or interact because the norm is the case. This is the equivalent to the denial of a need for rhetoric, and the loss of formal rhetoric in Western Europe from the seventeenth century is part of the stabilizing effect of ideology, and many political theories, not the least Marxism, can be read as an attempt to remedy the loss.

The rhetoric of the nation state structures its ethos simultaneously to build a norm as an artificial construction, and then to forget that it is artificial. Technically it works from accepted common grounds (corporate agreement), and uses a representative medium in such a way as to repeat without variation, or with as little as possible, which becomes increasingly realizable as technologies are developed to aid invariable and exact repetition. The result when successful is a commodification of desire and a retarding of responsive change.

Over the last century, probably because of enfranchisement, much commentary has been directed precisely at trying to articulate the strategy of this ethos and to deal with the fall-out. Engels and Marx writing on 'false-consciousness' articulate the nervous instruction of remembering to forget, that each private individual must carry out to be a subject true to the nation. Freud codifies the remembering to forget into narcissism (total amnesia), neurosis (ambivalence of memory), and psychosis (the externalization of the forgotten). Wittgenstein, after a slim volume that speaks graphically to the impossibility of stable representation, devotes his writing to discussing the ways in which we can begin to push language into articulating what is not 'the case.' Or there is Derrida on the difficulties of reminding ourselves to remember what we are trained to forget: aphasia, aporia, allegoria.

Many of these discussions are not all that different from those found in classical moral philosophy, politics, poetics and rhetoric. However, whereas the classical world is addressing a small privileged group in a slave state, these more recent commentators have been addressing the problems that arise when the rhetoric is widely applied to an enfranchised population, and more specifically, to an increasingly technologized print society. Canadian literary culture has responded vigourously to the different conditions and offers a multitude of strategies for articulating what is not the case, for reminding ourselves to remember the forgotten.

The alliance of capital and nation, and their joint dependence on the print medium, has interesting effects on 'writing.' The loss of rhetoric in the early modern period leads to the end of humanism as an engaged and dialectical mode, and its replacement by a classical education in the 'humanities' for the children of the powerful which becomes the primary means of forming ideological continuity.[4] Despite the loss of the critical engagement offered by rhetoric, those in power whether or not they agree with each other are continually aware that printed matter is rhetorically powerful. They control print in a variety of ways over the ensuing 400 years through guilds, machinery, censorship, taxes, sales, ownership and advertizing. And because of that loss of formal critical engagement, poetics and its associated commentary become a place where the rhetoric of the printed word is discussed and elaborated.

Nation state capitalism not only incorporates writing into the institutional discourses of ideology but also establishes a need for a writing critical of and responsive to ideology. This need has directed the work of poetics in the nation state as it has consolidated itself in different places during different periods of the last three centuries, and has become part of what we indicate when we discuss 'the canon.' From an outsider's perspective, while the structure of Canadian print society has several distinctive features such as modes of distribution, multicultural and crosscultural publication and others, the years from the 1950s have seen an enormous and swift expansion of print and publishing that acutely throws into relief certain canon-forming activities more quietly at work in other print societies.

When a nation is concerned to consolidate/ incorporate/ commodify a culture as part of an ideological project, it has to financially support the production and consumption of that culture. While social historians suggest that this was relatively unselfconscious during the early modern period, certainly by the mid-nineteenth century in Britain such support was carefully orchestrated, and has become a central aspect of the twentieth century nation state and is essential to policy making in education. The extent to which the Canadian state, both federal and provincial, has supported publication and writing between 1960 and 1985/90 has been remarkable. Over that period it has consistently defined and funded specific policy areas such as women, multicultural communities, aboriginal peoples, over which it perceives a need for control. This is not entirely a cynical story for that control enables the articulation of concerns. It is essential for a liberal and democratic state; it reduces the possiblity of confrontation; and it leaves the printed product indissolubly tied to an ideological project. But at least there is a product.[5]

The resulting literary cultures are often formal poetic and rhetorical responses to ideology: the canons, virtual public spaces where private readers and private writers may meet. They are deeply implicated in ideology while critical of it, and yet as canonical, they can be 'heard' by the empowered who are often deaf to other sound. While potentially subversive, printed canons are allowed because print is still largely controlled by government since the capital investment in any relatively large scale production necessary to profit requires subsidy, either from the government or from those with money to spare who are by definition part of the capitalist system, or popular sales. Furthermore, canons become a primary device for educating the populace into the ideology of the nation state.

Canons of culture, particularly literary canons in a print society, are virtually the only legitimating devices condoned by ideology that may also remind us of what is forgotten. Canons establish the common ground necessary to national culture, and within the nation state they are under intense pressure to maintain the stability of ideology. However, as the nation state gives away power to the multinational corporation it is largely transformed into a cultural artefact itself, so its canons take on a more pertinent activity: On the one hand they may become rigidly defining and be tightly linked to the educational program of the nation. On the other hand they may begin to be seen more widely for the limited representations of culture that they are. I take it that this is an area of political difference between modernism and postmodernism: first the degree to which a populace recognizes the limitations of culture and ideology, and second the degree to which a populace constructs agreements about acceptable limitations.

*

Canons may provide both supportive and subversive legitimating structures: both are profoundly ideological and dependent upon the educational program available to the public in formal schooling, informal learning through exposure to pervasive mass media, or domestic training from household members and affiliated relationships. Within a print society formal schooling is of great importance, and the focus of this part of the discussion will be on that sort of education, which is often to do with the generic status of kind and mode, as well as to do with issue or topic.

Canons are made up of works which address issues perceived to be relevant, in a generic mode appropriate to their status, and have to be accessible to the reading practices of the public on both counts. For example Harlequin romances address relevant issues but have the wrong generic status; Cohen's *Beautiful Losers* has the correct status and addresses pertinent issues, but is inaccessible in that readers often have difficulties with it unless provided with some kind of introduction to reading strategies. The more relevant the issue the less appropriate the status need be: for example a short-story for a popular magazine may be canonized not because it is well-written within a high-status mode but because it discusses an Aboriginal community or child abuse. Just so, the more appropriate the generic status the less socially relevant the issue need be: again for example one may find canonized a carefully structured poetic on the death of a dog. But works also acquire relevance by accessibility alone, simply because they are accessible many people read them and talk about them. Accessibility indicates the degree of intimacy with prevailing ideological patterns toward both issue and structure. Indeed an issue often becomes relevant and a generic mode or structure becomes appropriate through just this intimacy with ideology, as for example with the detective story or science fiction.

The activity of educational canon-formation goes on within the context of those who make the choices. The aim is often, but not necessarily, to provide a coherent story or theme that stabilizes the ground for ideology: that seems 'true,' reflects reality. Such choices about relevance and status are made by institutions without addressing issues of other groups—indeed alternative topics from non-institutional communities are not even perceived *as* issues as for example with the widespread avoidance by literature departments of tertiary institutions of literature by recent immigrants. The choices are also made without addressing issues about which it is too difficult to speak and for which there is no consensus, as with much overt gay/lesbian writing. Issues such as these disrupt the thematic coherence of the story. Choices made in canon-formation also seem to necessitate an exclusion of writing which engages in intense formal play, not only because it is in practice more inaccessible, with readers usually having to learn how to read it by exposure and comparison or by training, but also because learning how to read it *may* focus attention on underlying structure and again provide readers with the strategies by which to diverge from coherence.

If a canon is not directed toward thematic coherence in the first place it may be more open to the inclusion of writings which focus on literary and language structures. This is not to suggest that thematically focused canons are necessarily more closed than those focused toward structure. The activity of canons hinges on the activity of their relationship with ideology: whether it is articulated, in other words an attempt at conscious construction and addressing material conditions which challenges the stability of representation, or unarticulated and supportive of that stability. An unarticulated basis for a canon may well be more effective in the short-term or immediate context. But if it is accessible *and* unarticulated it is probably riding close to standard ideology; it does not require us to question and hence has stringent limitations of which readers are supposed to remain unaware. One example here might be Margaret Atwood's *Survival* which was widely-read, discussed and quoted at the time of its publication, and clearly addressed a set of models of power relationships whose relevance was probably foregrounded by the growing cultural nationalism of the early 70s. However, it dated quickly as issues and people moved on.

The more tightly ideologically based, the more 'adequate' to current representations of reality, the easier the writing will date; once dated it is irrelevant and needs new readings to bring it back. The result is often that there comes a vested interest in maintaining accessible readings without which there might be a risk of instability or incoherence. Yet maintaining the readings simultaneously maintains, however unarticulated, some of the ideological basis. A traditional example of this in British literature would be the work of T. S. Eliot; but recent attempts to re-read Atwood's *Survival* in the light of her later quasi-critical novels as a semi-fictional commentary, is part of the same process. Thematic canons tend to focus on social behaviour and are hence far more likely to be based on the for-granted ideology of prevailing humanism: condensed into the succinct 'I'm human too and therefore I know' argument. But they do not have to be. Thematic canons can also pursue activity which is socially unacceptable, disruptive of coherence: yet here again unless they do so in order to question ideology they merely titillate. For example, the use of sexuality in much writing from the 1960s treads a fine line between pornography and social challenge, just as the topic of 'aboriginal' does in many writings from the late 1970s and the 80s. Popular culture often sits on the thin line between delivering ideological images consciously and for subversive reasons, and unselfconsciously supporting the representative stability. The problem with it is that those readers who already recognize the need for a semiotic analysis are usually the only audience who read self-consciously. Popular culture too often not only speaks to the converted but inadvertently underwrites what it sets out to critique.

However, structurally focused canons, the few of them that there are, may also be closed. Canonical works which encourage structural discussion are rare in the English-language canon. One example might be Ondaatje's *The Collected Works of Billy the Kid*, where the structural play with photograph and film is accessible to increasing numbers of highly sophisticated television and film watchers, yet the writing is fundamentally romantic. Works placed in a structurally focused canon may be attempting the coherence of a 'plurality' story, as for example in some versions of postmodernist writing.[6] Some work placed in a structurally focused canon may be attempting to evade the social altogether, for example the New Criticism in the 1950s could be read as providing strategies for texts without context in order to protect them from neo-conservatism and McCarthy. Indeed, Warren Tallman's comments on the "anti-viciousness" of West Coast Modernism,[7] can be read against the Viet Nam War in a similar way. It does appear, though, that for many contemporary literary and critical discourses, once you choose to focus on literary and language strategies, semiotics and rhetoric, you encourage a questioning of system, of what we take for granted as readers and writers—as well as human beings. There is a tendency to forget that people learn how to behave appropriately, that they are socialized. In terms of learning, assessing, teaching and questioning skills within and for the written medium, this acquisition of behaviour is more apparent.[8]

The different directions open to both thematic and structural activity return to the question of an articulated or unarticulated ideological basis for the canon. This is a particularly important question for new canons which include living writers, because the topical issues they address are immediate and may, and indeed do, tend to dominate. Re-discovered writers move into and out of a canon more readily. Writings in the chronologically earlier canons of English-language literature appear, from looking at the shifts in the syllabuses of Canadian Universities, to be more open to change and to the incorporation of newly discovered readings/writings. This is possibly because in these older writings the issues are less relevant; the focus is on structural aspects or on overt strategies for recuperation. I am concerned more for emerging contemporary canons because canon-formation does define many of the conditions of the production of the writing itself. For example, Marlatt's writing is exceptionally challenging and fulfilling and the work is taught on a number of courses. More than once, however, I have heard educators trying to decide, due to pressure of time in the curriculum and in response to local dilemmas, whether to cease teaching Marlatt's work in order to include the writing of Gail Scott or George Eliott Clarke instead. Pragmatically such choices can determine and affect the willingness of a publisher to publish, the judgments and awards of grant-giving bodies.[9] And if it affects the availability of writing, what happens to reading?

*

From Britain, the formation of Canadian literary canons within education from the 1950s looks as though it has been driven by government support for writers and publishers and by the need for academic and critical secondary reading. For example, few Canadian universities in the 1950s or 60s offered courses on Canadian literature,[10] yet the university is a central location for the formation of canons and choice of literature because a formal canon is an expectation specifically of an educational ideology often with a nationalist bias.[11] The debate that has been going on between Robert Lecker, Frank Davey, Tracy Ware and others such as Barbara Godard and Lorraine Weir, has looked at what constitutes a canon, the Canadian canon, a plurality of Canadian canons, and why and how. Lecker's initial, provocative and rather casual claim that there is only one mainstream Canadian canon, and that Canadian critics have not addressed the issues surrounding the broadening of that canon, was immediately and effectively critiqued on the grounds of inaccuracy by Davey and latterly on the grounds of inadequate theoretical and critical context by Ware. But the debate was opened up and many contributors have documented the events behind the stabilizing of curricula over the last 30 to 40 years in Canadian universities and schools. What is undoubted is the intimate connection between canons and both educational establishments and publishing economics.[12]

My understanding of those events is offered here to indicate the context from which I am reading: To teach English-language Canadian literature within universities what was needed was a core of traditional scholarly aids: reference works, resource texts and learned journals.[13] Despite great unevenness that is still in evidence, this core was partially in place by the end of the 1960s. The enormous expansion of the educational network and relative economic stability went along with other cultural phenomena associated with universities such as small magazines, writing groups encouraging young writers, and reading tours for the more established.[14] During these years the growing publishers' support for Canadian literature was closely tied to contacts with the academic community, for example Malcolm Ross edited the NCL series and Robert Weaver worked with the CBC.[15] Furthermore, the government implemented the decisions of the Canada Council primarily through its jury system usually dominated by academics.[16] By 1967/68, which is apparently a catalysing year for the relationship between publishers, government and educators, the patterns are there. In the case of the formation of contemporary canons it seems that the cross-Canada activity may have been the agent that provided the confidence, but that the confidence also arose out of knowledge that the academic infrastructure and the scholarly resources were there.[17]

The 1968 Hall-Dennis report opening up the high-school curriculum to definition by teachers which simultaneously opened the field to Canadian literature,[18] and the 1969 Mathews-Steele report encouraging the government to implement a Canadian hiring policy,[19] can be seen as part of a long-standing co-operation between government and education as well as the result of fresh initiatives. Encouraged by institutional authorization at federal and provincial educational levels, publishers gave increasingly substantial backing to contemporary Canadian literature from the late-60s onwards.[20] Further, from 1967 on and often starting out from university sponsorship which tides them through to Canada Council grants,[21] a plethora of small presses such as Anansi, Fiddlehead, Talonbooks, Tundra and others, join the already established Coach House which focuses on new Canadian literature. Just as important, many of these new presses respond to their local literary community and begin the shift to a new emphasis on regional writing.

While there was the enlarging group of small presses, heavily subsidized and hence able to take risks on new writing, there does seem to have been a need for a stable supply of post-World War II literature, a supply that would not simply dwindle out after a first edition, making all the work that goes into the construction of a literature course redundant. For example ECW Press, which started out publishing new writing, shifted fairly quickly in the early 70s into providing primary and secondary texts for the contemporary canon. The market demand was perceived and ECW and other publishing houses such as Ryerson (later McGraw-Hill Ryerson) and General Publishing responded.

The early federal government strategies for subsidy and award in the 50s and 60s provided many of the first candidates for contemporary canonization. The speed with which these writings were authorized raises in a particularly acute manner the related set of questions about what the canonization of a living writer does to the work of that writer, and further how it affects the reader's response. Simultaneously, a complicated pattern of grant-giving bodies, providing the network of subsidy or (state-) patronage essential to any artistic community, develops during the 70s and early 80s. There is not just the Canada Council, but also there are institutional groupings such as the Women's Directorate, the department of Native Indian Affairs, the provincial government, or the Multiculturalism Directorate under the Secretary of State. Each of these groupings, which will be more extensively discussed in the following chapter, funds writing which addresses a specific audience and which tacitly holds a corresponding status within canon-formation.

With government sponsorship and publishing support falling into a particular pattern, the educational institutions were responding in a variety of different ways. In tertiary education, once a significant proportion of lecturers being hired is Canadian, it is reasonable to assume that emphasis on Canadian Literature courses will increase, particularly once interested high-school students begin to express willingness to register for such courses. Given the focus on Canadian Studies in general from the mid-70s,[22] Canadian literature is also an obvious area in which to develop a career. Topics for research degrees and career advancement cluster around monographs on little-known Canadian writers.[23] Nevertheless, courses are of limited length and only a small number of writings will fit into them. Despite the lip-service to Canadian literature it is clear that there has been considerable resistance to solving the problem by increasing the number of courses focused on Canadian texts. It was still the case in 1993 that people could take degrees in Canadian Literature, but study it only as a specialism within British Literature. Any English-language Canadian canon will necessarily be contesting the firmly-defined, dominant British or United States' ideologies that provide the larger virtual public space for reading and writing.

*

As if responding partly to the need for a national voice, but more urgently to a desire for a coherent story of any kind for the new writings, critics such as D.G. Jones or Atwood produced a contemporary canon that was not only author-based but strongly thematic with a representational bias.[24] Mythologizing, finding coherence, seemed endemic. As Weir points out, even N. Frye, who in a 1943 criticism of A. J. M. Smith's anthology of Canadian poetry, says that Canada is not a young country, that it needs no originating myths since it's as industrial as the next western nation,[25] cannot in 1964 resist mythologizing its destiny in the 'Conclusion' to *The Literary History of Canada*. These critics not only create a literary canon but they also canonize their own critical writing. A set of desirable readings is constructed that is predicated on the consumption of these interpretations, which are inexorably interlocked as they carefully establish their own authority by citing their extremely condensed lineage from other authorial texts.

A rather different critical canon, less concerned with applause than commentary, begins to arrive in the 70s from readers who respond to structure. Canadian writing has been rich with critical work emerging initially at least from academic sponsorship. These writers may be teachers of English, they may teach creative writing, they may indeed be critics or close friends with critics: and this criticism has responded with considerable care. Writers such as Davey and S. Neuman have outlined a potentially different contemporary canon of literature which includes writers such as Marlatt, George Bowering, and Robert Kroetsch, and have certainly generated a different critical canon from which recent strains of theory have drawn much.[26] Although lauded in Europe, many writings in these structurally focused canons have in Canada simply been ignored, or come in for adverse comment, been dismissed as abstruse, esoteric and more to the point, too difficult—but at least the writings get a look-in at the canon-formation which those in the next group do not.

The 1960s and 70s see the influx of many other voices, which could be defined as coming from those people who have not been accepted into tertiary education, but less cynically as those from newly immigrant populations, from the native community, from women. On the whole these writings do not appear to get easy access to the educational canon. One could argue that these voices arrived after the formation of the contemporary canons, that there was literally no room for more writing, but this is not entirely the case, nor does it cover up the tokenism of anthologies.[27]

*

Throughout these canon-forming responses which tend toward the thematically coherent and the mythological, people in education are interacting to some considerable extent with government and the publishers right through to the early 80s. The canons that were formed were at least informed by prevailing educational ideology, which is the sanctioned state site for discussion as well as evasion of ideological contradictions. But as that interaction weakened, partly because a canon was now in place (the publishers initially needed one to guarantee risk; the government to provide national validation), and partly because of the economic recession and conservative pull-back, the canon has become increasingly difficult to change and other related, worrying factors have emerged.

The first change that must strike an outsider is that the activities of the Canada Council have at present been subsumed into greater government control. Despite all the criticism of the earlier structure, the teachers and educators who had been involved at least provided a diverse and potentially questioning emphasis rather than the monolithic approaches of commerce and state nationalism. For example, the openness of the secondary school curriculum to definition by teachers is very important but problematic in effect. In Newfoundland the provincial education ministry has a firm policy of promoting Canadian literature, as well as Newfoundland oral and folktale narrative forms. Ironically, the Memorial University, which has a large folklife department will not accept the secondary school course in folklore as a major entrance credit. But in Nova Scotia, where there is a substantial black population particularly in Halifax, until at least 1993 a black literature course was not acceptable to the education ministry—nor for that matter was the Canadian literature course acceptable as a major entrance credit to university, although Dalhousiefor one had said that it would credit such a course.

This latter anomaly seems to be an effect of taking the canon formation through curriculum out of the hands of teachers and putting it into the hands of government. The resulting choices must have a considerable influence on factors such as the audience a local Nova Scotian writer such as Maxine Tynes or Susan Kerslake might expect to have, while their counterparts in Newfoundland such as Helen Porter and Bernice Morgan are included in the recommended text-books, thereby making a connection between student and writer that can only encourage public readings and new creative writing. Furthermore, in the areas where one has uninformed institutional intervention one also meets a great deal of censorship. The 'Challenged Book List' from The Freedom of Expression committee of the Book and Periodical Development Council lists writing from Callaghan, Geddes, Laurence, Munro, Newlove, Purdy, Richler, Mitchell, and many others.[28] Censorship, especially at secondary school level, is not an easy question: but properly maintained constructive discussion between government and teachers would help.[29]

A second area for concern is the publishing industry. As many book-publishing firms such as Lester and Orpen Dennis, under Free Trade and specifically the Baie-Comeau publishing policy, largely return to centralized and often non-Canadian control, they are in danger of losing contact with the very people who partly define their market: the teachers. However, these people define so small a percentage of the overall market that it is not surprising that large corporations are not bothered. Simple actions like curtailing reviews of books in newspapers such as the *Toronto Star* because managers or editors do not recognize the social relevance of issue or structure in writing, have

considerable effects: Innovative writers who depend on such response
to introduce their work to new readers get even less choice of broader
distribution and wider audience. Publishers will also be increasingly
less well-advised about writers from the growing non-academic field.
Despite the supposed commercial attraction of 'minority literature,'[30] it is
more often the case that most such writing is classed as unfashionable
and ignored. For example, the claim that recent writings by black
writers have been rejected by some publishing firms as not of general
interest is neither unique nor surprising in general publishing terms in
that evasion of similar kinds of new writing was a central problem of
60s to 70s canon-formation, but it could increasingly become the
case.[31]

Nevertheless, the educational connection has partly been responsible
for the problem of less effective involvement, possibly *because* of its
close relationship with the ideological institutions of publishing and
particularly with government. Whatever the web of relationship, the
educational institution has privileged a literary and a critical canon
heavily biased to thematics and to nationalist thematics at that. It is all
the more easy to fit this canon into the ideological control of an
unreflexive activity. Until recently, educators, among whom one could
place R. Lecker, have also avoided theoretical approaches which may
be able to insist on the historical materiality of writings, and keep the
questioning going. It is interesting that the theory that has come
forward to speak to many recent practical contradictions has largely
built upon criticism relating to the contemporary canon concerned
with language and literary structure.

Whatever the pressures, Canadian literature does now seem to have
at least two relatively stable contemporary canons, one thematic and
one structural, with a third less well-defined or taught group of
alternative writings. With a few exceptions, there does not seem to be
much encouragement in terms of teaching space on curricula for
expansion into a wide range of courses. So faced with a burgeoning
quantity of printed material, another acutely urgent question is how to
respond to new writings from the non-academic community, writers
such as Jacqueline Dumas, Erin Mouré, Thomas King, Silvera Makeda
or Isabelle Knockwood. These writings are often from communities
which have had difficult access to publishing, and are full of new
structures and strategies from different ideological sets, which are
sharply foregrounded in the context of Canada. But more immediately,

the writings are full of embarrassment because they insist on difficult and contradictory political problems and positions.

It may well be that these writings do not work effectively as part of the canon because they are not able to fit into the complicitous dichotomy of support and subversion which thematic-based material directly addresses and into which even structural genres find themselves caught. Simultaneously with the permission and encouragement that nation state ideology gives to canonical activity, yet frequently marginalized because of its difficulty of access to print, there has been a written discourse of public action outside the state in letters, almanacs, account-books, diaries and the like, as well as in written discourses from the newly literate, and some of the written discourses of popular and oral cultures.[32] Much of this material, some of which will be looked at in the following chapter, is neither educationally acceptable at the present time, nor published in high-status print objects, nor is it profitable. Yet the Canadian government policy of funding for printed writing has meant that at least some of it, for example writing from literacy groups, has become available. One difficulty then becomes whether or not to work on reading strategies for it, and recuperate it into a canon—which will of course weaken its alterity and subsume it within the stability of ideology.

However there is a larger difficulty that recasts this latter: We are not actually dealing with ideology any more, because state government and the individual have given way to global agencies, and nation states have become cultural artefacts. At the same time we are still dealing with an ethos that works in a similar way strategically: for example in the recent political theory of 'postmaterialist ' thinking and libertarianism which appear to operate in complete disregard of multinational economics in that they choose to ignore that they have already been commodified.

In this world canons may move toward the excesses of the nation state constructed as a private state and isolated by multinational market needs, in a manner analogous to the construction of the private subject by the nation state of the 18th to 19th centuries. This can lead to the national psychosis of racism or the obscenities of ethnocentrism which plunder the hard-won vocabulary of 'care' from women's studies just as the 19th century validated the private home in the name of women's worlds, forgetting the impact of the actual lives of women. But given that national culture is encouraged by multinational economics precisely because it stabilizes the market to some degree and makes profit possible, canons can also become like individual 'style' in the 17th century, the site for national cultures to contest the assumptions of multinational ethos. Here the voices of alterity become vitally important, offering the points of contradiction and difficulty that remind us to remember what we are encouraged to forget.

CHAPTER TWO

Alternative Publishing in Canada

A print society begins with education, with literacy, which gives technical training in both 'creative' and decorous writing and reading, as well as learning about the value and usefulness of communicating through words. Print society also supports all the aspects of production, publishing, distribution, marketing and sales, as well as the professionalization of writing, of authorship, copyright and censorship, and the formation of readerships, audiences, patrons, reviews and rewards. The centrality of print and of graphical communication means that many communities are effectively marginalized in society because of a difficulty of access to even just one part of the whole complex procedure: whether it be to those parts of production and dissemination of the printed product casually referred to as 'publishing' and operating under economic strictures, or to the more subtle strictures on cultural consumption.

Problems of access to print as a producer
The publishing edifice is not at all easy to shift because it is fundamentally tied up into the economic practices of a country, in this case Canada. Historically, since the fifteenth century and the start of the early modern period concurrent with mass, printed publication, the economics of print and publication are based on the primary fact that publishers are not altruistic. Publishing was one of the earliest capitalist ventures and has survived through a thorough understanding and exploitation of underlying economic practices of capitalism; printers simply run factories; booksellers will only stock items they think will sell, and that factor depends on readers with a regular disposable income. The only way to break this central control over

production is to publish writing yourself, or print it yourself, or sell it yourself. There are two provisos: first, you have to be sure of an audience, and second you need to be able to afford the cost of printing. The subsidy systems since the forming of the Canada Council in 1957 have meant that in Canada there has been an exceptional publishing world that has permitted many small publishers to behave 'altruistically.'[1]

The history of book production has been closely tied to the ups and downs in the cost of printing. Since the late fifteenth century there has been a decreasing emphasis on the costs of paper and of printing or the actual costs of production before profit, with more and more of the financial reward going to the publisher and bookseller with associated editors, designers, marketers and so on. Yet in Canada until the cyclostyles and mimeographs of the 1950s, access to print in any substantial way was not feasible for the majority of the population. Commercial enterprises could produce items cheap enough to buy and read, such as booklets, newspapers and magazines. It may have been possible for individuals to afford to produce one-off items. But to have regular access to production, to interact with a readership or an audience, was not feasible: printing presses even before the hugely capital-intensive power-driven presses which arrived in the nineteenth century were simply too expensive. More recently, with photocopying and computer-printouts, and now with desk-top publishing, access to print is broadening.

Problems of access to print as a consumer
There is no point having cheap, accessible print if there is no writer or audience. In Canada, literacy, or acquired skill in writing and reading, is the central aim of the educational system. This literacy may form the basis for learning in mathematics and science, or for skill in other communicative media, but in its primary focus on writing and reading the educational system is training people in the skills necessary for functioning within its print society. However, literacy is difficult to talk about, becomes problematic because desiring literacy presupposes a desire to be part of that society; it takes for granted a community of shared expression and experience that may well not exist. It is estimated that 25% of the adult Canadian population is functionally illiterate.[2] However, included in this number are those who are technically illiterate, and those who are non-literate in that while they can read and write they do not recognize or possibly accept that writing/reading

is a helpful way of communicating.[3] Accounts from literacy education programs speak of literacy work as one which not only gives access to an audience but can create an audience in the first place.[4] Many of those who do not communicate in writing and reading, or through the print medium which is the primary way we disseminate this expression, have no community—but it is a moot point whether they are non-literate because they have no community or whether they have no community because they are non-literate and excluded from access. Again, Canada has an unusual commitment to teaching creative writing throughout primary and secondary schools, and during the 1970s to 1992, to supporting literacy programs.

At risk of repeating a history all too familiar to Canadians, but to provide a context for this reading: In 1957 the federal government of Canada began a program of funding through the Canada Council for publishers and writers, although they chose not to fund readers directly through subsidy to bookstores. Later, in 1972 the then Multicultural section of the department of the Secretary of State was established, and in 1973 began to fund diverse groups, usually along racial or ethnic lines, for cultural expression including writing that other publishers would not publish. The Canada Council grants encouraged an increasing flow of slim volumes from the emerging public-private presses such as Coach House, Anansi, Fiddlehead, Sono Nis or Talonbooks, some of which derived from initial university sponsorship in the 1960s. From the 60s to the 80s, literary/critical newsletters, many started with grants from universities and some distributed free, could become a vehicle for an individual writer's entry into publication, and eventually gain them a Canada Council 'Explorations' grant.[5] Because the grants made it possible to produce these books cheaply, the bookstores were encouraged to take a risk on stocking them. However the access to a market was still restricted: Canadian books still only make up 20% of sales in Canada as opposed to the national scales of 90% in countries such as England or the United States.[6]

In addition, the Department of Multiculturalism, as it became, put questions of literacy and training on the agenda. Although there has been considerable worry about the aims of the Department of Multiculturalism[7] and indeed about the status of Multicultural grants, which both writers and publishers often take to misleadingly indicate second-rate work, this funding has opened up access particularly to communities outside the universities, and increasingly more people have begun to take up the opportunity. At provincial level and among many other programs, Alberta Culture, the Ontario Ministry of Culture and Communication, and the Cultural Affairs division of the department of Cultural, Recreation and Youth, Government of Newfoundland and Labrador, have all made direct grants not only to writers but to publishers such as NeWest, Coach House Press and Breakwater, respectively, often to fund books of specific social interest. Further federal steps which aided the development of publishing work from groups with otherwise marginal access to print were the establishing of the Advisory Council on the Status of Women (1973), and of the Department of Indian Affairs and Northern Development(1967) and the Native Citizens' Directorate of the Department of the Secretary of State (late 70s). Both sources were eventually able to encourage financial aid for the costs of publishing. The latter in particular was able to fund decentralized publication through the Band Councils, to presses such as Theytus and Roseway.

Provincial developments have been widespread, often addressing regional versions of interests funded federally by the Canada Council. But from the evidence of records of support indicated on the verso title pages of many Canadian books, Ontario and the prairie provinces have been the most active. The Ontario Arts Council, the Manitoba Arts Council, the Saskatchewan Arts Board, the Alberta Foundation for the Literary Arts, have provided extensive funding for a large number of regional presses including Coach House, Turnstone, Red Deer, Thistledown and Fifth House. In contrast Press Gang and Talonbooks in British Columbia, or Goose Lane in New Brunswick, usually indicate help from the Canada Council and not from the province. One result of the active and interventionist policies of the prairie arts councils has been to construct a prairie literary context, with writers and readers from different immigrant groups such as Icelandic (Gunnars and Valgardson), Ukrainian (Suknaski), Dutch (Vander-haeghe and Van Herk), German (Kroetsch) and many others. A literate community has been built in which people comment extensively on each other's work, and provide both secondary literature and reference material for prairie literature, enabling it to begin to enter an educational canon.

The provincial councils along with some municipal programs also support educational and literacy publications such as Toronto's East

End Literacy Press, as well as the establishing of creative writing elements in schooling from primary to tertiary levels of teaching;[8] and some provinces have provided support for specific groups through for example the Ontario Women's Directorate. Provinces have also been instrumental in funding posts for writers in residence at colleges and universities, for writers in libraries, and for writing instruction in community programs.[9] An example of one comprehensive program is that run by the Saskatchewan Writer's Guild which provides short term writer residencies in elementary and high schools, in libraries, in communities around the province, and an apprenticeship program "where a writer with some publications etc. is teamed with a senior writer for ... three months correspondence."[10] The Saskatchewan Arts Board funds the Sage Hills (formerly Fort San) writing school which offers residential courses for intermediate and advanced writing, and a manuscript reading service.

Summary
The result of these government initiatives to fund both literacy development and access to publishing has been an enormous growth of publications over the last 20 years from groups within the community who have in the past had difficult access to the written medium and its printed means of dissemination. That growth has not been uniform, and its differences highlight specific aspects of the problem of access that this essay will go on to discuss. It has also produced and is continuing to produce a substantial body of writing that is offering new ways of reading, new relationships between writer, text and reader that are outlining new genres and communities.

   This discussion is concerned with the development of access to publishing and to literacy in Canada since the late 1950s. It is further concerned with the effects of the marginalization of people from, and the participation of people into, the communities of Canada's print society. It is possible to encourage through grant-giving programs an easing of economic and cultural restrictions on access that may loosen the power structures of a dominant ideology. It is particularly possible to ease restrictions on access for writings and readings that understand and accept the aims and limitations of literacy and the print society that underwrites it. However it is far more difficult to ease restrictions on access for those people who do not fit into or may actively reject those aims and limitations: through participation in, for example, oral social media, through disagreement with the ideological implications of the dominant medium, or through lack of opportunity and support. These groups are often cast as fundamentally ignorant, whereas in effect their communication is being repressed. What is significant at the moment is that while access to production is opening up slightly to these doubly marginalized groups, access to writing and reading/consumption is being complicated by an inability on the part of trained readers in the institution to engage with and respond to writings from the newly literate community.

The opening discussion here will focus on the difficulties of access to production and print distribution to relevant communities, and briefly consider some problems of consumption, experienced due to language and cultural difference, differences of ethnicity and race, oral communicative culture, sexuality and gender. The discussion will then move on to look at some difficulties of access to production but more specifically to consumption in a variety of women's communities and in the recently-defined area of literacy and women, which describes a high proportion of newly literate writers, or people beginning to engage with Canada's print society.

Research on the relationship between publishing and writing/reading in the print societies of western capitalist nation states usually refers to periods prior to 1950.[11] In an effort to provide a methodological basis for a relatively new field of inquiry, much of the research, including that by members of the Bibliographical Society of Canada,[12] has been systematic, building comprehensive and coherent structures around available facts.[13] What follows here is, by contrast, focused on contemporary publishing practices and analytical of specific observed difficulties. Any such analytical approach must be general rather than abstract, and can only provide marginal commentaries with indications of further sites for study.

*

Language, culture, ethnicity and race
In Canada, probably the best-recognized groups of writers and readers marginalized from print are those of ethnic immigrants from Europe. Commentaries on this work have appeared with increasing frequency since the late 1970s; and while at first written largely by prairie critics such as Robert Kroetsch, Eli Mandel or E. Blodgett, responses have become more geographically spread.[14] Many members of groups such as those from Germany, Italy, the Ukraine, Poland and others, come from cultures firmly literate in a broad western rhetorical tradition,

and are highly educated in their own language and literature: They are used to a culture that values printed products—if not in all cases a print society which mediates its ideologies primarily through print—and they understand the acceptance and authorization that it permits/conveys to the written word and its author. Over the last 30 years, as the background lists from the Department of Multiculturalism indicate,[15] some of these writers acquire English or French and pass their writing on into translated work that then can gain a broader social audience. Certainly language is one of the most significant factors in their attempt to gain access to publishing. But acquiring the official language of the country is not the only problem of this community in relation to print.[16] The patterns of immigrant demography indicate that in most major Canadian cities immigrants with a language in common tend to live near to each other, often acquiring only a rudimentary or superficial understanding of the majority language.[17] This is particularly common among women who work in the home and elderly citizens, who do not have to go outside of a local neighbourhood. Here is also a pressing need for access to publication of work in their own languages.[18]

A pattern of moving from a beginning in local publishing that has emerged in the Italian-Canadian community is found in several other communities such as the Ukrainians in the prairies.[19] Many communities have produced mimeographed or photocopied material for local newsletters, carrying stories, poems, letters, local news and so on. Some people then go on to produce community magazines, or one-off books of specific interest to the area about family, history, biography or immediate pragmatic information, that are distributed in church basements, local shops, or through advertisements and notices in community and ethnic newsletters. As the producers acquire skills in the publishing process, some go on to form their own publishing businesses; and as the works produced begin to look like books of commercial publishing quality, the writers acquire authorized reputations and may be snapped up by other more established publishers—causing much resentment in the smaller publishers who took the initial risk on them.[20]

But it is clear that language is an important breaking point. A short bibliography of Italian-Canadian literature produced by Joseph Pivato indicates in its comparison of the original Italian-language publication with the invariably later English or French-language translation that

it is normally in the translated version that the work finds a commercial publisher.[21] Another form this phenomenon can take is illustrated
by *Ricordi: Things Remembered*, an anthology of short stories about
the Italian experience in Canada. Although it has already benefitted
from a grant from Multicultural that has made it possible for Guernica
to produce it, the two stories in languages other than English (Italian
and French) have been translated. This is not to say that commercial
publication of Italian- or other-language books does not happen, but
it is comparatively infrequent. A publisher is not going to risk money
on a commercial publication which may not sell well because it is
written in a minority language.

A recent, interesting development that underscores the problem of
language is that of the English-language writers in Quebec particularly
since 1976.[22] Several well-known English language writers, and
publishers who focused on English-language work, left Quebec during
the 70s. Many of those who remained or emerged subsequently often
felt obstructed from access to publication. The provincial government
gives grants less frequently to English-language writers than to
French, and indeed Italian and other language writers are even less
supported.[23] Both the majority surrounding French-language culture
of communication in newspapers, magazines and other media, and
even some of the English-language media that might have been
expected to provide a forum for reviews and recognition, have been
reluctant to do so. Just as reluctant have been the broader English-
language media in Canada as a whole[24]—to the extent that Linda Leith,
editor of the primarily English-language *Matrix*, states that in
interviewing,

dozens of writers, critics, editors and publishers in 1987 and early 1988 I
found an overwhelming number of otherwise well-read and well-informed
Canadians and Quebecers, French and English, unable to name even one new
fiction writer in the English Language from Quebec.[25]

There is now an organization, QUSPEL, which concentrates on raising
the public consciousness of English-language writers in Quebec. That
the cultural politics of Quebec is only to a lesser degree repeating the
marginalizing actions of those it intends to criticize elsewhere in
Canada, does not make it any easier for these writers or their readers.

Another group marginalized from access to publishing but also from
highly literate cultures is made up of more recently incoming
immigrant groups from the Caribbean, from Central and Eastern Asia,

and from South America. Attempts to break into the publishing ring of production follow roughly the same pattern from photocopied or print-out community newsletters, to magazines and specialized books, and to a certain extent to small publishing house. This movement from newspapers to magazine to book is also the pattern followed in many other parts of the world and at earlier times. Partly due to the intensely local interest of the newspaper which ensures a reasonable number of sales, this medium can have far less risk for the capital investor; and with the cheaper printing methods of today the risk is even smaller.[26] But apart from this rough consistency the immigrant groups have little in common bar their profound cultural differences within the majority society.

There are, of course, often problems of language and translation, which exacerbate publishing problems particularly in the area of Chinese and Japanese, which have respectively, pictorial and syllabic alphabets; Chinese has over 48,000 characters and computers have only recently begun to provide help at an affordable cost. Yet some of the most intense difficulties with access stem from Asian and Afro-Caribbean groups who have received at least part of their education in English.[27] While many of these communities have strong oral trad-itions, they also frequently have sophisticated, formal and literate cultures. But that they hold a language and literary tradition in common with the broader society serves to underscore rather than ameliorate cultural difference. The stylistic play of much of the writing foregrounds radical divisions between the traditions and expectations of the incoming and in-place communities. Because it asks for translation not from one language to another with the attendant acceptance of error involved, but within one language, there is no escaping the immediate implications for the host culture of the incoming difference.[28] Here again commercial publishers have been slow to take up writers, but not so much because of a language difference. The reluctance in this case seems to be profoundly cultural and at least residually racial.[29] While there have always been a few mainstream publishers who were willing to take on the work of writers such as Austin Clarke, more widespread access to publication grows in the 1970s and 80s with the emergence of newsletters such as the *South East Asian Review* and specific publishers such as Williams Wallace or Sister Vision who are committed to addressing this public.

From the outside the picture is complex: Multicultural grants aided both writers from ethnic European groups and writers from immigrant groups from the third-world, who would otherwise not be able to publish commercially acceptable products that can be sold in bookshops and kept in libraries. For many, the Multicultural aid is a stepping-stone on the way from local papers and self-publishing to being published by more established presses with aid from the Canada Council or from Provincial Arts' Councils. But there is still, within these communities, a substantial gender divide and an insistently rankling race and class divide that the applications of such aid have often failed to address, and indeed aid has not been forthcoming to all: the socialist feminist bulletin *Cayenne* appears to have published through the late 80s entirely dependent on subscriptions.

Oral Communities
A different set of difficulties about access to publishing emerges from the Aboriginal and the Inuit communities. For communities which have a relatively short history of emphasis on media for writing, offering print as a viable medium is not self-evident as a way to social participation. Furthermore, the communities are not primarily in the large urban centres of Canada, but spread over huge distances, and often without a readily disposable financial income. The pattern of self-publishing is similar to those in urban centres in that many newsletters and newspapers are produced, and a number of bands started publishing houses for book production, although some have closed; but what is missing from the urban pattern are magazines or other more substantial periodicals.[30] Magazines need a fast and regular distribution system and an audience with significantly more income to spend than on a newspaper. It may well be that the costs of transport into rural areas and the relatively small number of sales within what are small communities in any case simply make this form of publishing impracticable. Radio is a far more sensible medium for distance communication, as would be telephone-linked computer magazines in community/band centres.[31]

    Possibly more important is the question of the appropriateness of the written medium at all. Aboriginal and Inuit linguistic cultures were primarily oral until the twentieth century. The Moravian church missionaries established orthographies for several languages in the late eighteenth century, and in the nineteenth century syllabic systems were introduced.[32] But given the almost insuperable problems for the production and distribution which are necessary to printed publishing, which are posed by large distances and poor transport for heavy objects made of paper, and given the non-capitalist economics of hunter/gatherer society when capital is vital to the investment risk and profit-taking of the modern book industry, there would have been little use employing the graphic systems at all except where fixed records were perceived as necessary.

The concept raises a primary cultural contradiction between the fact-orientated denotative world of European informational systems reliant on and giving economic reason for the printed medium, with its associated modes of morphemic and syntactic copyright ownership and subject-based textual authorship, and a world of orally transmitted knowledge, with its modes of narratorial copyright and collective performative production.[33] The contradiction is extended into the controlling financial concept of edition: The fixed text or edition has allowed for the commodification of writing as well as for a broad social access that was impossible to an oral communication before technological media. It has engaged in a positive fight against censorship and information restriction, yet has also often become a tool of control. But if texts are to be produced appropriate to the contingencies of specific place, occasion and audience, then a fixed medium for the text is not suitable.[34]

This contradiction is at the centre of a dispute that rumbled during the 1980s throughout the Canadian writing community. Some Aboriginal writers were objecting to the use of Aboriginal stories and even to the portrayal of Aboriginal peoples by non-Aboriginals; while some, perceiving the value of at least raising the general social consciousness about Aboriginal communities, particularly in portraying Aboriginal peoples in film or novel, did not.[35] But there is a recognizable difference between the arguably racist portrayals of W. Kinsella's stories and the social conscience of Joan Clark's or Rudy Wiebe's work, a difference that has been taken up at a national level.[36] The depth of feeling on this issue is difficult for people with little notion either of the social responsibility required in the use of stories or of their sacred uses to understand.[37] A close translation might be to suggest that just as appropriation of an individual's words out of context may in Western European countries be considered libellous and defamatory to that person, so appropriation of a group's narrative out of context may be demeaning. The centre of such a translated debate is the context within which appropriateness (or not) is assessed.

To insist that the context should be that of the dominant social order is racist. At the Feminist Bookfair in Montreal, June 1988, the question came to an acute point: Lee Maracle, an Aboriginal writer, led an argument, saying that white writers of any kind should not use Aboriginal stories, against Anne Cameron, who is white yet married to a Aboriginal and with adopted Haida daughters. Cameron did "move over" from the practice and went on to write about racism.[38] The issue has since been widened out to other communities as illustrated by the text of a 1992 CBC debate "The Public Face of the Cultural Appropriation Debate: Who Speaks for Whom?" with participants from Aboriginal, in-coming and in-place communities.[39] More specific and detailed commentaries have come from groups of women writers from different social and cultural communities in collections such as *Telling It: Women and language across cultures*.[40] Broader questions about cultural representation directly linked to different media, have extended the issues from oral/print to drama and film: Productions of *Showboat* and *Miss Saigon* in Toronto during 1993 caused intense public response.

Nevertheless, participation in Canadian society is predicated upon written skills and the Aboriginal communities appear to be divided about whether they should be writing at all, let alone writing in English. The situation is compounded by the history of transmission of some texts which have been recently recuperated by Aboriginal writers: stories told orally in Aboriginal languages to nineteenth-century anthropologists and taken down by translation into written English have been translated back into present-day oral Aboriginal languages and then in some cases rendered into written syllabic form and published. The confusion of such transmission possibly achieves a sense of necessary collective authorship, and it also calls into question copyright of any kind. Other societies with a healthy print culture, such as India, which emphasize the importance of continuous translation to the written word, have managed to treat copyright in yet another way. But the apparent inadequacy of Canada's print society to Aboriginal cultures has permitted the federal government to be lax about support for publication, which in turn has excluding effects on social and political participation.[41] But over the last ten to 20 years, with an increasingly more book-educated populace, the Aboriginal communities have begun to get more involved in establishing some kind of access. Aboriginal papers such as the *Wataway News*, which is a bilingual English/Cree publication, often include poetry and short fiction as well as the usual news, sport and advertizing; and some initially Band-connected presses such as Theytus and Pemmican have become commercial publishers. But the problems that the Aboriginal communities have with access to publishing are particularly acute because there is no tradition of privilege for writing or authorship which has been the historical bridge between the individual literary communication and social participation.

Sexuality

Although each provides a different focus on the problems of access to publishing, the groups discussed above all have a fairly well-defined community and audience that is recognized by religion, language, colour or race,[42] and which is more or less susceptible to traditional modes of print distribution. But the moment that the location for community becomes nebulous, as in the case of individuals with a sexual orientation outside the socially accepted norms such as the gay and lesbian communities, questions of access focus on marketing and sales. Many members of these communities are again highly literate and formally educated. Language and writing are not the most pressing difficulties of access, although those factors represent an ideological hegemony which individuals may not want to be part of. The rejection of that hegemony has resulted in the emergence of some magazines focussing on linguistic and literary experiment.[43] However, the huge social rejection of homosexual behaviour in Canada does mean that there have been distinct problems in establishing a focused location for distribution of printed material: in other words where do lesbians and/or gays meet? and, is it possible to sell books in these locations?

For this community there are no necessarily common meeting grounds in places of religion, in distinctive areas of habitation, or in community centres. Furthermore, many commercial bookstores refuse to stock any homosexual publications and most certainly refuse to display them as such, often considering them to be pornographic. Mail-order distribution is one solution, if the publisher can purchase a relevant sales list or can rely on swift word-of-mouth information. That magazines rather than local newspapers are more typical of the community underwrites the appropriateness of mail-order sales which in Canada were favourable to this form of periodical publication until the early 1990s. Another avenue which requires considerable capital risk is the setting up of independent bookstores specifically to stock and sell printed material to this community. There are a few bookstores in Montreal, Toronto, Vancouver and elsewhere, which have been established to fill this gap in the publishing world, and which seem to have found a monied audience.[44] They have come to fill a social gap as well, in providing the urban community with a location or meeting place for the exchange of news and information, although rural individuals are still extremely isolated. But this response to access difficulties has not been without trouble. In the early 80s a Toronto bookstore, Body Politic, had its subscription list as well as much of its stock seized; and there have been a number of court cases involving bookstores and censorship prosecuted during the 1980s to 90s.

Given the social antipathy, which means that few grants are given to gay/lesbian writers or publishers *in support* of their social difference, it has also been difficult to establish commercial presses, most of which do need initial grant funding to start up. Some presses have emerged from the feminist community concerned with a lesbian agenda,[45] and some have arisen in response to the rather arbitrary censorship that is exercised on imports of printed material from the United States. Customs Officers are empowered to seize material considered by them to be dangerous or obscene, even from private individuals crossing the border. Although more research into the implications and results of this policy is needed, and not only with regard to the gay/lesbian community, it seems likely that one effect is to encourage the publication of such material in Canada itself.

Gender
Another group marginalized from the print society by the ephemeral aspects of its community within the current ideology of Canada is that of women. Well-organized responses to access have come from educated feminism and women within other distinctive groups, particularly those differentiated by ethnic origin and colour. In many respects these groups follow the pattern from newsletter, to periodical, to book publishing. One example among many is the small magazine *Fireweed* which was started by women who had acquired the necessary credentials to authorize them as publishers.[46] They were university-educated, some in the foreign universities of the United States which confer even greater credibility than those of Canada. They had gained experience by editing for major commercial publishing houses such

as Oxford University Press, or by working on established small magazines in Canada. *Fireweed* emerged into an authorized product through careful tending; it acquired grants and gained access for many writers from 1978 into the 80s.

Makeda Silvera's introduction to *Fireworks*,[47] a selection of essays from *Fireweed*, notes that the aim of the Fireweed Collective was to publish "works by a diversity of women" because "people not of the dominant culture have not had active participation in, or access to, arts journals, whether these have been part of the dominant culture or have emerged from the small presses" (8). But she goes on to say that in earlier issues of *Fireweed* "there were no articles by Native women and that pieces by both immigrant and Canadian-born women of colour were very few in number. Articles addressing the issues of class or by working class women of any colour were also rare"(8). Silvera raises the issue in order to underline that the selection in *Fireworks* will emphasize these areas of omission, and one contribution "Organizing Exclusion" specifically addresses the omissions. The issue is also related to questions of literacy that will be discussed below. Silvera herself now runs the press SisterVision, which concentrates on publishing writing by women of colour, and has moved to grant funding. The quality of production and scale of distribution, visibility for the sisters, and reward, has been substantially widened in the process; and the writers have far greater ease of access to audience.

The edifice of publishing itself and its complicity in the social fabric is far more difficult to question or shift. When its rules are broken, as they were when the Women's Press, which was specifically established to redress the omissions of the traditional publishers and the elisions of gender, decided in 1988 to drop three contributions to a collection of essays at the last minute, there was objection if not outrage. The reason given for dropping the contributions was that they were racist, although discussion of this difficult and embarrassing topic has been submerged under later discussions on the issue of censorship.[48] However the shock of the experience for those whose contributions were rejected also lies in the fact that an editorial collective had initially accepted their work, proofs of the material had been printed, and publishers conventionally don't pull out at that stage. In this case editor-writer relationships, guidelines for which have been in place for at least two centuries, were simply overridden. The Women's Press story is further complicated by the context of collective working and the potentially emotive issues arising from its aims of solidarity and political effectiveness. You may change what you publish, widen your net to include other groups/voices/ positions, but change of publishing practices, which in a print society often become naturalized into 'rights,' is shocking even to the most politically and socially flexible of writing groups.

What distinguishes the responses of these women is a deep understanding of literacy: the fact that reading and writing are the gateway into social participation and can create extended and supportive communities.[49] The larger, currently more disadvantaged group of women with regard to publishing access, is that of the newly literate or non-literate: the enormous proportion of the female population which does not communicate in the written medium. If literacy is not just technical reading and writing but also the recognition of the importance of writing and reading in forming communities, engaging with and participating in them, then many women are frequently only marginally literate. There are of course other ways of participating in broad social activities and other media for cultural communication, but none so central to the mediation of power in a print society.

Literacy
However, one of the primary reasons for a failure to take up literacy to the extent that other marginalized groups have done is that many women do not know how to break out of the circle of marginalization: If you don't recognize your position to be marginalized, or more important if you perceive it as necessary, you do not begin to articulate it in any medium and so you remain marginalized. The circle is re-duplicated with respect to literacy: If you are not aware of the social possibilities in reading and writing or again if you cannot see a way to participating in them, then you do not attempt to use the medium and so you remain non-literate. Breaking the circle is one of the central pursuits of feminism, and much feminist practice has been brought to bear on literacy. On both counts what is needed is consciousness-raising—a painful, lengthy and difficult process for many of us—and support. Given that marginality has been recognized, and that literacy is perceived as a means of addressing its disempowerment, the most urgent problems for this group are often time, and money. Most people within this group are working women hard

pressed at home, often with children.[50] Few have a readily disposable income that would permit them to enter the publishing world, which is the economic and technological medium through which literacy is currently effected in Canada.

This large group straddles a broad range of socio-economic strata, and represents the largest single audience for the products of the weekly and monthly commercial periodical market, which have a large after-sales circulation. But while there are many publications produced for this group, there are relatively few printed genres produced by it. Although it is difficult to estimate, the largest genre may be that of the PTA or community newsletter; another important genre is that of the fund-raising recipe book, where women can take the opportunity to share creative variations on changes in food pathways and domestic technology, in other words what is going into and out of stores selling household products. Other genres that emerge are often related to issues coming from consciousness-raising groups, such as natural childbirth, domestic violence, child abuse and general social feminist issues. One example here might be *The Midwifery Issue,* from the Midwifery Task Force of Ontario, which throughout the early to mid-80s was concerned with creating acceptance for midwifery as a professional body.[51] The newsletter was distributed primarily by mail-order to a membership list, reflecting the lack of sales outlets for such special-interest groups. It is interesting that the use of a computer mailing-list was considered highly sophisticated in the mid-80s, but by the early 90s was fairly common among other special-interest group publications. The *Midwifery* newsletter was still firmly part of a pre-Desktop publishing world, and was produced through typed copy and paste-up, unlike many newsletters in 1990 from, for example, the environmental pressure groups.

Publications from groups addressing specific issues are often funded by subscription, and in some cases from private donations. If there is no need for a sale, then one of the most important distribution points is the local library. Groups with more general interest, although dependent upon subscription, do seem to be able to find distribution in some stores. One example here might be the *Northern Women Journal,* costing $1.50 and collectively produced and published in Thunder Bay, which includes not only news and information but book reviews, poetry and short prose. Significantly, a more substantial periodical *The Womanist,* published from Ottawa, was initially free.

An early issue from 1989 notes in a request for voluntary subscriptions that "We are free because we believe that all women, whatever
their economic situation, should be able to get news about women ...
By being free we find that we can distribute *The Womanist* to places
where women are, such as laundromats, corner stores, and community
centres." But while they depended upon advertisements and subscriptions to cover costs, by 1993 they were charging a price.

This relatively recent publication is of course selective. If the
articles *The Womanist* prints indicate the breadth of its intended
readership, then it is clearly addressed to all women of whatever class,
colour or religion, who wish to discuss and debate issues arising from
a consciousness of women's position in Canadian society. But what is
then distinctive about the many publishers and publications advertised
in the paper is how few come from groups which identify themselves
as white working-class or women concerned with working in the home as
a community-forming activity.[52] There are advertisements from
publishers and bookstores representing lesbian communities, women
of colour, Aboriginal women, women of immigrant and visible
minorities: part of each of these communities already recognizes the
need to participate in the social medium of print. There are also
advertisements from feminist organizations and research institutes,
which produce valuable material analyzing the lives of women in
terms of problems and policy, and which aim particularly at those
people working on or interested in the interface with disadvantaged
and non-literate women, but these books do not appear to be written
for those women themselves and are certainly not written by them.

For many women, difficulty of access to communication through
print arises because the difficulty is not recognized as such to begin
with. Once recognized as a primary means to social participation,
there are problems of finance and problems of time: who will look
after the children? But this group has another problem that it shares to
a greater or lesser extent with all the other groups: That of literacy.

It is striking that many of the contributions to an issue of *Canadian
Woman Studies/Les Cahiers de la Femme* on "Women and Literacy"[53] discuss precisely several areas of this newly literate group, as well as
including many pieces of writing from people who are emerging from
it. This issue presents a valuable collection for literacy studies
everywhere, of scholarly research, bibliographies, commentaries on
social and political issues, accounts of programs in context, and a

critical look at contemporary practices. The editorial, from Rita Cox and Leslie Sanders, underlines the importance of reading and writing in a literate society where "the written word is the source of authority and power," and where literacy is needed by women "to function in the public sphere in order to provide for themselves and their children"(3). They also note that literacy programs provide the opportunity for women to gather "on their own behalf," to break their frequent isolation and establish community and support. But they end with a warning that literacy without a "challenge to the status quo" simply maintains faulty social structures. An uncritical acquisition of literacy may lead to uncritical participation in society. As Elaine Gaber-Katz and Jenny Horsman argue in "Is it her voice if she speaks their words," teachers of literacy need to develop a "critical pedagogy" (120) that will alert the reader/writer to the social, political and ideological dimensions of literacy practice.

While a critical pedagogy is important, it is difficult simultaneously to achieve practical skills and a critique of that practice: this process takes time. Further, there is the added problem of audience, that too strong a critique may produce writing so unconventional as to lose its potential readership. To start, the practical skills are needed so that at some point, sooner rather than later, critique may come. It is important to have the choice to be critical. Not to have that choice is, as Carole Boudrais says, "frightening":

I was illiterate. Being illiterate is the most frightening thing. It's like being in a prison of your own self. It's one of the deepest secrets that you keep hidden inside, out of shame. Not being able to read street names, medical instructions or menus pose a threat to survival.(72)

Certainly, as the Canadian Congress for Learning Opportunities for Women (CCLOW) notes, illiteracy makes it twice as difficult for women to get a job; and when they do, if they have less than a Grade 8 education, they make only 59% of what men earn compared to the 68% average of more literate women(27). Furthermore, not to have that choice is to be fundamentally isolated, from the social information given by of a newspaper about films in cinemas or local events, from the communication possible through use of a telephone book, from the work that children bring home from school: Indeed a number of personal accounts in "Women and Literacy" note that involvement in a literacy program began when the woman went to a parent-teacher meeting to discuss her child's work and revealed that she could neither read nor write.

Over the last 20 years literacy programs have begun to flourish all over Canada, from county and metropolitan councils, from public libraries, from community groups, from colleges, and from pressure groups for the disabled, for recent immigrants, for prison inmates. "Women and Literacy" raises the question of access for a large number of groups, surprisingly omitting the particular problems of the older generations, the senior citizens who suffer from many of the same disadvantages. Less surprising is the omission of the difficult area of children's rights to access, but the collection does point the way back to the problems of access to publishing once literacy has begun for the general community of the newly-literate. Literacy programs will not only provide a way to break the isolation by physically locating people with a common problem in one place where they can weave communities, but with a critical pedagogy, those communities can also move on to write about their focusing issues and produce material that can be read by others—extending their community by publication and broadening their social participation. What can be difficult at this stage for these groups, is entrance into the world of publishing. What is usually more difficult is for their writing to find and/or generate appropriate readings, in other words for some communication to be effected.

Publishing, as outlined previously, is a high-risk capital venture. To minimize risk, publishers and their editors, who act as ideological censors, produce writing that is acceptable to and desired by as large a market/audience as possible: a majority language, an unthreatening cultural perspective, conventional literary genres. Were publishers the only factor, written culture would have stagnated many centuries ago. It has always been the role of the patron—private or state and sometimes publisher *as* patron—to support the cultural explorations which effect change. The grant-giving bodies in Canada act in just such a role, but they do exercize criteria of evaluation which are rooted in the intensely literate traditions of most of both the early and later immigrant populations. For newly literate writers and readers there is rarely immediate commercial interest and there are few sources of financial support.

The writings reproduced in "Women and Literacy," such as "My name is Rose" by Rose Doiron and "My Story" by Olive Bernard, are funded by literacy programs, in other words indirectly rather than directly by the government. There is no conventional sales and marketing infrastructure for the products, presumably because the audience is perceived to be low-income. The writing does receive some circulation within literacy programs themselves, but there is little access to engaging with a wider audience. Unlike all the other groups, which get a helping government hand to step from newsletter/paper to small publisher, this group receives at best low-level indirect sponsorship. Certainly, the writing that is produced is not authorized as 'literature.'

An added difficulty emerges for those oral communities that want to gain some dissemination for their histories, traditions and stories, in the printed medium. The Storylinks project in Ontario, for example, offers ways for literate and oral texts to work in tandem. Its participants have worked closely on issues of orature, in order to find ways of writing appropriate to the skills, the techniques and devices of the oral text. While Storylinks has helped people from many oral cultures to write their spoken words into print without necessarily becoming literate, the 'double authorship' of such texts puts into question their 'literary' status: And so it should. These texts, just as much as institutionally conventional poetic experiments, are necessarily introducing new ways of writing into the culture that should alert us to the need for new ways of reading. However, in effect traditionally literate readers are less prepared to take the trouble to learn by engaging with such texts. Such writings are frequently classed as second- or third-rate, and projects like Storylinks lost a large part of their grant funding during 1992-3.

The Canadian government at federal and provincial level has, over the last 30 years, been encouraging in a number of ways both to literacy programs and to publishing circles. For whatever benefits to the state, it has enabled people to choose to participate in society through the medium of print. For a number of overtly cultural reasons it remains unaware of the communicative possibilities that are found in writing by newly literate groups, and needs to address this oversight. The Alpha Centre in Toronto has shelves weighted with material, but while new writers have been encouraged new readers have not.

Discussion

Groups with difficulty of access to written communication have a variety of problems. Those studied here relate specifically to the production and consumption of publishing, and to literacy as the recognition of the value of communicating through reading/writing. Canada as a whole is addressing many of these areas, and one result has been an explosion of writings over the last 20 years, which has begun to open up new strategies for social discourse. For example, there are the *SwiftCurrent* experiments of Frank Davey and Fred Wah, which from 1985 to 1990 used computer networking technology to provide a forum for writers. Davey's wish to drive a wedge between the capitalist basis of print technology and the medium of writing could easily backfire.[54] While *SwiftCurrent* II in particular gave evidence for a new and potentially far more broader-based technology for writing, it also indicates a potential for different modes of writing, especially the non-linear, and for new ways of establishing social groupings by way of writing. We must hope that more attention will be paid to the breaks in the literacy-publishing connection and that the new technologies for producing written material will bridge and enable rather than obstruct the possibilities for the formation of communities and their social participation.

Part Two

CHAPTER THREE

After Modernism: Alternative Voices in the Writings

of Dionne Brand, Claire Harris, and M. Nourbese Philip

As Lorris Elliott notes in the introduction to *Literary Writing by Blacks in Canada*, there has been an "outburst of literary activity by Blacks in Canada"[1] since the 1970s, and the three writers discussed here are part of that "outburst." Some of this recent activity[2] comes from Canadian-born writers such as Maxine Tynes or George Elliott Clarke, part comes from immigrants from the United States, from England, from South America and from Africa, and part comes from the community arriving from the Caribbean.[3] Dionne Brand, Claire Harris and M. Nourbese Philip, whose work is approached here, all come from the Republic of Trinidad and Tobago, and each develops a writing that raises three tightly associated issues: race, access, and the appropriateness of the verbal tradition, literary or linguistic, to their writing.

Race, and racism, is one of the most important issues for the black writing community in Canada, and any of its readers including myself. It underpins the questions of access defined in the previous chapter as the field of 'marginalized' writings: access to education, writing, to creative tuition in verbal craft, to publication, marketing, distribution, to reviews and audiences, and to rewards—the grants, tours, readings and all the publicity paraphernalia that makes the next book possible.[4] It also defines many of the specific grounds on which these writers discuss questions of literary voice, authenticity and community.

The complex process of learning about race and racism is intended explicitly to structure these readings as they engage with the skill and specific invitation or generosity of each writer, and it should be said here that no answers can be offered. It also needs to be said here at the start that the issue of access to literacy and print is of utmost importance,[5] particularly in the context of a Canadian education which provides extensive literacy programs,[6] and the possibility of training in creative writing and composition from primary, through secondary to tertiary education.[7] However what this discussion will focus on is how black women writers who have gained that access use it to develop a specific response to the problems of writing within a culture that is experienced as alien because of colour, gender and class; and how they balance the need clearly and immediately to tell and retell a history more appropriate to their memories than the one on offer from the culture in power, with the pressing demand to extend the processes of self-definition and authentic voice within current literary conventions.

Each of Brand, Harris and Philip is faced with the question of how to write within a verbal tradition that has never encouraged expression of their experience and indeed has often actively repressed it. Not only this, each writer also knows that to get published it is necessary to stay broadly within that tradition,[8] and further, that unless they stay largely within the tradition, their potential audience will be restricted, their traditionally-educated readers will not know how to read their work. But once access has been gained, there is an opportunity for trying out a new voice, making a new way of reading. Brand, Harris and Philip, address this possibility in different ways. Acutely aware of how language, narrative and poetics contain them as writers within the institutional structures that wield power, each is concerned to find a way to position themselves with regard to that power. In various ways, the works also make it possible for different readers to position themselves, and some those positions will be enabled and others alienated. Both are necessary to begin to extend friendship.[9]

The three writers can be read as starting with modernism's potential for generating 'other' communities and alternative histories, and as responding with a variety of literary strategies to the recognition of the problems implicit in modernism's universalism and claims to fixity and essential identity. In doing so each writer attempts a different stance than that called for by modernism. Modernism, and its outgrowths of postmodernism and neo-romantic surrealism which other Canadian writers have pursued, all depend upon writing toward the conventional expectations of an extant audience. While there is variation in the extent of the recognition of the limitations of culture and ideology, all these strategies work on an extensive corporate agreement about what is accepted. In contrast, the stance taken up by these writers acts toward the possibility of writing by interacting with an audience, constructing a stance out of its social immediacy and historical need. The stance outlines a different kind of community, not working from conventionally accepted grounds, but a community anchored as such by actual social problems often outside accepted grounds and hence a community that will necessarily change.

Each of these writers has a direct participation in particular social issues to do with race, the position of women, teaching, community relations, cultural power. They are at least partly concerned with writing for a broad audience, what Brand calls writing for a 'crowd.' So they are also concerned with an audience for whom conventional representation is, complicatedly, both profoundly habitual, universalizing and essentialist, as well as the recognized strategy for making 'reality claims,' particularly about history. This problematic raises a central issue in the study of any text or discourse: The 'reality' texts address is certainly there. Its representation is initially crafted out of an engagement between writer and reader based on an understanding that the conventional strategies that tend to habituate and make comfortable, need to be disrupted in order to address the social immediacy of reality. But that engagement can initiate strategies that may be carried on past the point of action and necessity, into a corporate agreement for dealing with issues that we do not want to, or have not the time to address directly—in other words they become the new conventions. This is an important sequence because becoming corporate is a helpful way of coping with our lives. Recognizing the limitations of the corporate is more difficult.

Disruption is the key term. The disruptions of modernism encourage a relocation into alternative histories which become corporate agreements difficult to dislodge. Postmodernism has attempted to encourage a continual dislocation, which can offer a rejection of history and make action on immediate issues impossible. Romanticized surrealism encourages a dislocation into the private, which invalidates discussion and rejects social immediacy, although sometimes claims the popular status of culture or fame.

Texts, in that they can make claims for history, may authenticate voices of unproblematic identity if their history is universalist and underwrites fixed communities and essentialist versions of self. But just as history and texts are also social realities, anchored in material needs if also constricted by ideology, so 'authentic voice' is a way of describing the necessarily different self that emerges from the discussions, decisions and actions instigated by addressing social realities and the communities that form in response to those realities. I use the terms authentic voice and community in the latter sense, with an acute awareness of how that responsive stance has the potential for increasingly corporate habituation precisely because it is historical and social, but with an equal awareness that the evasions of the corporate in postmodernism and the surreal lead to a rejection of historical and social reality.

I am also aware that this literary historical outline evades the primary social immediacy of questions of race. It is to speak as though the racial divide between black and white critical positions did not exist, as though a white critical position with respect to text, history and social support and trust, could be drawn unproblematically from these writings by Afro-Caribbean Canadian women overtly concerned with a specific history and the social reality of race and racism. There will be necessary differences between any position I could take as a white critic and those of these Afro-Caribbean women writers. Yet there are points of contact, critical readings made possible by these writings and the way that the texts interact with some common historical grounds that bring the possibility of socially immediate and radically engaging stance to feminism, at the same time as opening the door on the reality of racial difference and the history of problems that it carries. The stance could address those problems and make possible another discussion within feminism about race.

To be open about what I here intend: These writers write about issues I recognize intimately when they write about their position as women, as lovers, wives, mothers, daughters, women at work. I read these issues differently depending upon the availability of common ground offered by the texts. That common ground can be radically displaced by the difficulty of my own understanding of race, yet where the grounds that bring women together can be articulated, it can provide a place for talking about precisely those difficulties with race that separate us. When a familiar common ground like mothers and daughters, which women might expect to remain stable or at least recognizable, is suddenly refracted through racial difference, the effect is often a radical impetus to extend discussion. In a practical way the points of contact, like Philip's floor for her "sisters to dance on," constructs a community out of the needs of the problematic. It brings together people to discuss the grounds for action within the current constraints.

*

Claire Harris provides some context for understanding the historical specificity of these writings in her essay "Poets in Limbo,"[10] where she talks about the educational background of Caribbean, here specifically Trinidadian, writing in English. She talks about the educational indoctrination that students in Trinidad experience, an indoctrination into Western European language, culture and tradition: "We learnt English folk songs, put on Gilbert and Sullivan. British gym mistresses taught us Morris dancing among other survival skills" (117). The pupils were also forced to learn huge quantities of English literature by rote—Chaucer, Wordsworth, Arnold—an experience that Harris says can be "terminal" for a potential writer. Yet the oral folklore "saved our imaginations." "We remain" she suggests "...poets whose sense of the art is essentially rooted in the English tradition. When we turn away, that is what we turn away from. What we turn to we have essentially to make ourselves" (118).

Harris goes on to suggest that what the tradition most comfortably gives writers like herself is a way to "seek wholeness in the landscape," which is an activity that her own earlier poetry does attempt. Turning to what they have to make for themselves, she offers a number of different approaches that present responses to the stylistic and topical conventions of European literature. She speaks of development of dialect representation and of the poetic fracturing of the traditional equation between word and image, but points out that both stylistic devices risk not only alienating but permanently estranging the audience. In contrast, responses to topical convention are possibly more immediately enabling. She notes here that there is a pressing need to sort out the relationship with Africa, by implication with re-tellings of origin, history and the present culture that are highly problematic. It is important to counter the ideological presentation particularly of the physical self, and hence a need to challenge and reject "names." To do so writers typically ransack their colonial childhood for different images. Writers should also make use of all the available materials about Black experience, "Journal entries, newspaper clippings, pictures of horrors, reports of Amnesty International," that yield "material for collages" so that at the least partial, pasted together realities can be constructed, and Harris experiments

with precisely such a structure in the short story, "A Matter of Fact."[11] For
herself she says "Personally I am content to try to write well and to
trust to the authenticity of image, content and perception to see me
true" (121).

The potentially essentialist vocabulary of "natural landscape" and
"authentic image," belies Harris' own poetic practice. What Harris, a
linguist and teacher of literature and language, doesn't tell us is that
the literary tradition that she, Dionne Brand and Nourbese Philip
appear at first to be most deeply rooted within is the modernist poetic
whose purpose is already to fracture the conventional discourses and
to construct different connections and communications. In other
words, these writers are already part of a profoundly dislocating
stylistic, albeit one with a firm historical backing that poses specific
problems for their writing. Like the reworking of modernist poetics
typical of the work of many contemporary Canadian writers, each of
these writers answers the alienation that results from modernism's
inappropriate history, with a particular poetics of her own. Rather than
pursuing an ahistorical postmodernism or the romanticist individual-
ism/heroics of the surreal, these writers offer a set of historically-
based alternatives that shift away from the heroism of alienation
toward questions of authenticity that deal in engagement and social
support that generate questions about trust: trust in ideology, in
history and in language.

The pursuit of authentic voice and image has become a contemporary attempt to speak of experience that is denied, oppressed, subtly
distracted and disembodied by modes of representation coming from
politically and economically dominant cultures. The attempts have
engaged with many of the elements of representation that Harris lists
such as storytelling structures, dialect, media, verbal and technical
strategies. But above all the attempts have engaged with the
overwhelming conventions of realism with its currently broad claims
to adequate representation. However the engagement is ambiguous:
if your reading community accepts the realistic convention as the
appropriate medium for recording history, for conveying event and
experience, for persuading, then as a writer you take a chance that any
transgression of those conventions will invalidate your account. At the
same time an uncritical use of them may simply valorize some
nostalgic desire for an essential and different past world. Yet the
writer can also overwrite realism as if it were a palimpsest, can

conflict with it, or connect glancingly with it. What you cannot do in the contemporary context is completely reject it, or the literary community breaks down; communication becomes impossible and the audience cannot hear. Harris's trust in the "authenticity of image, content and perception" indicates a trust that somewhere in the craft of writing a different, more appropriate and understandable representation can be made for her community.

Harris also offers a trust in "natural landscape" which is as ambiguous as a trust in writing. Yet the physical world, even more than writing, is resistant to conventions of representation. Perceptions of the natural landscape do change, but landscape also constantly engages with those perceptions by way of a physical actuality. The writer's engaging with this resistance, like that with the elements of representation, can work in a number of different ways. There can again be a simple valorization of some pre-colonial native/natural land which attempts a naive recuperation of a lost origin. But the historical resistance of the landscape to representation can provide a useful place from which to write about the resistance of a community to representation. As Noubese Philip discusses in *She Tries Her Tongue,* no history is possible without memory, and physical reality is akin to the body both in its resistance to remembering and in its ability to remember. The body, the physical world and the community can each resist and remember representation of authentic voice, landscape and history, not just as identity but as commodity, or reflection, or difference from, or difference within, or deferral or différance.

Modernist poetics, with its initial engagement with and resistance to realism, and with its attempts to articulate the subject and speak of private individual experience, is thoroughly bound up with the later pursuit of authentic voice. But modernism looks inward for self and position. Its attempts to lassoo the significant moments, the isolated epiphanies of experience where we seem to find our selves, can underwrite many of the limiting qualities of fixity and inviolate essence that the word 'identity' calls up. On rare and enduring occasions modernist writing looks inward and sees nothing. This is the moment of existentialism which can direct the private nothingness of identity to loss, representations of which may be found in both postmodernism and the surreal, or toward social being and authentic voice.

The modernist poetics of identity are concerned with 'difference

from,' with the intertextual ride against fixed representations of the
individual, and with dislocations of those representations. The poetic
requires an agreement about literary, cultural and historical
conventions—linguistic, stylistic, logical and topical—toward which
the activities of allusion, fragmentation and so on, move. However,
the problem with this agreement is that it may enclose the writer
within tradition and convention; isolate the writer from the social and
communal which continually reworks and renegotiates reality. This
may end in the continual deferrals of postmodernism, found for
example in the writing of George Bowering in the late 70s, which
render the construction of self as necessarily inauthentic, always
hegemonic and compromised, never conflictually resistant or
potentially changing. Many Canadian writers in the post WWII period
have been dissatisfied with the apparent agreements of modernism.
While some have evaded it in the ahistorical postmodern, others have
attempted to collapse it into the surreal. Surrealism constructs the self
as heroic individual, treading dangerously along the rim of chaos in
order to convey significance onto self. Constructing and meeting that
terror can be therapeutic, but the satisfaction of private need for terror
is a privileged activity that has little effect on poverty or racism.

The transposition of modernist poetics by romanticism into
surrealism has a quite different activity to that of the postmodern. The
process of romantic symbol is to engulf an event or person within a
representation, so that the necessary inadequacy evident from the
clash between symbol and actuality becomes the ground for
communication: a negative capability.[12] The romanticization of
modernist poetics consists of making a metaphor of its dislocation of
tradition, extending the symbol of dislocation surrealistically to its
limits so that it breaks down. The importance of the surrealist
extension of symbol is that just before it breaks down it is at its most
disturbing. The clash is no longer the point; the representation of a
necessarily inadequate ground for communication is no longer the
activity. Instead it is the perception of chaos lying beyond the
symbolic that becomes the central concern; alternating a deep trust in
the control exercised by representation and a deep fear in the chaos
lying beyond it. Here we can walk along Ondaatje's edge between
dream and nightmare or to the early boundaries and white places of
Atwood's page.

What is significant for the purposes of this discussion is that Harris,

Brand and Philip, in common with some few other Canadian writers, move to alternative strategies for writing which are neither surreal nor postmodern. This search, which embraces the positive gifts of so-called chaos, otherwise called the world outwith dominant cultural representation, and which embraces the social resistance of authentic voice, is of immediate importance to the broad literary community working with the English language. It raises wide-ranging questions about the limits of ideology, about the possibility of re-gathering history, and for writers, about the extent to which their written medium and its language can be trusted to re-present the people and communities who have been written out.

Aware that the modernist tradition is inadequate because it falsely assumes too much common ground and initiates complicity into structures people may wish to oppose, change or refuse, what do you do? Do you give people fables because in practice you cannot give them another completely different language, but you can provide the incidents and events to remind them that literature and its language only speaks for a few? Do you arrest language so that the reader may release its significance, as with many recent reconstructions of modernist imagism or the phonetic deconstructions of bpNichol? Do you hold the ideological structures and metaphors so tightly by the throat that they speak with a strange voice, such as the attempts to strangle and twist cultural icons like the 'cowboy as hero' in Kroetsch's writing, or the drifting landscapes and maps in Bowering's later work? Do you turn to your own myths/ghosts/memories but make sure that their complicity in the ideological is foregrounded, for example in the potentially sentimental return to personal folklore in the work of Laurence or Munro, that must be consciously artificial-ized in order to clarify a present, contradictory, position toward it? Do you turn to the most elusive words, the ones that you use to friends and do not think about, not the cliché but the earth of your language: no longer only playing with the fictive in the powerful/powerless dichotomies of convention but with the syntax and structure of these few words that reach out into the needs of your community of friends, finding in their bodies spaces and openings that they had not realized were there? The literary developments of each of these three writers are enabled by a growing awareness of the possibilities for communi-cation generated by talk with and to their own community, particu-larly other women.

*

Claire Harris is one of the most elegantly precise writers out of the modernist tradition. Her work indicates an immensely skilful and rigorous practitioner who also has something to say: an unusual combination for modernism that makes her a particulary significant link in the wider development of the tradition. But the published work indicates from the start the tensions of working within that poetic. Of the many women's experiences recounted throughout the poems in *Fables from the Women's Quarters* (1984),[13] perhaps the phrases "flesh is not civilized flesh is not haiku" (30) from "Blood Feud" re- mind the reader most of the intensely intellectual and language-centred tradition of the writing. However, in these poems, curiously, it is the brain and the intellect recalling "the bittersweet pervasive ache of the women's quarters" (16), that fail to "innoculate" her against the demands of men. Through *Translation into Fiction* (1984) to *Travelling to find a Remedy* (1986),[14] the demands of men remain uppermost but the intellectual poetic tradition gradually becomes itself one of those masculine demands.

The poems of *Translation into Fiction* present fiction both as a mask bereft of power and as the language of those in power. This double edged activity of all ideological constructions becomes the informing movement of many different verbal translations into fiction: white/black, man/woman, youth/age. People use words to bring reality within their control. Here the control is that of romantic symbol, explosive with the tension of inadequacy, presented as the fertile control of the gardener—her father—who is at the same time terrified by the anarchy of imagination. But for Harris "translations" are also specific to the printed medium for language that she uses. In "By the senses sent forth ..." the writer chooses to present a three-strand narrative emerging in typographic form as fragmented prose on the left opening, and two strips of poetry on the right. The right opening is composed of modernist verse, often mythically allusive, in italics and ranged to the left margin; it is opposed by shorter, metaphorical, more intense rhythms of verse, in roman type and ranged right. The three strands could each stand alone, but as presented they intercomment upon one another as if the writer is admitting that she cannot speak adequately and is giving us three stylistically different versions.

The typographically fragmented technique is common to much of Harris' work: from verse with footnotes, to haiku with narrative, imagistic with descriptive, and in *The Conception of Winter* (1988)[15] postcard fragment with commentary. It is as if the modernist and the romantic landscape describer are standing off and commenting upon one another, not meeting yet self-validating. The fragment, acknowledgely partial, presents those things we cannot make sense of and/or cannot articulate because they are either too alien or, perhaps, too familiar. In contrast, the story given whole represents the things we can make sense of. It provides simultaneously the ground that makes the fragmentary bearable and the ground to be fragmented. As the poetry develops, this technique becomes both less discursive and less sparse, as the poet increasingly integrates the images and trusts the audience.

Harris moves from a highly individualistic concept of the writer/ fictionalizer as especially gifted to be "stricken by and seeking" reality in *Translation into Fiction*, to a re-drawing of the romantic poet in terms of moral responsibility in *Travelling to Find a Remedy*, to a rather less heroic and far more thought-provoking set of questions about the helpfulness of the writer in expressing experience as against the articulations of those who do not use words, in *The Conception of Winter. Travelling to Find a Remedy* is a key work whose opening and closing poems examine the process of writing, and enclose more fables/reports from Black history. "Every Moment a Window," which opens the collection, asks how we, or the poet for us, open the window on reality. Both the images working within smaller parts of the poem and the overarching allegory critically rework the cruel and persistent romantic metaphor of woman as source of poetry and man as articulator or poet. Here the speaker/poet is presented as two people mediated by the shifting gender of pronouns. At first significantly male, the speaker enters and places her dried heart in the sink of her life/memory from which she surfaces as youth and poet, foreign to and stumbling among words that acquire coherence from the web of our response. A poem is an accident, a seeding, a machine: it is "bits and pieces/never the whole story" (11), memories, ghosts of what the writer earlier, in *Translation Into Fiction*, called the "aborted / dreams" (71) which "I slipped / casually into not being," and myths. Myths become the "small control" in the ordered chaos of a world where we have no "natural claim / to anything save / death" (14). The speaker is a Prometheus, stealing words like fire from the gods both for the survival of human beings and as an anchor in our separateness from each other. At seven she is horrifed by the immediacy of the real that myth permits her to feel; but by eight the horror has failed, the myths have passed into recognizable order, the window is closed. And at the end, there sits the initial speaker, dressed in white and waiting for her, reading *God and Physics*. It is as if the white, intellectual, male tradition of verse and poetic gives her a window on reality at the cost of dessicating her ability, her capacity for experience.

The concluding long poem "Peter Petrus" is a mystery story where things are both revealed and hidden, while the writer plays phonetically and syntactically around the dual petrifying images of horror and stone. Peter Petrus is the Poet, the Peculator of other people's myths, the peripatetic tourist (postcards) who is petrified from his perilous/parlous/ period into stone. His language is signified by the typographically capitalized or doubled "P" or "Pp" as in "escaPes"; it is a visual Protrusion or eruPtion that alerts the reader to the arbitrary structure of words that is yet responsible for signification. It alerts us to the difficulty of meaning as we read these bizarre eruptions of the arbitrary/chaotic letter into the conventional structures of our language. In contrast to Peter Petrus, the language of the Witness is standard.

The immediate mystery of the poem is why Petrus throws himself out of the window, but the effective mystery is what lured the Witness into his room to witness his jump and what effect it has on her. Terrorized by the immediacy of the real, Peter Poet has gradually hardened into Peter Petrus. The dried onion skins of his petrified flesh rasp, "thin and insidious" reminders of Coleridge's imaginative "I AM". As if the stone has consumed nearly all the flesh and he needs an heir, Petrus "oPens door to the corridor" to seduce in the Witness for "she has Possibilities pPetrus has/heard the sand shifting in her the layers forming/being stone sober pPeter p pPetrus wills that this/be given to her" (67). And as he leaps from the window, a window on reality is opened for her, and she then tentatively engages with the poetic discourse of Petrus, the double "Pp" intruding into her language from the moment she sees him jump.

The poem presents a deeply ambiguous image of the poet indicating reality only at the cost of consuming her/himself, at the same time as making a necessary self-sacrifice into stone. The ambiguity is redoubled by the conflation of an overtly Christian metaphor of self-sacrifice onto a version of the Medusa myth which warns the powerful about the dangers of ignoring the disempowered: as if the human turns to stone because the emulation of god-like activity necessarily destroys them. Further, the entire allegory is called into question by the vocabulary of violence and the implicit entrappment of the Witness: as if the Witness is being coerced into the position of victim to perpetrate systems of poetic power. And that is where the poem, on the penultimate leaf of the book, ends. The Witness is the next Petrus, caught into the traditions of poetic structure and language technique that will only permit her to engage with reality through channels that will destroy her. The book itself ends with a haiku.

Despite the continual reference to women and to women's experience, the touchstones for event in the early books are often male. In the poems of cultural inquiry enfolded by the studies of poetic at the start and the end of *Travelling to Find a Remedy*, two of the more immediately demanding focus on men as husband and father. The title poem presents Africa as a man who wants the speaker to have his children. But there is too much of the Middle Passage to slavery and out, in the history of the (presumably Caribbean-Canadian) woman, to allow such an easy "grip on my hand." She says that she dreams "in another tongue" (26). Further on, in "Black Sisyphus" the writer reaches out to her childhood and her father. It is a poem concerned with post-colonial contradictions, framed between the Church institutions and her father's own beliefs. Within that tension he too grasps her hand and wants to "refashion" it, with all the complicated duality of caring and power that parents exercise. But in *The Conception of Winter* Harris turns more and more to the community of women. At the same time she increasingly turns away from the concept of the poet as mask, as hero, as sacrificial victim, to the poet as sharer: In a sense she speaks less of her own hand being taken and how she rejects that "ownership" or possession, and instead she offers her hands to the reader, still very tentatively and with enormous caution, for she has every right to fear us.

The open invitation into *The Conception of Winter* offers the reader a different kind of poetry where the writer speaks less of the significance of words and trusts more to their activity. The long opening poem "Towards the color of summer" begins with a study of three women as tourists, one of whom is the speaker, going to Barcelona. Tourism, as we all know, is at its best in the Travel Agent's Office where the wish-fulfilments still seem entirely possible. Harris

describes the moment of escape in the airplane, saying "I become blue
meaning by this a measure/of release what I imagine the soul feels//as
it escapes drained bone or pained/medieval angels suspect who long
to escape//strictures ..." (3), and later "too far above ground for traps
in such blue/I float suspended disguised in my favorite self" (3).
Tourism is the world of licensed anarchy which allows us to permit
ourselves to be other people, to transgress our personal codes. We
travel to places which have different social codes of behaviour, both
frightening and passionate, a world of liminality, of adolescence,
where the strategies for maintaining survival can be self-enclosing or
self-destructive, curiously mimicking the activity of colonial power.
The tourist may feel threatened but also knows that in the normal run
of events money, passports and embassies can intervene—which is
why we feel so acutely shocked when diplomatic protection for the
tourist fails. At the same time the tourist is profoundly involved in
exploitation.

These shadowy social implications permeate the personal
transgressions of the three women who refract and disperse their
images of self through this alien culture, stumbling upon the more
deeply embedded structures of identity that resist new angles of
vision. The poetic begins by setting off the descriptive verse against
the "postcards."The latter seem at first to yield the flat banality and
ennervation of reality that the tourist postcard imposes; but against the
description, which re-does or repeats the images and lends a verbal
density to their sparseness, the postcard verse becomes compressed
haiku that sever their content from causality. The haiku provide the
image yet the response/significance becomes the reader's; they
provide an arrested reality that flowers only if the reader cradles the
seed, the bits, relates the fables. Just so, the women can at first detach
themselves from the visited world, watching its severed surrealist
concepts or abstractions from behind their foreigness, but gradually
become implicated into it. The speaker says "But this is not why we
came here / three week exiles we have chosen to lose // our place in
the world three women searching / a ledge for freedom excitement for
self // (and I am here where the rivers grief / and blood rose think of
it //"(19). The speaker opens up for herself image by image, the
connections of Spain with Africa and with slavery, she establishes the
substratum of fear and pain and rape that this city, that first sent out
Columbus to the New World thereby initiating the slave trade, has for

her underlying the sun and flowers and people.

Then, as with much of Harris' work, death intervenes. Death walks relatively lightfootedly but pervasively throughout her writing and is one helpful guide to the direction of her poetic. The early poetry gives us accounts of war, of private and public cruelty, that are particularly atrocious in the controlled violations that the verse permits. Much of this transmutes into a more private and intellectual study about a sudden visibility of death in "Coming to Terms ...", from *Travelling to Find a Remedy*. The verse is phrased in a tense counterpoint between just-voiced questions answered by jagged, almost cacophonous essays into articulation.

The Conception of Winter moves into far more personal response. But whereas the earlier writer might have been left vulnerable and the reader embarrassed, this poetry trusts to the community of the writer's audience. When, in "Towards the Color of Summer," the three women on holiday are arrested by news of the death of a friend back home, the speaker places herself both in the first person singular and in the plural. Echoing her earlier release into the sky at the start of her trip, she now asks in presence of death "how to save ourselves who no longer believe//in winged souls caged in flesh nor yet//believe in shared rounds in organic growth/and becoming" (25). Together, the three women "Dissipate Grief" by buying things, by consuming their emptiness in acts of monetary expenditure that only reinforce that emptiness. Here the writer allows the emptiness to grow in between a ranged-left, clipped, fast-paced short-line narrative poem, and a ranged-right, end-stopped, series of images of death, that begins:

We hustle in and out of shops	*and this is what happens*
bustling to buy	*when you die*
everything	*first you uncoil*
we say "it	*the guts of pain*
is cheaper here"	*where it leads*
we point at things	*you gather yourself*
	(26)

After this story about the impossibility of articulation, comes the title poem "Conception of Winter" during which the three women, again together, "become sad" for "here in this place in our determined joy/we find ourselves fearing the birth of winter" (28).

What the poet has been keeping at arms' length is of course her own death, and in the concluding long poem "Against the Blade," an elegy for her mother, she seems to find again in the community of women, that is this time the difficult identity with and difference from her mother, words that can be shared with her reader. At one moment in this careful but moving study of a parent's death, the speaker says, "now sometimes / i came upon her suddenly / and in shadow / now perhaps my grave's clarity / resolving itself / i understand / what passion forged the cool smile" (51). The shadow of the mother, at the same time in life obscures the speaker's grave yet clarifies it in death; it also obscures both the mother and child in life and helps to resolve, find resolution and focus for, each in death. Within the context of this poetry whose cool smile is also forged by passion, the reader can watch the poet describe her mother who "lived language" (44), and watch her faced with the "victorian silence" of the mother. The poet brings words back from abstraction and isolation into lists of events, descriptions of the mundane, accounts of personal history, trivial actions weighted with too much significance like flowers brought to the hospital that are "stricken like this verse/extinguishing what is left of her/that is wild and full of grace" (58). The movement of the earlier long poem about the three women travellers is rather more generous in its search for common grounds—but then it can afford to be. With this concluding long poem, the risks the poet takes with the death of a mother are far greater. But overall, in *The Conception of Winter* the poet offers with immense control not the attack of precisely transgressed tradition, but a tentative movement into a common language for articulation that arises from the women's community about which she is writing.

Harris talks in a 1986 *Fireweed* issue of "the way language is used to shelter the deformed morality of power".[16] She is constantly aware both of the large and sometimes deadly structures of that power, and the immediate and powerful realities of everyday life. Given that for Harris the problems of marginalization are the defining conditions and content of any poetry or any writing, her assertion that one cannot solve the deformations of power with a poetry of revenge, not even revenge upon the traditions of language and the poet, becomes a statement of her political position. Recently it is as if the immediate realities have become pressing, and her poetry must look toward community and authentic voice rather than the opposing dualities of tradition and an essential individual.

A parallel but different response emerges from the work of Dionne Brand, as she too works away from a tensely executed modernist poetic toward an alternative voice. Politically the most assertive of the three writers discussed here, Brand is poetically the most traditional. The poetic of *Primitive Offensive* (1982),[17] a history of racism in violently ambivalent Poundian cantos, torsions modernist verse in on itself. The fragmented modernist image or allusion works by being able to refer to an understood continuum, a shared history or literary tradition. Unlike Harris who initially deals with this structural and epistemological need by continually providing parallel discourses, Brand's early poetry[18] chooses not to address the problem that much of her potential audience, defined by the use of a modernist poetic, will be unaware of the particular history of oppression, slavery and colonialization to which she refers. By this, I do not mean simply to suggest that readers do not know the facts about these events, but that the average white, western-educated, middle-class reader does not have a literary or linguistic or cultural or folkloric tradition that could foreground their repressive elements/referents. For example, the speaker of Harris' "Towards the Color of Summer" finds protruding into her Barcelona holiday rivers of grief and blood. When the associated image of "men with net and chain//and coffle" who then "slaved and died" emerges into the high tourist bureau landscape, it provides a startling and disruptive link with the slave trade and European neo-colonialization. Columbus for many is long the explorer and discoverer of school history, and only on prompted conscious awareness, an exploiter. However, having read Harris' poem, it becomes just that bit more difficult to eradicate the history of slavery, specifically the vocabulary of "net and chain and coffle," from the repository of allusions clustering around Spain. The history of slavery offered by western education is not the history offered here. One of the distinguishing features of the reworking of modernist poetics by these writers is that they have to both rewrite the history and the shared literary convention, and simultaneously allude to that rewriting as if it were traditionally received.

The sparse imagism of Brand's early poetic lacks such an allusive repository although the writer is aware of precisely this problem. Her use of modernist dislocation moves with a trust that such activity will find another more appropriate history. In the attempts to redress the undercoding of the reader with respect to this history the writing occasionally overcodes, labouring the detail into necessary overemphasis. But the series "Winter Epigrams" (1985)[19] and "Chronicles

of the Hostile Sun" (1984)[20] on the Grenada invasion, both respond to the
semiotic demands by opening up the poetic to conversational rhythm,
dialect and more personal accounts of everyday event. "Winter Epigrams"
is a long series that constructs its own narrative background as it proceeds.
An early epigram reads simply "they think it's pretty, / this falling of
leaves. / something is dying!" The sequence of familiar urban experiences
that follows allows the reader to contextualize "they" as white (wintry)
Toronto and to recognize the dry humour of the observation, while at
the same time retain the initial, rather sinister, ambiguity of the
isolated stanza.

   Chronicles of the Hostile Sun goes much further. Separated into
"Languages," "Sieges," and "Military Occupations" the sequence first
establishes a narrative and realistic vocabulary, then explicitly
problematizes the apparent directness of its description before it
proceeds to recount the events of the invasion of Grenada.
"Languages" leaves the reader in no doubt about the skill with which
this writer can employ the conventional literary devices; the voice is
familiar with racist ideology, with the colloquial and the cocktail
party, with song and with newspaper code. Yet, in "Sieges," under
siege by this language as if it is a man demanding sex, the writer tries
to negotiate a voice that is, if still bound up in convention, at least
direct. In "Anti-poetry" the speaker says that this poetry is for a
"crowd" and unlike other poets who "don't feel the crowd eating their
faces / I have to hustle poems between the dancers and the drummers"
(30).

   These first two sections, "Languages" and "Sieges," attempt the
double activity of establishing a ground for communication and a
distrust of that ground, while not dislocating the voice into incom-
prehension. In other words they attempt to establish a voice that can
be trusted to tell this newly gathered history, on a linguistic and
literary ground that must be kept at arm's length. "Military Occupations"
can then offer a series of commentaries on the effects that the invasion
has on the speaker and the local community that elide from the
recounting of immediate events to the necessity for speaking of those
events to the "waiting crowd." The fragmentation of convention
increases as the writer moves away from recounting the events and
toward recounting the recounting, for example in the section "four
hours on a bus ... " which is a relentless unpunctuated prose
monologue. But the voice never lets go of its commitment to telling

this history in a manner that both questions literary conventions while using them to reach as wide an audience as possible. The first stanza of the penultimate poem reads:

The varnished table
beside it, the shortwave radio
the foreign news ricochets off the white wall
behind. Spotted at dead mosquito intervals
I listen for what europe is doing. Voice of america is insipid
The BBC tells me when they will attack
disinformation about more killed / under the curfew.
We know that they are coming. (73)

There is a stasis achieved by the isolation of table, radio and wall at the end of the first lines, by the odd qualifying phrase "Spotted ... " that precedes "I listen," by the grammatical precision of "The BBC ...." Yet within this stasis there is the loud, "ricochet" of news, the implicitly violent killing of mosquitoes, and a vocabulary of war: attack, disinformation, killed, curfew. All of this detail of impending destruction is set against the stasis of "We": the "we" "know that they are coming," the "we" tensely waits. And the rest of the poem follows the sudden imbalance of action and counteraction that happens when the invasion brings the promised destruction and breaks the stasis.

The poetic of this stanza and those that follow inscribes the unusual detail remembered from moments of intense stress, through the immediacy of physical images and precisely controlled disruptions of grammar and syntax. At the same time, the memories are given an unmistakable broad referential backdrop of political and military event. The ambiguity of the final three lines to the opening stanza underlines the distrust we need to bring to language as it reconstructs history. Do they "know" the americans are coming as a fact separately from the radio report? Or do they know it because the BBC gives a time for attack? or is that time "disinformation"? or is it the recognition of something as "disinformation," for example false figures about those killed, that provides the knowledge that the Americans are coming? The multiple ambiguities from these three lines alone as personal memory narrates chronological event, is there to warn any attentive reader about the inadequacy of representation. However, the fact that invasion happens; the fear of Europe, America and the BBC as a "they" ranged against an isolated "we," and the presence of the personal in all this, is clear and immediate.

The collection of short stories *Sans Souci* written between 1984 and 1988[21] pursues the narrative impulse to conventional communication, and the early poetics begin to breathe more freely as the writer relaxes, albeit slightly, into prose. The stories present a mixture of voices or histories of the experiences of black women in the Carribean, and of those who have chosen to leave and go to Canada. The histories examine why they leave, looking at the structures and pressures of both societies, and why sometimes (rarely) the women return. These fables also look closely at the inhuman expectations of the people who employ the Black women, at the families they leave behind, the *other* children they care for instead, the abuse they receive, the fear they feel, their pride and the necessity/obstinacy of that pride. The writer makes her salient commentary on the cultures by taking epigrammatic density and extending a descriptive ground for it to build upon. The narrative structures are simple but the prose allows for an expansion of and anchoring in context. For example "Photograph" is a narrative excursion occasioned by looking at a faded photograph of her grandmother, which tersely put is saying that her grandmother acted as her mother for many years while her mother was "away" earning money, and that on her mother's return her grandmother shortly died. Phrased epigrammatically it is a story about the complications of familial love and power. The epigram-matic here is extended by a sequence of recountings, remembered incidents that emerge through analogical links. These inner stories or memories are not accumulative in the narrative sense; they do not lead to a conclusion about guilt or blame. Rather their procession accretes a verbal and literary density in the initial descriptions of the speaker's relationship with her grandmother, that is disturbed and contorted upon the return of the mother. The resulting responses of both speaker and reader are complicated, intentionally and purposively difficult to analyze.

Similar expansive remedies of epigrammatic density are made possible throughout *Sans Souci*. The story "I used to like the Dallas Cowboys" has a terse structure that runs like this: The speaker as a young girl used to like the Dallas Cowboys American football team, partly because football was *not* the local sport of cricket and partly because her in-depth knowledge of football proved her worth in a man's world. But, she is later in Grenada at the time of the invasion and she recognizes in the American war machine many of the elements of the American football team. The concentration, the end-game direction, the ruthless beauty of their occupation into the game, is transferred onto the precision of the military operation. The story then becomes a study in sport and war; it foregrounds the brief epigrammatic structure and contextualizes it, thereby re-grounding the potential for cliché in the contingencies of an immediate re-reading. The reader is encouraged to invert the parallels back onto the questions raised by cricket which is the slave master's game, played always at the ready for a riot, as well as onto the young girl's attempts to compete within a man's world. What happens is that the image begins to carry the larger ideological allusions along with it and the reader learns the social references.

These stories are skilfully executed essays in history, written to present the problems of marginalization as social and political, and as something that one must act on from the ground up. Their activity is underwritten by Brand's experience of grass-roots community work,[22] her writing on racism[23] and her studies at OISE.[24] Her work is firmly assertive with an anger that readers either immediately recognize or need to make a place for: the necessity of voicing the fears, reactions, rejections that are tied up in the Black experience of Canada's racism. Brand's militant assertiveness, if not her formality of style, is echoed in Nourbese Philip's work on racism and access. But in apparent contrast to Brand, Philip is an institutional fighter recognizing that the social and political roots of marginalization are something that in Canada may also be changed within the institutions of power themselves: witness her fights about racism with PEN[25] or with the Writer's Union or the ROM exhibition "Into the heart of Africa"[26]—or indeed her apparent despair over the controversy at the Women's Press (Toronto) that split the Press collective.[27] Philip says that she writes "To witness; to bear testimony and build a tradition: 'So that you may dance (my sister) / I will build a floor for you'."[28]

Philip's published literary writing begins not with the fragmentations of a rigorous modernist poetics, but with the Canadian reworking of that poetic into romantic metaphor and with the resultant surrealist stress on the imagery of estranged dream. An early work such as "Salmon Courage" depends thoroughly upon the full metaphor of the returning salmon: to leave and to return and to return only to die, but here somehow to be reborn. The image is not dislocated; the reading here needs to know and understand the reference to the

salmon's life cycle. Yet the biological metaphor is both stretched
against the tension of bureaucratic millstones that drag one to the
ocean and the physical magnetism of the lodestar pulling one back to
the river source, and is also extended within the strange terrain of the
"huddled hunchbacked hills" "humping the horizon." The image of the
salmon becomes surreal as it is extended past conventional literary
comprehension: The place to which one returns is never the same, it
will always have moved on; and so the person that one returns to be
is not/cannot be there. There can be no whole recuperation of the
natural landscape; and yet a trust in it offers the place for Salmon
courage, which is to swim against the tide, to die to be born into a
possibility of change. Increasingly since the mid-80s Philip has
combined this metaphorical stress with experimentation in syntax,
phonetics and sound, moving swiftly toward representations of dialect
versions of Caribbean English, and with manipulation of generic
conventions in both poetry and prose. Both developments, within
language and literature, can be read as attempts to build bridges to
new audiences.

    In *Harriet's Daughter* (1988),[29] Philip is brave enough to attempt
to address the experience of that most difficult of audiences, the
adolescent reader, within the context of the Black community in
Toronto. The book was apparently rejected by Canadian publishers
because it did not have enough interest for general readers, or as
Philip herself states elsewhere, because it had "black children" in it.[30]
Only published in Canada after Heinemann in Britain picked it up, it
is an example of the "access" bias besetting the Black writing
community, about which Philip has written much.[31] It is also an
unconventional piece of writing. The narrating prose from the
adolescent character Margaret/Harriet is curiously flat and holds no
hostages to fortune, as if the writer is afraid to patronize or
unconsciously reinforce through stereotypical representations the
structures of power being criticized. In contrast, direct speech is
rendered in a representation of dialects which is vibrant and active
with conversational rhythm. The contrast has a profound effect on
how the text is reconstructed in reading: the rather distanced
witholding position of the main narrative is interrupted by islands of
stories, conversational duets, that place a firm emphasis on the
primacy of spoken communication.

    Within the observed adult community the experience of the

adolescent girl is rendered as hesitant and externalized; yet the moment she speaks, or is involved into direct communication with her friends or other adults, the character flourishes as obstinate, clever and thoughtful. The technique is strategically very sensible but it does have disadvantages: the long sequence of description concerning the "underground railway" game played by the children, which is presumably given so much narrative space partly in order to focus on the personal worlds necessary to young people particularly so they can build a personal history, is distanced with coolness; and accounts of other events also suffer. Yet the technique comes into its own when it gives a tense and half-understanding purchase to the problems of gender and family in the adult community that accumulate toward the end of the novel. The writing stalks a difficult line always in danger of falling out of kilter with convention, and some of the questions raised by the book are very much to do with the need for genre experimentation and the danger of providing something too different that the audience rejects. However, the book is an attempt to build a bridge to a new audience in a manner quite different from modernist and post-modernist strategies. As Philip addresses a Black, female readership, specifically dealing with adolescence to arguably set a new lens on the adult community, she is also addressing the problems of another generation. While it is necessary to remember the history of Black slavery, of Black immigration from the United States, and of the civil rights movement, for the daughters of those events the questions are also those of race and culture, class and gender.

Philip's attempts at bridge-building are immensely generous. The sequence "...And Over Every Land and Sea"[32] proffers an arching image of a parent (mother)-child connection, how to find without binding, how to leave, how to cope with the adoption of other families and not lose one's own or oneself. More broadly the image narrates a story of displacement from one culture, here the Carribbean, to another: "Stateside, England, Canada" (107); and the poems move from a dialect representation into modern standard English repre-sented through a more Latinate, multi-syllabic vocabulary as the displacement proceeds. The early sections of the sequence use dialect to play with cultural ambiguity, with the double meanings that words acquire in the mouths and hands of people from different societies. For example, the word "with" is rendered as "wit" allowing for extensive interplay along syntactical and semantic lines: The

conclusion to the first poem "grief gone mad wit crazy," can be read
at least as "grief / gone mad wit crazy," "grief gone / mad witcrazy,"
"grief gone mad / wit crazy," and "grief gone / mad wit / crazy." Much
similar subtle doubling and folding of language occurs in these
opening dialect sections.

The central metamorphosing poem is "Dream-skins," which the
writer specifically sub-titles "in two languages" as she leads her reader
from one culture to another. The poetry is opening a door onto white,
Western language and tradition for culturally displaced readers, but
at the same time it opens that door for white Western-educated readers
as well. "Dream-skins" alternates between dialect and oral englishes,
at first focusing the dialect stanzas on "she" and standard stanzas on
the connection between the speaker and "she", until the final duet
within the poem of "Blood-cloth" and "Blood-cloths" which is the only
dream for which the writer provides expression in both languages.
The poem raises profound questions of the structuring and acquisiton
of cultural identity. At first "she" rises from the sea with emerald skin,
akin to the lime-green skin Philip gives her Black women elsewhere,
yet simultaneously both "she" and the speaker are "white" and swollen
with womanhood, "with child." After birth, after the recognition of
both traditions, the speaker is locked into a struggle between the white
breast and the black, but when a hybrid plant seems to sprout from her
throat it is taken out by "she," released into "split of throat / silence."

The speaker is left with, first, the dialect "Blood-cloth" in which her
woman's "blood-rush" at least can be called upon; yet even here "wit
some clean white rag/she band up mi mouth/nice nice" (109). Then,
"Blood-cloths" in the different language sends the reader out into harsh-
ly distinct images of "sand/silence/desert/sun." Here the "blood
of rush" writes hieroglyphs, in allusive reference to the Egyptian
sources for Judaeo-Christian culture and for written language and
poetics as it has become in the Western world. Here the inscriptions
again are bound up, this time as wounds, and carried by a "broad back
/ hers." This binding, like that of the dialect "blood-cloth," is not just
to constrain and keep in but to provide some security: it is about baby
binding, finding voice as the mother's voice teaches the child, but here
there are two voices. The painful transition into white language is not
however simply loss. Philip is trying to build bridges, trusting in an
understanding of the ideologies. The speaker in the sequence goes on
to attempt "sightings" of other cultures, other mothers, with a feeling

that there was once an image that gave "she" a name, perhaps a smell. She is left at the end in "Adoption Bureau Revisited" with the constant revisiting of the possibilities of birth, and of living.

The study of displaced culture and social construction which "...And over Every Land and Sea" presents in terms of a search for the mother, has a companion-piece in "Cyclamen Girl"[33] which foregrounds not language which carries the doubled tradition, but ideology which tries to shape and possess. "Cyclamen Girl" presents a far more formal and traditionally accessible poetic about conversion, communion and puberty onset: being reborn into the institution of the Christian church, at the same time as into a man's world, into a white world, and often also into womanhood. The poem offers a study of the way that womanhood can work against the institutions of a white world, how it can be both a preservation from and an opening up into differences from the white world. Here the bridge the writer builds for her sisters crosses all races.

Philip's emphasis on metaphor, her evident trust in the broad back of language, goes hand in hand with her generous invitation to a wide range of readers. For all the immense gifts in such writing, there is a potential drawback in the apparent wholeness it presents. This poetry trusts to broad cultural and social references of parenthood, authority, childhood, gender and other metaphors, but in this openness the issue of race and Philip's black heritage may be passed over. For all the abrupt elisions and under/over codings in Brand's poetry, through their embarrassment the reader is made aware of her own ignorance, of incomprehensible space. Philip's poems extend in significance even further when re-read against the experience of reading the more socially and politically explicit groundings of metaphor and allusion, for example in that of split and displaced families, in work by other Black women writers such as Brand or Makeda Silvera.

Philip's more recent work makes a significant shift in both poetics and narrative prose. It engages with quite different aspects of extending the bridge between languages and between language and the world. An extraordinarily powerful piece of prose, "Burn Sugar" (1988),[34] which extends her bridge even further, is concerned again with metamorphosis and transformation but is here explicitly located in particular experience. The voice of the narrator is an immensely sophisticated textual weave, that interlaces present, past, historical present, dialect present, oral performance present and narrative present. The movement of child to woman, woman to mother, mother to daughter, black to white to black, is set against the metaphor of following or reconstructing a recipe from memory. The woman speaker in Toronto, displaced from her Caribbean home, is trying to make a cake traditionally made each year by her mother and, since she emigrated, sent to her by post. The cake invariably arrives slightly mouldy, and this story is about her attempt to make it for herself. At the pragmatic level there is the range of transformation as sugar amalgamates with butter, eggs reluctantly mix in, sugar—that ambivalent commodity emerging from slave ownership—delicately and precisely burns from white to black to provide the essential bitterness of this cake. And all is beaten, beaten, laboriously, back-breakingly, into one.

In another mode, the narrative is about a central cultural experience: the transformation from oral culture to written through memory, in the focusing image of recipe recreation. Recipes are traditions, cultures, historically grounded in food pathways and economics. They are also often familial, handed down patterns for performance that are never uniquely repeated but central to survival: as so often, the culinary is a discretely exact analogy for social and cultural construction. The child's voice moves from the "Mother" of her memory to "Mammy" as the mother we make for ourselves as we learn the necessities in our history as well as the changes, as we learn to live with and speak to a community. The process of recipe reconstruction provides a sense of how the child learns both language and survival from the mother: by example, by wanting to do so, by being included, by training, by being able to repeat, by being able to produce and construct for itself in another world, with different contingencies. Each of the transformations is unpredictable, each carries its own resistance and describes the difficulty of bringing different cultures with different meanings, up against one another. One of the differences is that between the work of the Mother and the work of the speaker/daughter: The speaker's work is to render into language, even into written language, to find significance, not to avoid but to take risks with communication and culture. This particular work is necessary because for the displaced, gaining access to the primary means of communication is one of the most important ways of making a community. Philip, from her years of hard-won access, here extends both the literary and linguistic features of traditional prose out into techniques, strategies and genres drawn from the topic of a women's audience and community.

Even less trusting of ideologies and intimately part of Philip's approach is the poetry in *She Tries Her Tongue, Her Silence Softly Breaks*. Here the writer faces head on the problem of speaking/writing in a language "not only experientially foreign, but also etymologically hostile and expressive of the non-being of the African,"[35] and the problem of making a language to express the personal memory and authentic experience that build history. In "Universal Grammar" Philip takes on the entire linguistic debate about natural language and turns it into an anguish about speaking within pre-defined language. The operative irony here, as the writing presents dictionary definition setting itself against practical language eliding into poetry, is that the 'natural' ease of language arising from its potentially 'innate' quality is simultaneous with the ambiguous 'incorrectness' of the necessary transposition of these 'innate' grammars into another language. You can indeed transpose noun and verb, speak 'incorrectly'; but you are still wrapped up in verbs and nouns. The writer transforms the acres of dry disputation surrounding this debate into the tensions of the body that initiates a series of tense repetitions that attempt to dismember language while "the smallest cell remembers" (67). The sense of 'always already' being defined has led many into the sliding signifiers of post-modernism. Philip is led to "Mother's Recipes on How to Make a Language Yours or How Not to get Raped": that if the word "does not nourish," "Spit it out/Start again" (67).

The way that words and topics accrete historical meaning through body memory is pursued in "The Question of Language is the Answer to Power" as a direct proposal of a stance different from the modernist directive to "Make it New" that is left "floundering in the old" (71). In a rhetorical debate that verges on the epideictic, Philip fits the question around the history of Black slavery and how an understanding of that slavery can be re-made as a history relevant to contemporary race relations. The underlying logic is that when the empire colonized it lost the language of the "other," and the "other" were deprived of their language. This of course is the starting point of much postcolonial theory of discourse. But rather than become lost in multiplicitous images of self, Philip structures the next steps in terms of the physicality of language. Answers are not provided, but questions (helpful and not) and commentary are offered: "Facts" may claim that "words collect emotional and physical responses" (72) yet

you may also ask "Do words collect historical responses" (74) and
"how." *If* "Anxiety to convey meaning often results in over emphasis
and emphasis as a way of conveying meaning means that you are
unconsciously holding on to meaning and limiting it" (72) (sin for the
postmodern), *then* "By holding on to the meaning of life, did the
slaves unconsciously limit it—or merely the word?" (74). These are
tough and necessary social and political questions that do not often get
asked in literary circles. They replicate in intellectual discourse the
tensions of speaking to a crowd described by Brand: how to trust
language while keeping it at arms' length.

The final, title poem, "She Tries Her Tongue; Her Silence Softly
Breaks," fuses questions of language, ideology and history by taking
up the comments Philip makes in her introductory essay, "The
Absence of Writing or How I Almost Became a Spy," that "The only
way the African artist could be in this world, that is the New World
was to give voice to this split i-image of voice silence. Ways to
transcend that contradiction had to and still have to be developed, for
that silence continues to shroud the experience, the image and so the
word" (16). The writer suggests that "each word creates a centre / circum-
scribed by memory ... and history / waits at rest always // still at the
centre" (96). Language and the body of each individual are the place
where words and memory meet and can re-member the verbal. "That
body should speak/when silence is ..." (98) is of utmost importance to
those people whose memory/history, whose control through language
has been effaced or obscured not only because of the resulting
disempowerment within the dominant society, but because the ability
to build an immediate community is taken away.

*

If there is an attempt to break the silence, to write another self, where
is that self found? This is of course one of the central questions of
recent discussions on race, literature and language, not the least
because self-definitions can so often hold the beginnings of further
racism. Self can be the contradictory self-identifying modernist
identity that ends in existential nothingness. It can be the continually
compromised image that emerges from self as 'difference': difference
from, difference within, difference deferred, difference as chaos. For
the disempowered, the effaced/defaced, an important place to build
self is in community and specific social movement. Sometimes the
definitions can move out and act more broadly in social policy, begin

to affect the larger social and political structures. At the moment, within the literature and language of English, one of the most effective strategies for this building of story and movement out into social recognition is conventional realism. However, just because of its social acceptability realism easily becomes reductive; just so, social policy can swiftly become anachronistic and authentic voice quickly turn into stereotype. In order to understand and control these casual slippages the detailed procedures of language need to be scrutinized and thrown forward to the reader. What each of these writers does is both locate and build a common ground on which to write and read, and simultaneously encourage the words and the reader to make commentaries on those grounds.

As Claire Harris states "The problem is one of audience. We all know *for whom* we write; the ambivalence, and it is a dangerous one, lies in *to whom* we write."[36] Each of these writers is concerned with writing for a community that needs their words. Having access, their work can be seen as a series of attempts to locate and learn from that community, which in turn learns by responding and constructing itself as a community in that shared response. Perhaps that recognition will allow, or encourage, both the community and the society within which it operates to proceed with coping with the fact of racism.

CHAPTER FOUR

Postcards of Canadian Culture

Current Account

I have taught poetry and writings of George Bowering and Frank Davey and others from the TISH group,[1] in Britain since the mid-70s. From here, what has been compelling to watch is the way in which the initial attractions of the fear of referentiality in language became informed by the complications of a parallel fear of political referentiality. The two have pushed at each other and in the process established various agendas for literary criticism, theory and politics. A fear of the referential and a fear of politics are two aspects relevant to a definition of postmodernism. Postmodernism provides a basis for the validation of late-twentieth century western capitalism with its so-called service society. At the same time it provides a basis for a critique of the modernism that underwrites that society. The curious doubleness of interest in the apolitical and the political leaves the works of these writers open to readings that engage with a variety of strategies for theorizing about/dealing with current contradictions in many western societies. More directly put, Canada is externally often constructed as an apolitical, apathetic, populist country, and this is frequently associated both positively and negatively in its literature with the strategies and techniques of postmodernism. What I'd like to explore is whether this is a helpful reconstruction and how the work of these writers relates to it.

As many commentators have by now pointed out, a postmodernism that turns on the habitual image restricts itself to surfaces that appear to be ontologically free-floating and it invents games. This of course can appear to be a kind of mindless fun that gets people into trouble because it does not appear to question the way in which the design is itself constructed. I emphasise 'appear' because it seems to me that within a local and specific community this fun and games can, initially at least, have a radically unsettling action. But in order to engage with that action people do have to recognize the significance

of the chosen image and context; and Canadian critics, particularly
Linda Hutcheon, have frequently commented on and theorized from
this position. Hutcheon notes that postmodern art "is paradoxically
made the means to a new engagement with the social and historical
world."[2] Without context postmodernist strategies create a patina of
mindless pluralism. There may not be an essential ontological origin,
but there is an originating procedure or rhetoric, and it is with this
activity and its validation that postmodernism can be engaged.

To talk about postmodern strategies, this discussion will start with
realism. As suggested in chapter one, realism is a canonical strategy
that is implicated in ideological structure but nevertheless critical of
it. Its devices are inextricably dependent upon techniques made
available by way of print technology. They include the construction
of culturally appropriate verisimilitude with a focus on written
representation of the visual, the establishing of enough common
ground with the audience to convince them of immediate parallels
with its own life, and the claim that the re-presented world is
complete. The devices construct a self-sufficient world that can be re-
read and will remain stable, that the audience accepts as 'realistic' at
the same time as it tacitly agrees not to infringe or shatter it with
examples/knowledge from the actual world.

Through these strategies, realism offers one side of the Janus-face
of the rhetorical stance of fantasy, which uses exactly the same
constructions and differs only in that the audience accepts the self-
sufficient world as plausible/possible rather than 'realistic': true-to-
their experiences. In some ways, realism is the fantasy of the
corporate public audience. But fantasy is more important to those
individuals who need to satisfy their desire for a separate private
space: the medium of the book allows for groups of isolated
individuals to share, separately, alternative private worlds. The
construction of an overt or hidden public audience is necessary to the
working of either realism or fantasy. Both have to be socially
immediate, yet both always retain the potential for merely being
reductive and banal. Just as authenticity can switch from the socially
immediate to the banal, realism and fantasy and other associated
genres become banal when they try to derive from and play toward the
private individual. You can anchor the socially immediate only when
you recognize that individuals are not just private.

To pick up another thread from chapter one: the structure of nation state ideology, which creates the possibility of the private individual, also creates an isolation that problematizes all social discourse. 'Realism' can be read as a set of devices that stabilizes an increasingly large and diverse audience, and fantasy as the reverse side of it that allows for the development of concurrent, stable, isolated worlds for groups within that audience. Both encourage the audience to communicate within the nation, and especially within one language. Both underwrite the need for a set of cultural common grounds. At the same time, the strategies also allow for a generic diversity that ranges from the novel to the scientific paper, from Gothic to the detective story. Indeed the generic flexibility, while dependent upon the printed medium, permitted a market explosion of published books. Historically, realism dominates the publishing expansion of english language books in the eighteenth century, thereby acquiring currency but also and increasingly, notions of representational adequacy. While realism is a set of strategies for conveying the socially immediate world, its historical concurrence with the development of nation state ideology that needs representational stability above all else, encourages both writers and readers to take the strategies as adequate to private experience, as banal.

   This process of descriptive theorizing is moving closer to a study of realism and fantasy as a way of producing commodities, which is unsurprising given that capitalism also emerges concurrent with the nation state. Despite the questionable axioms involved, particularly the concept of language as inadequate rather than necessarily limited that the following chapter will pursue, what I would like to do is refract the discussion through the specific terminology of fantasy in order to reach the postmodern. The structure of fantasy invents strategies to construct and maintain a sense of a private isolated world, and its primary problem is to suppress any infringement from the outside, from other places that might shatter its plausible completeness. And this suppression is carried out in different ways and to differing degrees. The dominating strategy of total repression of the outside world is the narcissistic gesture of fantasy that reifies the isolated world into commodity. Fantasy can also retain a sense of social immediacy by constructing an ambivalent hover, elsewhere called a neurosis, over the moment of isolation and repression, that foregrounds precisely what is lost in agreeing to suppression of the other world. However the defining movement of fantasy that infuses the postmodern is the psychotic displacement of the other into the fetish, which precisely replicates the two-way switch of the realism between constructive awareness of inadequacy, and banal reduction to commodity. Postmodernism can be taken as a fantasy stance through which, historically, elite small groups construct isolated worlds to satisfy control and power; and as this discussion will go on to suggest, contemporary popular culture can be taken as using postmodern strategies by which large groups construct isolated worlds to satisfy desire.

Postmodernism is a set of strategies that responds directly to nation state ideology. Like the ethos of ideology, it builds worlds which remain stable by becoming isolated and systematic, yet its impetus is to foreground the artificial conventions within realism for potential critique. It can move to both constructive and banal fetish. At the same time postmodernism has largely found its public audience in a small group of people educated for many years precisely in recognition of the cultural common grounds which are held up for critique. While it allows for the formation of limited communities within that public and produces a political pluralism, it leaves them subject to broader ideological and economic effects.

Postmodernist strategies are fragmenting/ary. From the outside they are perceived, as all new strategies are, as difficult to read and esoteric. From the inside they lead to challenge, they ask for engagement. All strategies begin work on a community level, with small groups of readers. They can become elitist if those people are in a position of power, in a position desired by others; or if those people gain power and become an object of desire (commodify themselves and achieve fame). You could say that as larger groups of readers learn how to read, the strategy loses elitism and becomes popular: a movement that has happened with much other new writing. But postmodernism as a political gesture sets out to control popular response, to maintain isolated groupings.

The maintenance of isolated and particularly small groupings has in the west conventionally been favoured on the basis that only within well-defined groups can you have an immediate address to the specific needs of the community, looking closely at the contingent, the material.[3] At the same time isolated groupings also permit the broader structure of current capitalism: defined markets maintained by the satisfaction of discrete desires.[4] The larger the group the greater the financial reward but the more difficult to maintain satisfaction. Postmodernism is not operating to find a new, broad consensus, but to satisfy smaller immediate needs. This is important: You can argue that postmodernism works positively because only in small isolated groups do fundamental challenges to the dominant ideology get a chance to define themselves and emerge. But you can also argue that it works toward the banal both because in small isolated groups there is continual self-justification and validation, never any change impinging on the outside world, and because the isolation radically separates each group from an other. This separation enervates any attempt at dislocation on the part of a single group by leaving it apparently superficial and extraneous to the practical needs of the broader society.

The problem with postmodernism is that because it is after the radical disjuncture from ideology, there is no way for it to claim a common radical disjuncture, nor is there any clear methodology for how it is to construct after it has deconstructed. In the meantime it is extending the sanctioned strategy of working within isolated worlds, a strategy which encourages the neurotic worlds of desire serviced by discrete technologies that typify the power structures operated via rationalism on behalf of humanism in late twentieth century capitalism. It is because of this radical complicity with the isolating and fragmenting structure from which the coherence of current technology and capitalism derives that those advocating postmodernist strategies need rather more urgently to define their stance.

Nation state ideology is no longer the only or the main site for power, nor is the private individual the main site for the construction of desire. To return to the work of Frank Davey and George Bowering which initiated this theorizing, the discussion will follow readings of their writing as exploration of and movement through the postmodern, first to strategies of the provisional and the intertextual which haul the potential for psychotic commodity back to a point of radical ambivalence, and then to suggestions of how to move on through postmodernism. The internal tensions of works by both writers are central to the political problem of postmodernism: In the dislocated and fragmented world that has emerged as a challenge to the dominant ideologies, what validates action? Postmodernism challenges ideology by dislocating realism's potential for control through isolation and satisfaction. It works as if realism were always banal, always directly referential. The initial anxiety, therefore, is with the political power of the referential. If much of Bowering's writing focuses on a fear of the referentiality of story, and leads him to sophisticated intertextual devices for commenting on the artificiality of story, Davey's writing indicates a fear of where the stories come from: the referentiality implicit in the process through which societies accept myth.

Davey: Appropriating common ground

Bowering constructed one Davey as a leading post-thematic critic in the early 80s, and more recently Davey has been modelled into a scourge of thematic criticism on the basis of Barbara Godard's authorization of his essay "Surviving the Paraphrase" (1976). What Davey suggests by the word "paraphrase" is an unreflexive thematics that takes cultural icons as givens. The article is specific enough to make a number of coherent readings about what Davey does not like, but we are left with the question of what he does want. Indeed much of his subsequent critical and editorial work has moved toward attempting definitions and strategies for alternative approaches that he perceives to be more valuable, and which provide points of departure for a commentary on postmodernism.

Davey's intellectual curiosity is recorded in detail in *TISH*, in the several series of *Open Letter*, and is anchored at moments by *From There to Here*, *Surviving the Paraphrase*, and *Reading Canadian Reading*. Godard contextualizes "Surviving the Paraphrase" in terms of the western tradition of popular theory,[5] and in providing a context for it builds a kaleidoscope of opportunities for literary critical discussion in general. Davey takes a rather specific line through the offerings, that is charted with some clarity in his own response to Godard in the title essay of *Reading Canadian Reading*, in which he positions himself as concerned with "interest" and "contradiction" while being wary of pluralism (3-7). Yet his concluding "Preface" underwrites provisionality, not position. The tenuous line between provisionality and pluralism is, in itself a thoroughly postmodern dilemma: pluralism being the commodification of small group response, and provisionality a way of insisting on its relativity or ambiguity.

"Surviving the Paraphrase" is not a particularly sophisticated piece of criticism, but it is one that in the early 70s brought widely used criteria to Canadian Literature. It is a seedbed for Davey's concerns, but what is interesting is that the essay needed to be written at all, let

alone that it should now be considered such a landmark. What the
work does attempt is to uncover the ground, expose not only the taken
for granted cultural icons but also the rooted desire of the critics for
such icons, for such complexes of metaphor that achieve cultural
stability because they underwrite ideological demands and concerns.
In the essay the proposed alternatives to the thematic and pragmatically sociological focus on "the form—style, structure, vocabulary,
literary form, syntax—of the writing" (7) and generate a variety of
criticisms: historical, analytical, generic, phenomenological and
archetypal. In *Reading Canadian Reading* the direction of the
alternatives is re-defined as semiotic.

What semiotic readings are concerned with is finding the story: Not
underwriting the story as ideology, but finding and analysing both it
and the processes of its acceptance. "Surviving the Paraphrase" lies on
the border between Davey's early approach to stories emerging
somehow unprocessed from the real to his later stance which presents
stories as a construction of societies, cultures and communities. While
the earlier concern was with the ways in which the writer could re-
present reality without being dishonestly referential, the later concern
is with understanding the terms of that dis/honesty.

What is common to both the earlier and later concerns is the fear of
referentiality and the power structures referentiality implies: that
words refer to objects, that symbols refer to fixed and definable
cultural manifestations such as guilt or emotion, and that human
beings can know and manipulate these connections with explicit rules
about referentiality. Such structures underwrite a validation of
mathematics, science and technology that has made possible the
growth of industrial capitalism.[6] The recognition of the inadequacies
of such claims is a central feature of western humanism, and for
various reasons primarily to do with the history of rhetoric, ever since
the Renaissance poetics has been one of the primary sites for
discussing the alternatives. These alternatives, however, have always
been complicit in nation state ideology, and have usually diverted
poetics into forms of heroism.

A contribution by Davey to an early issue of *Open Letter* indicates
the extent of complicity, but more significantly, the emerging need to
displace the assumption of a common cultural continuity. The writer
notes that what is needed is a "Jessie Weston," a bibliographer, a fact-
gatherer for Canada, so that Canadian writers can, like Eliot, write

through "things that bear reality" of their own world: things such as "place names" and "tales of shipwreck": their own stories. This "reality" of place is, however, in the service of "epic ... [which] has always been our final goal."[7] In the following issue, March 1966, Daphne Marlatt immediately responds by pointing out that the heroic is egoistical and uninteresting, "The single point is the place"; and Davey, who has not yet learned to change his mind—something he does with the regularity of grace in recent years—ties himself up in a series of knots in order to appear to defend himself by agreeing.[8]

Later that year he elaborates, again in the pages of *Open Letter*, tying a rather more complicated knot in the name of the phenomenal world. He says that poetry testifies to:

What happens in that imaginary garden of the poet's mind when those real toads—the things, events, facts of the phenomenal world—hop their way into it. For things ... take on significance only when they impinge upon consciousness, and it is in his fidelity to his own consciousness, in his ability to perceive objectively what this imaginary garden in his head does with the toads ... that the poet encounters the real. The ego has little to do with this interaction ... that the world of poetry is man-centred is not to say that is it ego-centred.[9]

What is really in question is drawn more explicitly elsewhere in this issue of *Open Letter* when Davey criticizes the surrealist's words that "communicate only himself—and not the real world," that are "private (like Hitler's vision)" (8), not reality but a symptom of reality. As he strains after immediate materiality rather than the banal, he writes that he is objective in capital letters, "EVEN TO THE EXTENT OF SEEING MY OWN SUBJECTIVITY AS A COSMIC FACT" (8). The heroic achievement of the individual recognizing the private self is a new kind of tragedy only possible within nation state ideology: that the moment of recognition is the moment of underwriting the individual as a subject, under the control of and in response to the ideological.

However the writing is traversed by fault lines that indicate that there are more than a few problems here: how do the toads hop into your head? who built the garden? what is ego if not consciousness? what is objectivity if not ego-centred? Yet there are a lot of open doors: significance is not fixed but arrived at in the act of becoming conscious; consciousness impinges upon the real; consciousness impinges as ego-centred: a private Hitler's vision that dominates over and re-defines the real as self; consciousness impinges as man-centred for the writer has not yet recognized women. The claim for objectivity is a response common to many of those who want to stand outside ideology, who when faced with the breakdown of human control, reach in a panic for for the cosmic fact of being. But as long as you hold on to this cosmic fact of being, you will continue to reinscribe the complications of heroism, which will reassert the problems of an essentialist, uniquely identified consciousness that retains the power to define, dominate and control its world. Furthermore, you will continue to need stories of private identity, unique to subject, nation and state.

The writing in these early *Open Letter* issues is happy to discard those stories attached to nation and state but not those attached to the subject, and is also apparently aware of this. Working out of readings of McLuhan that document a version of the breakdown of rationalism and romantic humanism, another piece from an early *Open Letter* castigates the tendency for Canadian critics to insist on the authority of the poet as writer.[10] But against their "false image of the poet composing by imposing" (27), what is offered is the poet who "submits" to the "laws," "directions" and "disciplines" of the poem itself. The deferral of authority onto the "word" presents an attempt to de-centre power from private human beings; however somehow the "true" poet still has the unique ability to use his body as a physical medium for presenting the actual. This essentialist alternative is problematic, and the following two decades of Davey's critical writing locate that problematic as the central contradiction from which the writer derives a theory of a constructed subject that is quite different from the cosmic objectivity of being.

Modernism is, as Davey recognized, based on a tradition that validates reference, authorizes action by claiming essential authenticity. The moment you question that by discovering/desiring the need for a different tradition in a different culture, you upset the premise of essential authenticity. If you don't reclaim it you have to move on into other structures. Early western twentieth century moves provided pragmatic essentialist responses like solipsism, or club responses like nihilism, dada, surrealism: all increasingly more compromised approaches that saved the body but also all very private and difficult to translate into community, although it could be argued that existentialism does exactly this: creates communities of private individuals. Chronologically parallel responses such as marxism and freudian psychoanalysis permit a validation of action in terms of a constructed referential code, and are concerned with addressing the problems of groups defining society within non-traditional decentred power structures. Marxism critiques the status of the private self and thereby undermines the entire structure of stable representation needed to maintain the ethos of the nation state. In contrast, freudian psychoanalysis denies the wholeness and completeness of the private self, thus denying the totalizing aims of ideology, at the same time as offering a theoretical vocabulary for analyzing how the private self is constructed within the nuclear family. Postmodernism can be read as a more recent response directed to addressing similiar problems in terms of the individual attempting to define a self within such structures. What is interesting and problematic about postmodernism is that it allows for the formation of limited communities in order to encourage the idea of a local and participatory construction of individual self, while leaving those selves or subjects vulnerable to larger economic effects.

From There to Here, Davey's 1974 review of contemporary Canadian writing, extends his quest for story into the political and arrives at postmodernism. Modernism is cast as "essentially an elitist, formalistic, anti-democratic, and anti-terrestrial movement" (19). It abandons both the material and processual worlds: what the writer refers to as the phenomenal and noumenal. In contrast, Canadian writing is held to recognize the discontinuous and post-logical operations of reality. It is phenomenological, unprocessed, pre-reflective: all criteria for the central topos of the body which has become so important for recent theoretical discourse; it turns to image and stimulus, not to idea. At the same time myth is held to be innate in the everyday.

Lacking any kind of theoretical base for materialism, the argument here clings on to the compromises of objectivity by insisting on pre-reflective origins and innate mythologies. It is an argument that is reiterated in a roughly contemporaneous article on Gwendolyn MacEwen, in which Davey comments that her characters incarnate the imminent word. They involuntarily relive myth much as the characters in his own *King of Swords,* also published in 1974. But parallel to the comments on innate mythologies, is an emergence of a political sensibility. *From There to Here* indicates an attempt at defining the pluralist politics of postmodernism that have arisen from the decentralizing activities of technology and an enlargening power of the individual. Again from McLuhan, but here not ironically, the writer indicates analogies of form between politics and style, where he allies the business report with world-wide domination, and his own mythological patterns with individual recognitions of alternative structures. Yet in 1973 Davey had published *The Clallam. King of Swords* and *The Clallam* stand off against each other much as Davey's cultural commentary stands off postmodernism against a growing awareness of marxist economics and the world-wide structure of capital.

Earlier twentieth-century movements within art/writing indicate similar responses to a growing politicization that often derives from changes in cultural position and educational background. As the politically marginalized sectors of society which have always had a written and oral verbal culture moved into political enfranchisement, particularly in the nineteenth and twentieth century, there have been complications. The structure of poetics has been implicitly political since the Renaissance, but when faced with direct political involvement, the writer is faced with group rather than individual action. The problems that this may raise have become the topics for much twentieth-century writing as it has explored the conflict that has emerged between the writer, used to dealing with a personal poetic that deconstructs authority, and an enfranchised responsibility for engagement with that authority. The recently marginalized are often unaware or afraid of the possibilities for power; they are also often worried about compromise. It is only when it is recognized that the more insidious compromise lies in not taking up that power, that anything can change. It is here that theorizing on popular culture is particularly helpful. Postmodernism arrives in the afterbirth of modernist poetics as an elite, middle class, restrictive activity, but popular cultures can be read as the poetics of the recently empowered. Both are subject to the switch between constructiveness and banal commodity, but the power relations are quite different because postmodernism focuses on individual desire while popular culture deals in group desire.

The comments in *From There to Here*, on technology and on the parallels between style and politics, indicate a tension between an increasing consciousness of broad political implications and a fear of jettisoning the unique self that western poetics have since the

Renaissance posited in opposition to the faceless dehumanization of authoritative power structures. On the one hand the position denies the existence of the "totally integrated whole" of modernism, yet on the other it states that "The tightly controlled, formalistic, and elegant poem shares formal assumptions with a company directorship, while the loosely structured film or lifestyle shares assumptions with the commune" (14). Davey's postmodernism is at this time thoroughly tied up into a form of Canadian nationalism that validates Canada in the name of the counter-culture, the (implicitly heroic) anti-hero. This counter, which was oppositional and therefore complicit in the structures it criticized, is later reconstructed in "Reading Canadian Reading," as a challenge to a dominant Canadian culture within the context of the early 70s. In either reading, the contradiction of the denial of essentialism running hand in hand with implicitly essentialist statements about form and politics underwrites a form of individualistic pluralism.

Snapshots
There is an unusual opportunity for the reader to follow a movement from this complicated and superficially utopian frame for late-twentieth century artistic activity, from the isolation of postmodernism to a broader political perspective, in the series of seven runs of *Open Letter* which have been edited by Davey. What is of significance is the way that the pages of *Open Letter* move through linguistic and narrative experiment, to a multi-media environment that attempts to break down media divisions, to postmodernist excesses, to a sudden politicization in the early 80s, to an incorporation of theory. The politicization indicated from Davey's own writing continues through the 80s with attempts to link the production of writing with materiality by constructing a theory of genre—writer/text/reader interaction—out of the criticism of thematic interpretation. It is a development that runs parallel with attempts to link the reproduction of writing with an economic materialism in a growing recognition of the historical conditions for the making and distribution of books. The interest in publishing history foregrounds the immense importance of popular culture, while the critique of genre makes a cultural study of the commodification of theme. The developments describe two very different attempts to find a story adequate to the construction of the subject and its contingent materiality within ideology. Davey's poetry, from *Edward and Patricia* to *The Louis Riel Organ and Piano*

Company and *Post Card Translations,* provides an alternative site for reading about these attempts.

"Reading Canadian Reading" reconstructs "Surviving the Paraphrase" as semiotic and discourse-focused reading that has become the commonplace of cultural studies, in conflict with the consumerist concept of reading held out by thematic interpretation. Thematic readings are ignorant of ideology; they take theme and significance and meaning for granted as if they were innate. Thematic readings explicitly reject the theoretical, but in doing so enter a tautological world where the interpretation is validated by finding just what it writes into its assumptions. This process is the classic construction of post-Renaissance fantasy, based on an unreflective referentiality that attempts always to satisfy desire, even if that means the pre-definition of satisfiable desire.[11] The article goes on to criticize these readings not only for their literary referentiality but also for their unitary view of Canadian culture, their insistence on essential Canadian identity.

The commentary is particularly helpful on the topic of the commoditization of literature, both through theme and aesthetics, and their relation to the canon, in the article "Recontextualization in the Long Poem." On the one hand, "aesthetic commoditization occurs when a canonical text is no longer capable of producing meanings compatible with a society's dominant ideological formations"; on the other, thematic commoditization "is most likely to occur when a new or non-canonical text is perceived capable of producing meanings that aggrandize one or more of a society's dominant ideological formations."[12] Yet here, in 1985, the commentary also goes on to give Steve McCaffery's work as an example of writing that "minimizes both aesthetic shape and denotative content to ensure that his text has values only as writing, that its 'truth' or meaning are inseparable from the play of its language." In contrast to Dudek and Milton who "seek an encoded meaning," McCaffery seeks a "textually-produced" meaning.

The differentiation begs the question of of how text alone produces meaning. Meaning derives from the ideological training of education, through the media, the institution, domestic habit, all in recognition of significance. Textually produced meaning derives from encoding as much as thematic or aesthetic. However, elsewhere in the writings there are more instances of what the commentary may be getting at. Recalling the toads in the garden, the essay "The language of the contemporary Canadian long poem" in the collection *Surviving the Paraphrase*, speaks of the way that Canadian writing deconstructs the European myths necessary to modernism by substituting texts of "low cultural standing" (186). More importantly, there is no substituted transcendent, no "host" as in Duncan, nor even Spicer's angels and martians. Instead this transitional criticism posits writing which conflates the phenomenal with the noumenal, claims that the actual is real and ready to explode with "magic."

Technically, magic is fantasy based on extra-human authority somehow acquired by humans. It is the lurking underbelly of the essentialism predicated by cosmic being, and a retrograde step for a materialist because it is even more displaced from contingency than the innate. This recognition of extra-human reality is in strict contradiction with contiguous statements that the "low" subtext of popular culture is not a counterpoint but a challenge to reveal meaning; it is not making way for magic but for opposition. The contradiction is further reinforced with the comment that the "reality" of writing is a process that is not solitary, independent or adversarial, but a reliance on surprise from "outside" the poet's conscious self. Not yet having a way of speaking about the constructed self, the commentary is still tripping over ego.

Davey, and Bowering, both emerged into writing at the same time that the Canadian government began indirectly and directly to fund writing and publishing. Concurrently the costs of multiple print reproduction were becoming smaller with the advent of mimeographs and photocopying. Davey was quick to make use of the newly accessible media and makes a note in *From There to Here* on the way that "correspondence poetry" burgeoned during the 60s. His energetic editorial support for a series of projects from *TISH* to *Open Letter* to the computer-networked *SwiftCurrent*, testifies to a continued awareness and clever use of the media. The comments in *From There to Here* on the appropriation of the media by national interests mark an early attempt at theorizing this awareness, an awareness that emerged quite firmly in "Writers and publishers in English-Canada" (1987), and "Ideology and Visual Representation: Some Post Cards from the Raj" (1988).[13] The studies of the interaction between literature/writing and economic materialism that result indicate the immense significance of technological processes for an understanding of verbal communication. Here however, technology is not described as something that underwrites pluralism, but something that makes possible the construction of isolated worlds necessary to political and ideological control. It is here that the pursuit of ideology has started to work into the network of social and political context which begins to describe the garden, the referential reality of power. And what is said about the economic garden and about the commoditization of the toads is in radical contradiction to what is concurrently said about how they resist economics and ideology.

While the commentary is unusually helpful about the commoditization/commodification of literature and criticism, it is continually straining within contradiction when it attempts to speak of the resistance to it. The outline of postmodernism in the Canadian context "Some. (Canadian.) Postmodern. Texts." (1989), underlines the dichotomy. Reconstructing *From There to Here* as a text that described the sociological tendencies of postmodernism toward both totalization and decentralization, the extension of the commentary into postmodern literature moves topically, although not by name, from Saussure through Althusser to Habermas. In order to emphasize the construction rather than referential transmission and/or interpretation of texts, the essay outlines a background: Language is not an instrument but a system of continuously modified codes; humanity is not essentialist but constructed; there has been a fragmentation of public discourse so that there are no longer any authoritative voices for large communities of belief; hence the arbitrary can be a useful social construction. Writers such as Nichol and Marlatt provide examples of language which has been treated as political and semiotic, not metaphysical; they are not concerned with external authority or the pain of its collapse: but with the construction of meaning.

This is a particularly helpful up front outline that invites engagement with a story about ideology and the constructed subject. But while it describes the positive values of postmodernism in terms of decentralization, it neglects to look at its totalizing effects: almost implying that postmodernism is in contradiction to totalizing, that totalizing is a remnant of modernism that postmodernism has dealt with. What it neglects is the garden, about whose construction Davey speaks quite differently in his work on the implications of the processes of print reproduction. The problem with the arbitrary is that it can use its arbitrariness to neglect the need for self-reflexivity or positioning. The writer is happy, in *Reading Canadian Reading*, to encourage the reader toward "reflective critical reading" for the identification of ideologies and interest, but is less open about helping the writer to position the stance of the text. The valorization of provisionality in the concluding "Preface" to *Reading Canadian Reading*, underwrites this potential for evasive action, as if Davey is still worried about taking specific political action in case it becomes totalizing.

Desirable Economics / Economical Desire
Davey's *Popular Narratives* (1991) openly faces contradiction between systems of power and the work of the writer, between the political materialist and the semiotician. The text does both Marxism and postmodernism. The fragmentation of the latter is filtered through the discourse of cultural studies, and the determinist structure of the former is recast in terms of popular culture. Cultural Studies as a mode of analysis frequently elides into talking about power rather than working on skills to recognize and deal with the structure of power. Just so theories of popular culture frequently focus on the consumerist aspect of desire rather then the ways people negotiate value through desire. The seven sections of *Popular Narratives* take topics of popular cultural significance such as cars, cemeteries, postcards, romance, and through them explore issues of sexuality, death, foreignness, commonality. At the same time infused into each discourse is a metacommentary on cultural difference, local and national and global, which questions how we form and agree to those topics, even how we examine the construction of those issues.

The opening sequence, "In Love with Cindy Jones," is a fugue-like set of exercises on the construction of adolescent sexuality. With familiar postmodern strategies it unpacks the cultural clichés of romance, ironizing the young boy-man's attempts to articulate desire, mapping that desire onto the commodities of cars and performances like sport or music. The Christmas gift for Cindy, by which the boy-man will articulate desire, is hidden, lost, not given, given to someone else—like any good floating postmodern sign. But there is no sense of parody, or that common postmodern response, cynicism. The present voice builds connections with socially conventional responses as it follows the gift around. Yet these are continually problematized: they are passed through a variety of non-chronological time-frames as if to focus on the fictionality of coherent development; they are interspersed with other narratives of adolescent desire that confer peer status or that result in pregnancy, neither of which are fully connected to the desire of the boy-man, although he is aware of them.

Indeed, once the reader begins to try to understand the difficulty the boy has with articulating his desire, giving the gift, we also become aware of the difficulty he is having with making any coherent sense out of heterosexuality: he knows something is going on but can't work out what it is, what he wants to do about it, or what other people expect him to do about it. Women, girls, aren't as predictable as cars; they aren't kewpie-dolls because they have babies. These apparently self-evident elements of society and culture are loaded with difficult but powerful significances for the young, which have to be learned, negotiated, worked through in far from self-evident ways. The reader is not handed a character, nor deprived of one. Instead we are encouraged to work with what we have in common with the elements of popular culture, and concurrently build a critique of the character. The most important aspect of the metacommentary, to the complexity of which this reading does little justice, is its ability to re-incur both the bewilderment of youth in the face of sexual desire and the willingness of the happily amnesiac adult reader to engage with the immense difficulty of that bewilderment.

"Postcard Translations" works with a different emphasis exploring the ways in which cultural commodification of tourism reduces the representations of a country to banalities. As the shift occurs the relation of the individual to the nation must change, for there is no longer a need for the private subject whose isolation maintains the ideological stability of the state. Indeed the nation can be read as taking on the role of a private, isolated unit necessary to maintain the markets essential to the viability of the multinational. The readings of postcards offered in this section look at the ways in which individuals find common ground among the cultural differences of other societies. Although we can guess the tourist commodity of each postcard, we are given a cultural analysis of it which provides a plethora of signs from which we could construct a response.

If we take the short sequence "The View" and "The Post Office" as a point of reading: Both "postcards" are made up of one paragraph of writing and a single line, italicized list of condensed icons connotative with it. The title to each offers what the picture on the postcard is 'about': mountains, imposing 1880s post office buildings. Contained within a "3 by 5 field," mountains are humanized, controlled, given museum quality. The traveller sending the card is sucked into "a large role in the packaging of nature." But people don't let themselves get used to commodify nature unless there is something in the process for them; implicitly, here, the overwhelming "bigness" of mountains seems to initiate an inarticulate desire to spectate, to allow the "spirit" of such hugeness to "rise toward" us, to cease work and stare. Yet the moment desire is recognized it can get trapped into culturally specific modes for realizing it, possibly to provide ways of communicating about it, possibly to stabilize a potentially violent re-presentation, but largely because popular culture gets harnessed by economic power. The moment it does, it also becomes subject to the economic power: it becomes a market. If the market is perceived to diminish or not bring a large enough profit, then the modes for satisfying that desire are withdrawn: the dome car through the Rockies is stopped.

Nostalgia and sentiment are the ways we remember satisfaction of desire through commodified processes. What is cheerful about Davey is the lack of cynicism he allows to this area of potential regret. It is made quite clear that the cultural mode for realization is constructed, that we should be aware of this at some time as enjoying the satisfaction it yields. And if it is withdrawn, well, then we need to move on. The counterpointed, italicized lined of potential icons, focuses the reader on our ability for creating new modes. Here it reads "The local. A grizzled trapper. Eggcups. Man and nature. Museum quality." (41) What you do with this is reader-specific. For example, I question whether the eggcups sit before the writer as he gazes out towards the Eibsee; or whether they work like small inverted mountains; or whether, like a storm in an eggcup, they contain immensity for the individual that is otherwise trivial or banal to others; or ... . In this process we both realize significance and build meaning, against the context of the accompanying paragraph.

The postcard "The Post Office" discusses the way that communications systems in "advanced civilizations" simultaneously play upon the need/desire of people to exchange news of themselves, such as "I miss you and the children, but I feel sure that you are looking after them well," and commodify that desire into units of power. They claim to themselves the status of past ecclesiastical theology, the ideology of the church, by mimicking its architecture; they claim the "glory of Greece" in their inexplicable splendour of the Ionic columns. Yet communication resists commodification: literacy may create the "illusion of objectivity" but "writing is a waterbed of irony." Writing itself is a culturally specific mode for realizing desire, yet it has immense potential for making significance beyond the meaning of the words. The person who writes "I miss you and the children, ..." then says not "and," but "but I feel sure ...," conveying anxiety and an assumption of individual control over the family situation that is deteriorating in the writer's absence. Further, although the person may miss both "you and the children," the concern is overtly for the children, that they are being well-looked after, or it is that this writer knows that "you" is in good health/spirits if looking after the children well, that this is the primary way "you" works? Nevertheless, the sender of the postcard participates in the economic system of the post office. It is not merely that these systems commodify individual desire, but that they acquire economic power by way of that commodification. Yet "every dog must have its day" and the Post Office will go, perhaps more quickly, just as the power of the church has receded.

If many of the postcards explicitly address the complicity and resistances of economic power and popular culture, they also frequently raise the immediate issue of cultural domination and exploitation. An individual may come to terms with a mountain in Canada or Germany or India, in much the same way. But if nature is packaged by commerce to satisfy the Western tourist, then modes for realizing desire in say India, become a version of western cultural domination. Yet how can we make sense of, understand, speak to, communicate with, other cultures without re-packaging each other into inadequate commodities? In an answer, the writer juxtaposes, in the "Elgin Marbles," "The postcard hereby becomes an important vehicle of exchange and a foundation of the shared values of human culture," with "You should see the African collection" (57). Despite the "universal" values of the Elgin Marbles at the British Museum, "You should spend as little time as possible in Athens," because of pollution. Despite the Attic grace, "these peoples were also "scandalous, barbarians."

The italicized counterpoint makes the paragraph resonate with Keats's "Ode on a Grecian Urn," which itself raises questions about the validity of western metaphysical traditions, and how to cross cultural, social and historical difference. At the same time, the question of who 'owns' the Elgin Marbles raises issues of cultural ownership. The writer notes the idea that only one copy of every book should receive subsidy. If this is the one that sits on public access in the British Library, then in a sense it is owned by the nation, but it also could make it unnecessary for any individual to 'own' a book. The whole publishing industry splits between small print runs of significant influence, and mass production of "light" reading. While these are determined largely by the extent to which their texts commodify popular desire, why does Athens want the Elgin Marbles back? Is it because there is only one copy and it should be a national resource? That the acropolis functions to define part of the cultural specificity of Greece, and that the Marbles are in London is a sign of continuing cultural domination? Perhaps, "You should try fibreglass" and produce many replicas, just as books are multiply replicated writings? this might circulate the image more widely, like a suddenly popular work deriving from a small but significant publication. At the same time, entrance into the world of commercial commodification will release the cultural sign into uncontrollable global significance.

The readings these postcards release indicate a number of important developments in the current struggle for national determination. Just as in the early days of print, when Erasmus turned Agricola (an oral master) into a star of the written word,[14] learning how to build fame and charisma for replicated images of individuals, just so nations today have to deal with constructing viable national characteristics that can be replicated on a global scale, in a medium with at least the flexibility of writing, if they are to respond to popular desire yet avoid the excesses of commodification.

On a more intimate register, Davey pursues many of these issues in terms of local communities and individuals in several other sections of *Popular Narratives* The concluding piece "Dead in France" is among other things a study of the cemetery Père Lachaise in Paris, and how the bourgeois creators of this nineteenth-century cemetery chose to represent themselves with specific icons of death. The love of Héloise and Abelard, and of Rodin and Claudel, are presented as discourses of petit-bourgeois France, the 'master narratives' of their nation. Davey's semiotic structures are not codes with answers but invitations to make significance, and these romances define possibly for the nation but certainly for foreigners the cultural signs of gender, sexuality, art, belief—but not class or race: these latter absent discourses being the problematic areas of political reality.

Yet this piece is also an elegy for bp Nichol. The two romances replicate a pattern of couples who have some great passion for each other, and then one of them dies—in both cases the man. This obvious redoubling is echoed by other patterns including the highly controlled references to the "Bride of Christ," the wife, the church, who lives on after Christ's death, never having had sexual relations yet paradoxically involved in lovemaking. The writer suggests that paradox may be oppressive. But what's a paradox but a cultural knot that contains and releases energy? The intercommentary of the replicated passions draws on this concept of paradox, constraint and desire, contextualizing it within an openly fictional re-presentation of historical and social issues that leaves much ambiguous except for the energy. On Abelard's death Héloise brings his body near her; on Rodin's, Claudel is physically shut away but also released from oppression. And we passionate readers of Nichol's writing, engaged in the lovemaking, the adrenalin surge of seeking significance, what do we do on his death? Like Abelard and Rodin, Nichol has a life after death, has access, albeit problematical, to discourse, but this is fundamentally different from being dead, the sudden absence of a body for which we grieve. Replication of cultural patterns of grief may ameliorate or intensify the inadequacy of discourse.

Popular Narratives looks at the ways that common cultural ground gets fragmented and how it is held together. If you do a postmodernist version of culturalism and break up the common grounds of social discourse, how do you prevent the unthinking re-establishing of cliché, or, how do you take action in the absence of any common ground? If you do a Marxist reading of popular culture, and focus only on the economics of commodity, how do you account for the energy of desire? Both postmodernism and popular culture question the banal reduction of common ground to cliché or commodity, at the same time as they retain the potential for dealing, through that questioning, with a constructive awareness of the inadequacy of language and discourse. For the first time, Davey openly looks at both the dangers and the appropriateness of these approaches, and is concerned with the ways that common culture not only separates us from other culturally different groups but also holds groups together. Although he seems worried about the latter in particular, he does not merely talk about power, but works through to offer practice and skills with dealing with it. His essays in *Canadian Literary Power*, published in 1994, extend these issues into theoretical and political commentaries on literary critical institutions in Canada, and critique their practices explicitly in terms of the doubleness into which post-modernism has been constituted.

Bowering: Appropriating the Body
Where Davey is acute on the identification of cultural story and helpful with textual strategies, George Bowering's concern is continually to evade the story, and he is far more useful about what writers do than how stories emerge. Davey manages to sort through questions of consciousness and ego and move on to look at toads and gardens, at materiality and ideology, but Bowering really isn't interested in toads or gardens or, for that matter, in stories. What Bowering implicitly and continually returns to is consciousness and ego.

   If fear of the referential and commodified in Davey's writing directs it into a study of where the stories come from and how they work, fear of the referential in Bowering's writing appears increasingly to have led him to attempt to reject story completely. In the former, what is indisputably there is culturally accepted myth whose artifice must be indicated. The rhetorical discussions of the strategies necessary to the construction and deconstruction of these commodities are written with the precise skill of a text that could as easily manipulate and appropriate as expose and indicate. What is just as indisputably there but far more difficult to speak of, is language: rhythm, rhyme, syntax, morpheme, line and letter. While Davey produces awkward, contradictory discussion of language as rhetoric, Bowering rejects this as yet another story and turns instead to enactments and descriptions of their production that have different contradictions and are valuable for entirely different reasons.

   Bowering operates, superficially at least, as if consciousness were not problematic, as if the hero as ego can simply be dismissed. Davey's easy claim that the Canadian writing he cares for is processual and pre-reflective, which he later came to recast as semiotic, is something that Bowering lives in the middle of and for a long time sees no apparent need to foreground/ discuss/ artificialize. The result is quite curious. If process remains unforegrounded, if its artificiality is taken as a given/ground, if process simply 'is,' how can the reader learn to read? Bowering suggests that the words and letters will open up and tell us, that there's no need for the writer or writing consciousness to lead the reader since this would be manipulation.[15] There

are at least three readings that result. The first is an idealistic account
dependent upon some transcendent authority informing the meaning
of words, in other cultures this could happily be reconstructed as
'magic,' but it is not an advisable mode for a highly technological
society with an ideology already sophisticated at masking its
dependence on service states. The second is a cynical suspicion that
the writer is a precise manipulator covering all tracks of making. The
third is a non-idealist account of the postmodern process of fetishization: that if we attempt to learn we end up imposing already-known
structures on the material world and don't learn anything we didn't
know already; and that if we try to let the words act without being
specifically directed to this or that meaning then we might end up
reading in a different way. However, the postmodern banal is that we
simply will not know how to respond to the immediate demands upon
choice and action.

How the West Was Won / Over
To raise questions of choice, is once more to raise questions about the
political. Unlike many writers of the 60s contributing to *TISH* and/or
Open Letter, Bowering's early work often speaks openly about war,
party lines and national identity. Yet during exactly the same
chronological period that Davey was finding ways to speak about
politics, Bowering was finding ways to displace his political
commentary. He was consistently criticized for the naiveté, crudeness
and directness of his political poetry,[16] yet it is extremely difficult to
find a line for political commentary in the enfranchised but largely
unpoliticized world of late twentieth century capitalism. *At War with
the US* (1974), one of the last openly political poems, is an extraordinary piece of war poetry, commenting implicitly on the internal
Canadian conflict focused rather drastically on Quebec and the War
Measures Act of 1970, but explicitly on the emptiness, futility and
"few churrs" of the Viet Nam war. For whatever reason, possibly the
ineffectiveness of individual protest during that war, possibly a
transference from federal government actions toward Quebec on to the
marginalized position of the west coast (with which, despite 80s'
parody, the 70s' writing was obsessed), or whatever speculation,
Bowering begins to shift toward less explicitly political language and
the need for writers first to effect change through the processes of
writing.

Bowering's divergence from the referential into looking for contradictions within language itself can be placed in the context of the way he describes his attention to language: In *Errata* he notes that he needs and enjoys the easy, consolatory, comforting reading offered by many books (78), but that he takes writing itself as making a challenge, searching for contradiction. If we construct this back onto the political directions of his work, we can study his readings of others (criticism) as continual play with consolations, and the writing (poetry) as often going looking for resistances, ignoring story or context. The split that this suggests[17] emerges subsequent to *A Short Sad Book* (1977), which itself could fairly be called a scourge of thematic criticism and a scourge of politics as a specific party line: which definition of a fear of referential politics lingers behind Bowering's work over the following decade.

A Short Sad Book writes a fragmented discourse of dead ends and red herrings. The narrative voice, which is the only consistent line in the 56(-1) section work, sets out to put us off the track, to evade the hunter, the critic-detective looking for meaning. Taking up the national 1970s' obsession with the 'Great Canadian Novel' that will speak for Canadian Identity, the voice opens with a catalogue of ideological markers: geography, history, myth, sport, all of them capable of providing thematic coherence. But, gradually insistent, comes the recognition that meaning is reserved for those in power. The text turns its attention to readings of other writing and speaks first of the split between the novelist who makes romance, makes the consolatory mountains for the reader to hide in, and the novel itself that is writing and process (80-1). Just so history is not the happened/written event, but making history: "history [is also] filled with mistakes & most of them are written by poetry" (103), because poetry constructs. "The novel can only sit back and try to understand" (103) and sometimes "go to war again": as Bowering does here despite all.

The text is particularly interesting on the postmodern novel which forgets history and so history forgets you/it (107). Postmodernism offers a double-edged movement that at least residually allows for a writing that does not control publically recognized historical event, but conversely that movement away from control implies careful individual organization of the arbitrary: postmodern writing that shuns the social becomes a private puzzle. By contrast, Black Mountain writing is a mystery. But in either case there is no solution for

Canadian Literature; it is neither puzzle nor mystery. To contribute to
it we should be writing, not thinking. Once again there is the
implication that to think is to fall into the referential, to think is to
write "a mirror on the floor" (134), but to write is to construct
(somehow) from the real, "as if it is there." The writer here puts the
writing outwith both. The Great Canadian Novel is neither a mystery
story about a detective who confronts Tom Thompson in London,
Ontario (the body at the bottom of the lake), nor is it the written
currently departing utopian vision of Evangeline who leaves in good
science fiction style, as does the writer, on the last page of the book,
trailing surrealist clouds of oddly Kristevan feminism and mythic
time. What the reader is left with is the book, no more no less. Only
we are in fact left with a lot more because there were a few great
similes along the way, and Bowering did go to war.

   A simile works because it permits the reader to make comparisons
with a known event or experience; it is roundly referential and
associative. And the procedure of *A Short Sad Book* is to dislocate that
habitual tendency to the commodification of language to which most
readers move. In many ways, despite Bowering's own definition of the
term, the book is an exemplary attempt at a postmodernist text. Come
at from outside the community that supported its production, it reads
as fragmented from the perspective of narrative, theme, grammar and
syntax. It can reduce the reader to playing games with numbers: of
chapters (one missing), of pages in chapters (2 or 3); with structures:
of character (how often do they appear, when do they appear first, are
they encoded in the names of other characters), of plot (should we just
rearrange the sections, is one story prioritized); and so on into other
reaches of litcrit exercise. In other words it sets things up to get the
reader to move the counters of literary expectation, but there is no
particular end, no way of winning the game and reaching a conclusion
or answer other than a set of plural possibilities. Not only is this kind
of strategy frustrating because it denies reference and the conventional satisfaction or fulfilment of desire, but it is profoundly
abstracted from the materiality of the world, from reality.

   But, from within another context, the text is a tightly constructed
catalogue of questions directed toward literary devices. It opens with
a quotation from Alain Robbe-Grillet, which immediately provides an
intertextual discourse with other strategies for dislocating readerly
expectation in an attempt to artificialize the search for answers.

Generically, the work takes the ideologically bound romance devices of the roman à clef, the detective story and the science fiction plot, as the most fruitful place for disruption of narrative convention. The writing chooses to displace the cultural icons and images specific to works of literary criticism published in Canada during the immediately preceding decade. The writing offers a series of points of contact with narrative, generic, cultural and other expectations which work intertextually rather than referentially because they ask both for the recognition of those links and for the dislocation of those links. But of course in each case the reader needs to be part of a particular literary/cultural community to appreciate the dislocation.

For that community the work is also a political commentary on the marginalization of Western Canada, from the Ontarian centre: the story of an internal emigré. It talks about the limitations of Canadian nationalism and the frustration of regionalism. It provides a focused analysis on publishers, writers and grant-giving systems, on the literary expectations of the educational system, during the 1970s in Canada. It is at times bitter and rude, patronizing and evasive, especially when the writer allows himself to honour his own heroism: "You learn it in writing poetry you tell it in writing prose" (89), which complete eradication of the reader returns us to the problem of the unproblematic conscious.

Embattled by Ego
Bowering's fear of the referential in language translates into a fear of the political referential, that turns *A Short Sad Book* into a tangle of conflict and opposition, without the necessary climax of a nice heterosexual book. The writing comes out the other side into a number of writings that implicitly admit the necessity for some semiotic in that they are, simply, easier to read, and that rehearse the topics of *A Short Sad Book* from a conversational stance that the writer develops in order to be able to justify "leading" the reader. In the process the writer attempts to net the political down under the immensely sophisticated and patterned constructions of language. The commentary is in a sense won over to the postmodernist artist who is described through Davey in *Craft Slices* (1984)[18] as one who "does not believe that he can absorb, structure, organize, and discourse definitively on the universe" (141). Bowering says that the best poets in Canada believe that:

the animator of poetry is language. Not politics, not nationalism, not theme, not personality, not humanism, not real life, not the message, not self-expression, not confession, not the nobility of work, not the spirit of a region, not the Canadian Tradition—but language. The centre & the impetus, the world & the creator of poetry is language. (140)

And he goes on to describe these poets as children, without power over language, letting the language speak. Unlike bpNichol, who also focuses poetics in language, Bowering both denies the mystical and evades the explicit idealism of the materiality of language operating without human control.

In contrast to Davey who virtually begins with the deconstruction of the individual consciousness into the constructed subject which encourages him to concentrate on ideology and its relationship to the real (garden and toads), Bowering concentrates on the existential control of the private individual or subject. Hence he has to distinguish between ego and consciousness but translates them into thinking and writing: respectively, language which is controlled by human beings (the unreflective garden of referentiality and content: ideologically coherent) and language which speaks through the human being (the unreflective toads appearing, mystically, from the actual through verbal process). Bowering is always trying not to be 'heroic,' but to write where/what is within him that his heroism springs from. The poetry and much of the other writing is attempting to do without story or reference: which may be taken as an idealistic and humanist trust that we can read without story, or as a non-idealistic, materialist, meditative recognition, rooted in the local, struggling out of specific experience of repetition and contradiction which is a version of constructive postmodernism. The latter is, in Bowering's poetry, a detailed act of provisionality, but it runs alongside the possibility of the pluralism of the former, and this doubleness is particularly clearly enacted in *Burning Water* (1980). Bowering's writings are both heroic and effacing of the hero: For all his rejection of politics and the knight who seeks the grail he is an errant writer, and as Marlatt also notes, arrant. The errant knight finds/completes the errand only by mistake, by erring and by implication never. But that the knight engages in the errand in the first place is an indication of arrogance and self.

The commentaries of Bowering's *Errata* bend modernism and postmodernist theory as defined by Davey toward the concept of potentially heroic self merely through the omission of any discussion of a constructed subject or consciousness. Modernist writing is set squarely in realism, and attempts a set of referential techniques. In contrast, postmodernist writing resists the referential and welcomes "stray" material (13). Reference and realism are made "purposive" by those people who do not recognize their accidental basis, and blindly accept the conventional as essential (93). So far, so good. But then we find that "stray" material is somehow a non-conventional revelation of reality, specific to the writer; the accidental is only apparent coincidence (6). The postmodernist writer is out to trick reality into revealing itself (19), to trick the idea into being so that it can then be dismantled, for the "art" is in the dismantling (55). It is as if the commentator on this activity fears the power of the conventional, of the ideological, of the symbolic order that defines consciousness, because once acknowledging it he may lose articulacy, lose the ability to see and speak from strange places.

In *Errata* we find out most about the process of this postmodernist writing from the notes on intertextual reading that offer a commentary on the provisional activity rather than the banal pluralist activity of *A Short Sad Book* and several other writings. Rather than being a consoling recognition (78) that is a performance of re-reading (3), reading should work by breaking habits (10), by finding discontinuity. The reader should notice rather than buy/consume thought (18); thought should be discarded to allow for disunderstanding, dismantling, deprocessing (55). Intertextual reading here becomes analogous to articulating the world/reality. Reading, or tracking the real, is the writer's first action (91), yet the writer is able to read things "invisible to the rest of us" (91). There is some moment when the writer can evade the stories of ideology and see the real. And while in writing the craft may be visible, the referent remains invisible.

As a generic description for the necessary misrepresentation/apprehension of reality, the intertextual ties in well with many aspects put forward by other commentators concerned with the problems of reference. But Bowering presents it in *Errata* as a heroic or prophetic role carried out by "writer-poets." He says "Socially and politically I am a romantic leftist; but when it comes to the composition of literature I am an elitist" (22). Disregarding that "romantic leftist" can be glossed as "right-wing anarchist," what is interesting about the statement is that Bowering apparently thinks that the intertextual reader/writer from the real is part of a small group which is distinct from the popular desire for consumable re-readings. There is a lurking implication that postmodernism can never become popular because, apparently, it is not consumable, specifically it is not referential. This openly evades the popular reception of postmodernism in pluralism, which is exactly referential.

Errata also offers the comment that literature has "a social responsibility. But it does not owe its forms to the state" (51). Well, yes, it does. Elsewhere this writer says that politics begins with language, and that too is so.[19] But to evade any clear choices in language in order to deny the power of the referential may generate not only a personal politics but also the pluralist. The distinct fear that the political positioning might entangle him into an ideology, a state story, seems to have enclosed the writer in an oppositional conflict of consolation and intertext centred in the individual which, as in *Kerrisdale Elegies* (1984), can only be lived with by continually trying to displace what is recognized as the self. Bowering's trust that there are some people who can read without any story could be interpreted as the complete narcissistic totality of blindness to convention, or as the non-idealistic, local and long-term struggle through the disunderstanding of allegory that Davey puts forward as the positive material awareness of writers such as Nichol and Marlatt.

Unsung heroes
Just as Davey is concerned with toads and gardens, with materiality and ideology, so Bowering is the gardener or ideologue: Indeed he makes play with "bowering" and gardens in *Errata*. He is inside the garden which is inside him: constantly handing over/offering over his body as pre-reflective and unprocessed/able. Davey offers the reader a constructed subject that is producing theorized commentary on where/what we have forgotten and marginalized in literary produc- tion. Bowering structures the literary production to invite recognition of the need continually to defer the stasis of the consciousness that defines the constructed subject. But with the 1987 novel *Caprice*, while he retains the focus on the individual, he begins to look out at the landscape beyond the garden.

It is all too easy to read *Caprice,* to look, with "ordinary Eastern eyes" (33) on the landscape of a genre familiar as the "western." In- deed the back cover of the Viking edition described the book as "a great old-fashioned yarn." This particular version of the novel could be called "The Woman who never bounced" and carries an erotic charge from the primary device of cross-dressing. The title character Caprice is on the track of the man who killed her brother. Since the agents of justice seem not to be concerned with bringing him to book, she is going to do so herself. The plot follows her search for the killer and her romantic involvement with a teacher; it is interwoven with a variety of subplots that revolve around the desire of various men for her, and is interspersed by commentary between two Native American Indian men who observe the drama from a distance.

Caprice is constructed out of an assembly of cultural signs recognizable to anyone who has watched or read westerns. She is the tall, silent, stranger, who looks like a boy or young man, carries a bullwhip, and to mark her mysteriousness, writes poetry, drinks China tea and reads Goethe in restaurants. Her androgyny, initially clustering around the definitions of her as cowboy / cowgirl / cowwoman / bullwoman / bullgirl (4-5), echoes the clichés of desire in much western popular culture from the 80s, but is also necessary to lines of gender definition in the novel. If she were unquestionably a woman, her vengeance might be that of the furies, the women on the other side of chaos whose eruption into ordered society must be stopped. Yet here, the androgyny allows the men in the society to admire her, think of her at some times as "one of them," indeed think of themselves as her. This is the desirable not as 'other' but as 'self.' It is the contained, narcissistic gaze of approval transferred onto the self as hero who deals with the bad guy who everyone fears but no one else is prepared to face. It's a clever feat: being able to write an image that allows one to desire the self—an immensely satisfying narrative technique.

Counterpointed with the story is a narratorial voice concerned to talk overtly about "the west." While well-integrated into the narrative landscape it can speed by as description, this voice coalesces about half-way through the novel (108) by way of an extended commentary on the lack of irony in the west, the way that the west works through a continual nostalgia for pure origins that is gradually having to give way to the East, to Europe, to men in suits who have irony. People with irony always know there is another story; people with irony always write with the ambivalence of the other story in mind. In contrast, as one of the motifs is at pains to suggest, writers in the west, without irony, are poor poets. And Caprice is a poet from the East, whose poetry deserts her as she becomes a western hero (201). Heroism and poetry are closely connected here, as in other areas of Bowering's writing. For example, Caprice finds herself using the same strategies to pursue her brother's killer, as she would find her way into writing verse (225.) Finally, she realizes that she pursues the killer in order to end the poem (226). It is at that point that she also recognizes the radical difference between writing and life: one being an area where humans control and direct the words, and the other being a place where we may decide and act, but can never control: C'est stupide, she says of her quest.

Similarly, she can be a poet just as she can be a hero because she is supported by money. Unlike other western heroes who have to rob banks and kill people to survive, she can be a good hero because someone else is paying. The discourse about "the west" is extended through a counterpoint between the narrator's discussion of irony (108) and the Natives Indians' discussion about action and thought (189) in the west. The idea of "the west" is tied up with exploitation, robbery, or overt theft; and exploitation is possible as long as there is only one story: irony stops all that. When exploitation stops, sometimes because of recognition of another story and sometimes out of necessity when there is nothing left to exploit, then "the west" stops. When you acquire irony, you acquire a future, you have to think, to choose, to act not conventionally but upon decision. When exploitation ceases, work starts. The gender shift from man to woman, externalizes and makes easier to analyse the desirable elements of the heroic; it also makes it easier for Bowering to write the character of a woman which he elsewhere finds difficult. But it is also implicitly a commentary on women becoming men, being poets, and making the same heroic mistakes. Who precisely is this woman from Ste. Foy, Québec (the Québecoise feminist being a powerful icon in Canadian culture)—this caring *heterosexual* woman, who acts like a man, this Amazon with Medusa snakes in her hair?

There is a quiet erosion that takes place as the reader sees the surface of the novel 'crumbling' away from generic meaning. One of the most carefully structured techniques to assist the reader is the use of the detail of familiar objects contemporary with our own lives like chocolate bars, black tape and baseball, that normalize the past into a place of present significance. This normalizing is generally read as anachronism, and unless playing simplistic postmodern games writers are careful to avoid it because it doesn't matter whether those objects actually existed at that time for they are conventionally read as not being so. The self-conscious use of perceived anachronistic detail allows the narrative to frame modern gender roles allegorically; at the same time as we look with curiosity at past events, we can invert the lens and look at ourselves. This is exactly what the two Native Indian men do in their interspersed observations for, "Curiosity was to be expended on the white men" (34).

Through the Native Indian eyes the entire novel becomes an exercise in observation, as the older mentor tries to teach the younger man to observe, to be fastidious and precise about use of words and stories, to distinguish between habitual action, thought, imagination and fancy, to use memory and history to understand culture, and to learn that living is "being funny" (229). The observations provide a device for metacommentary, that works particularly clearly by being openly about teaching and learning. The understanding of another culture is the final step that the younger man must take before he can be fully responsible within his own society. The presentation of the two Native Indian people works fairly untheoretically with a set of white clichés about Native behaviour. The reader can follow the double movement of a society both historically at the point of being fixed in the colonizing gaze, and anachronistically in control of the clichés that will define that gaze. In order to be recognized by the powerful, you must give back to them their image of what you are—so the mentor teaches the younger man about white fascination with Indian religion, about facial expressions and body language. At the same time, to counter or at least meet the powerful within their own world, you must simultaneously be fully adept at their language—the younger man also received a full education in Coleridgean aesthetics and pertinent areas of western metaphysics: Although at times it is difficult to assess whether Bowering is offering Romantic responses to sublime grandeur as serious challenges to the excuses of humanist control or ironic reaffirmations of western consciousness (198).

In contrast to the whites who remain unchanged, the two Native people learn how to learn. Their educating process is dependent on assessing knowledge, building a sense of respect for the craft of living, acquiring skills of observation and interpretation, becoming able to criticize, and joke, and to turn the teacher into a friend (279).

It is at odds with the procedure of Roy Smith's "Industrial Residential School" which he knows are inappropriate(232). In both societies, art and poetry exist alongside education as ways of controlling responses to the world. But while the Native Indian education does not here extend control to life, western education does. Western education teaches "sanity" (249); it constructs individual consciousness and motivation that encourages people to define self rather than learn about others. This is pertinent commentary on the action of the novel, and sees Bowering beginning to explore how the ego could work if there were no need for the private individual, albeit by way of another radically different society.

Yet for me one of the most appealing readings of the novel is the way it makes available an unheroic masculinity. Who would read a book about unheroic men? It's as if Bowering sets up the bad guys and the woman as hero, precisely in order to create a space for "ordinary" men. We get glimpses of their clichéd responses to male power in the doctor's pornographic book, the attempted rape of Caprice, the lust that lurks via the narrator in so many eyes. We are explicitly told that women are commodities, prizes or breeders (183). At the same time, the narrative goes out of its way to insist on the politeness of most men, their reluctance to fight. Roy Smith is of course the archetype: gentle, intelligent and capable of love/sex as "an expression of care" (75). He is a baseball player and a teacher of children—children who we are also told, either "wanted to be heroes. They longed for myth. They didn't want to be children. They wanted to be immortals," or children as children: "reminders of change or potential" (145), of a future (217). However, the writing stops short of male domestic conversation. It hangs implicitly around various characters but is only voiced through the discussions of mentor and student. This could be read as a failure of nerve on Bowering's part, but also a tacit admission that white, western men have lost much of the conversational discourse that is the ground from which non-ideological discourse works.

While *Caprice* in many ways allows itself to be read as a series of contending cultural clichés, that can reduce it to banal manipulation of the discourses of desire and power, at the same time it provided parallel texts that ask the reader to work intertextually, to learn how to read the various generic and narrative strands. Bowering here takes the obsession with individual consciousness and the heroism of self-identity, and explores both the constraints on the individual and the narcissistic strategies that build the totalizing world of the hero. He also acknowledges a community, he helps the reader read. He is the teacher/mentor and the learner.

Material Canadians
Both writers are concerned with the adequacy of the referential and its potential for banal commodification, and with dislocating it and moving it on. They are concerned with breaking down the patterns of language and literature that permit us to speak to each other in the encoded language of our society, because of their potentially totalizing effects. In that breaking down they initially engage another set of strategies which are far more local and immediate: the provisional and the intertextual. These strategies, built partly so that we may say to each other things that as members of the immediate community we need to say to each other, things that may not have been spoken before, can become both exclusive and appropriative.

Reading the work of both these writers throws forward the problems of political empowerment. If you've ever been on the margins, you are always aware of how other people's positions of power oppress. If the marginalized gain access to power there is no point denying it and laying claim to pluralism. Constructions of the Canadian postmodern which emphasize process rather than product and have an apparent bias to the anti-referential and anti-political can be diverted into an increasingly inadequate pluralism by the same interests that have diverted the materialist agenda of deconstruction into the Chinese box game. Both Davey and Bowering offer recognitions that postmodernism is just as open as realism to the banal. They suggest that to control the potential in postmodernism for commodification you have to move through the plural politics of the provisional to specific instances where cultural difference and gender definition present immediate social locations for materiality.

I am conscious as I write that it is easy for an outsider to see Canada itself as a cultural fetish, a commodity, since I am not part of the social immediacies. It is easy for outsiders both to turn Canada into a banality, and to turn Canada into a constructive example of responses to multinational globalization, which is how I teach this writing. More difficult is the sense that radically to challenge the multinational, this cultural tourism must be resisted because it's already in terms of the powerful.

CHAPTER FIVE

Bodily Functions in Cartesian Space

Since the late 1970s at the least there's been an undercurrent rumbling about theory and language-focused writing, and the high profile that this writing appears to maintain in Canadian literary culture. To an outsider listening casually to conversation in a variety of literary sites in Canada from writer's workshops to libraries to academic institutions, this rumbling has centred on the erstwhile Canada Council grants system and particularly on the makeup of its juries. Another crude analysis will throw forward the unusually close connections between tertiary academics, small publishing houses, and language-focused writers. This chapter will not attempt any detailed historical analysis of this background, but the frequency of related comments indicates the problems of socio-cultural reception encountered by such poetics in Canada. What I am particularly keen to study here is the way that women's 'language-poetry' in Canada has been traversed by the politics of Freudian/ Lacanian language theory and its associations with recent French philosophy. I am not here concerned with commenting on the poetic texts themselves, but upon the philosphical and cultural filter they acquire in critical and academic responses. The discussion attempted here assumes that philosophical thinking is always a political act, with a greater or lesser social effect.

An Analysis
The debate between language-focused writers and generically accessible writers involves the public perception of a number of issues on both sides. J. Marchessault in "Is the Dead Author a Woman?" suggests that the two are oppositional.[1] She notes that "the critique of realism that evolved out of psychoanalytic feminism in the mid-seventies was an essential step in confronting the oppressiveness of prevailing forms of narration and representation.... Our thinking continues to be informed by the rigid opposition of realism and modernism, of truth and its negative" (87). Yet an analysis of these,

indicating quite similar constraints on each, could proceed in the following way:

a) Public perception of philosophy
b) Public reception of language-focused writing

OR

ai) Philosophy *as* philosophy: logic-chopping, male discourse
aii) Philosophy as Freud/Lacan: focus on language

bi) Language-writing as difficult
bii) Language-writing as male discourse

BUT

ai) Philosophy/theory needs to be seen as site for work on articulation, therefore a moral site bound to daily living
aii) Freud/Lacan is part of Cartesian space, and relegates the woman to the silent or sacrificial. There is a need to work through Cartesian space to the other side, and find other images: not for the sake of new metaphor/metonymy but for the sake of moral action/stance

AND

bi) Language-writing is not difficult in itself, but in its shift of naturalized common grounds. All writing does this, and language-writing needs to be seen as a site for work on articulation, a moral site.
bii) Language-writing's alliance with male discourse ties it to Cartesian space and collusion in women's oppression. There is a need to take on the authority of the voice in order to have effect, and to work through it to other sites: not for the sake of authority but for the sake of women's oppression.

AT THE SAME TIME there is a problem with

c) Public perception of women's discourse
d) Public reception of culturally-foregrounded 'genre'-writing

OR

ci) Women's discourse as private, intimate, with no valid broad common ground cii) Women's discourse as 'genre'-writing, &/or personal autobiography

di) Genre-writing as easy

dii) Genre-writing as culturally safe discourse

BUT

ci) Women's discourse needs to be seen as non-institutional social action: a site for the extension of political rhetoric parallel to the nation state.

cii) Autobiography (intimate) and Genre-writing (grand cultural gesture) are accessible and open to complicity. Accessibility and popular culture are places where we could find a place to value women's daily lives. We need to do this not only to be oppositional nor to replace the institutional with a new framework, but also for the sake of defining another discourse field where other things can be said.

AND

di) Genre-writing and autobiography are seen as easy because they are accessible. All ideology is accessible, work with these writings needs to be seen as a site for dealing with the sophistication of institutional discourse.

dii) Genre-writing/autobiography, because they dealing with institutional discourse, are collusive in women's oppression. They need to be taken on despite their collusion partly because of their wide audience and learning potential: not because they are populist but for the sake of articulating a world in which women work, so that it can be spoken, critiqued, changed.

Both language-focused writing and autobiography/genre writing are weakened by their potential complicity in the institutional. Both are strengthened by their commitment to the community of women from which they draw their alternative discourses. Here I want to focus on some of the problems deriving from both the public perception of philosophy and the public reception of language-focused writing. The institution of which I am part, and of which some of my audience will be part, has been deeply infused by the attitude to philosophy often used to anchor language-writing and to the particular post-Cartesian theory of Freud/Lacan. Much of the authoritative language/vocabulary used by institutional commentators on feminism is still part of this psychoanalytic discourse field. I want to examine the grounds, work through them, and discuss some of their implications as they emerge in feminist discourse in Canada surrounding language-focused writing.

An Opening

The curious oxymoron,'language-focused' writing, usually refers to writing that radically disrupts the current conventions of verbal linguistic graphic expression. In Anglo-American criticism, commentaries on it have leaked into the gaps left by the narrative impetus of much structuralist and post-structuralist theory dominating literary and cultural analysis since the 1950s. Yet a number of Canadian writers and critics have been particularly responsive to the need for some kind of discussion and critique; for example, the Toronto Research Group papers in the issues of *Open Letter* 1973-78 are substantial contributions to the discussion.[2] More generally, the philosophical field of literary and linguistic theory has come to be seen not as engaging with the devices of 'language-focused' writing, since both have the common concern of working on historically appropriate articulations, but *as* language-focused writing. Criticisms of the poetry use the theory as ammunition, and *vice versa.* As a result, despite contributions such as those from the TRG, there is little assessment   or critique of either except to dismiss their political effectiveness. Any one theory, from for example J. Derrida, J. Lacan or H. Cixous, is taken variously as a) prescriptive and speaking in jargon, b) processual and trying to avoid meaning or c) temporarily interruptive and chimerical.[3]

During the 80s elements of this debate transferred into the commentary of women writers, particularly acutely in Canada where for a variety of reasons a number of women writers have chosen to develop their craft in this way. Erin Mouré speaks about the suppression she experienced when writing "anecdotal/conversational poems without reversal (which is to say, without the language confronting itself and its assumptions in the poem)."[4] Several accounts are brought together in Smaro Kamboureli's "Theory: Beauty or Beast? Resistance to Theory in the feminine," *Open Letter* 7:8 (Summer 1990) counterpointed in the same year by Libby Scheier, Sarah Sheard and Eleanor Wachtel's *Language in her Eye: Writing and Gender.* None of this story is straightforward. Part of it is related to a separation between generically specific (and therefore easily publishable/consumable) and generically non-specific (and therefore 'difficult' to read) writings. Generically non-specific writing works largely within techniques and strategies that the society takes as 'naturalized'; its actions are capable of inverting, displacing, changing, the cultural commonplaces of language or linguistic object in ways that call for radical response because they unsettle tacit agreements about communication that are frequently taken as self-evident, or axiomatic. For some women writers this generically non-specific writing promises a useful ground for speaking of different lives. Gail Scott for example speaks of the need to write against the "reader's line of least resistance."[5] Smaro Kamboureli calls contradiction in language a political act.[6] But allied to this promise is the difficulty of getting the writing published.

Part of the story becomes tied to an anglophone Canadian perception of Québecoise language-writing, which appears to get published and win respect.[7] The early Tessera editorial collective is at least partly attempting to duplicate not only similar concerns with poetics, but also the publishing platforms their Québecoise sisters set up during the 70s in for example La Nouvelle Barre du Jour. In anglophone eyes Quebec has an intellectual community outwith the academic institutions that dominate English-Canadian intellectual products and which are predominantly male.[8] For anglophone women therefore, there is by example a promise of an alternative community for the poetics of difference.

The story is complicated by the increasing numbers of women who entered Canadian academic institutions in the 80s, many of whom appreciate and indeed practice generically non-specific language writing. These women, and the few who preceded them such as Shirley Neuman, Barbara Godard, Lorraine Weir, Sherrill Grace and Linda Hutcheon, see the success of the tactics of their male colleagues and work on the authorization of this poetics through criticism. More helpfully, they work on teaching strategies of reading that enable readers to take the chance of commitment to a text, to find ways of reading appropriate to these ways of writing. The story is further complicated by a broader movement in western feminism in which the univocal presence of the articulate largely white middle class women of the 60s to 70s makes way for / is shattered by newly articulating voices from different races, classes and genders. This shift, which has been well-documented, often places the 'authorizations' of women's language writing in a discredited field of masculine poetics, whereas some of those authorizations may also be read precisely as attempts to save women's language-writing from accusations of racism, exclusion, and class blindness.

As with any attempt at an alternative movement there are necessary engagements with the dominant modes of power, and neither the anglophone women writers until recently, nor their authorizing critics, have addressed that complicity directly, nor do either clearly attempt to assess how the writing is positioned in the social. The antagonism they set off is understandable.[9]

*

What is interesting to note is that the impetus from Québecoise writers occurred at a time in the late 70s when French feminist theory from H. Cixous, J. Kristeva, M. Wittig and others, was becoming available in English translation.[10] This language-focused theory, implicitly and explicitly offering a Lacanian analytic, was profoundly influential on the development of western feminist discourse especially that focused on writing. However, Québecoise writers such as Nicole Brossard had already worked through this analytic to a critical and more materialist basis by the early 80s.[11] Brossard's work was available in translation from 1975,[12] but it is unclear how widely read and critiqued her work and later work by Cixous and L. Irigaray,[13] also critical of Lacanian theory, was until the end of the 80s. As a result the authority of a Lacanian analytic far outstayed its helpful stage and added to the negative reception of women's language writing. The conflation of women's language-writing with Lacanian analytics has brought immense criticism from socially based women's studies theory, and has led to unnecessarily prolonged divisions.

Many of the negative accounts from Canada condense into an argument that a set of women writers, including Daphne Marlatt, Gail Scott, Lola Lemire Tostevin, Betsy Warland, Kamboureli herself, and others, are too language-centred, too theoretical. What seems to be signified is that this writing is prescriptive, particularly about the need for women to find a different language for expression, and that this writing is difficult to read. Specifically translated, the objections are *first* with the writing's often overt connection with Lacanian feminism and *second* that it is part of an experimental graphical poetic related to concrete/breath poetry that is merely relativist and with no social relevance: either it's process only, with no immediacy, or it's unnecessary because language is neutral so there's no need for 'feminine' writing. The underlying argument is *first*, that if these women are the avowedly feminist writers they say they are, then their theoretical jargon/complexity and their linguistic obscurity/difficulty, put them so far away from the usual concerns of women as to make them useless.[14] And *second*, that it's worse than this: the theoretical concerns of graphic linguistic experiment are part of a masculine tradition and the engagement of these writers into these concerns compromises their work and places them in collusion with women's oppression.

In effect we can take pieces out of the poetry by writers such as Marlatt, Scott, Tostevin, Warland and Kamboureli, and indicate the apparent separation of the words from the concerns of most women in Canada—or elsewhere. And of course it is just because of the decontextualizing that the pieces appear to be neutral. For example there is, from Lemire Tostevin's *Gyno Text*[15]

mute
skeleton
moves
to
muscle
string
pulled
taut
from
A
to
Zone

or, from Warland's *Proper Deafinitions*[16]

induction

showing "our sexts"

women's texts subtext
between
            the
                                    line
context pretext *text*:
"in the original language, as opposed to a translation
or rendering"

pre-text
mother tongue:
"a language from which other languages originate"

But, there's not a single writer here who does not engage in a narrative that can provide a location for the neutrality of out-of-context settings. This writing also tells stories, not merely as a strategic sop to narrative expectation but as a necessary link to practical issues.

In this, the pieces are supposedly unlike comparable writing by male writers such as Steve McCaffery or Christopher Dewdney, although this apparent masculine neutrality has increasingly been questioned and challenged, including by the two cited writers themselves, in the pages of *Boundary*, *Open Letter* and *LANGUAGE*, and in a number of recent articles and books.[17] Betsy Warland explicitly comments that the motives moving language poetry by women are different to those for men. While for women it's a matter of survival, for men it's often a game lacking any root analysis of patriarchy. She lists the adjectives 'aggressive,' 'cynical,' 'witty,' 'enervated': which are the melancholy points to which the gamesmanship of postmodernism rolls. But for Warland this is not an essentialist split where women go looking for a biologically feminine sentence, but where we all look for the disallowed language appropriate to our needs, our 'dialect.'[18] For example, there was/is bpNichol as a male writer with an ability to critique gently, to "circumvent the despair of the dominator's role" and to "delight in the daily world as a co-inhabitant" (292). All that Warland says generally about male writers is repeated by others about women language-poets. And her conclusions on Nichol can aptly guide the reader to commentary on herself.

*

There are problems here raised both by the notion of 'poetic' and of 'theory': I will begin with those clustered around poetic, and follow them into theory. If we take a step back from the debate, it's possible to recognize it as part of an on-going anxiety about any poetics in the post-Renaissance western world. A problem with a new and challenging poetics is the need for mediation into that poetics: first time readers of Dryden or T. S. Eliot typically have similar problems. Poetics have always separated, untied, dislocated the *loci communes*, the topics of society, that keep that society bound together. The activity of poetics described here is specifically relevant for western

European and hemisphere societies and their affiliates, that have depended upon a classical education in rhetoric which provides the methodology for all social agreement from consensus to totalitarianism. Alongside rhetoric, poetics work to open up the verbal media, but poetics are also learned in a historical context, they are not natural. Poetics and rhetoric are learned by both rhetor/writer and the audience, who both need to be able to assess relevance, and for today need particularly to address graphic poetics as they have developed since the Renaissance within a very small class-dominated context of power, education and publishing: what is called 'literature.' In that context we need to ask: What is the relevance of a writer's craft developed within a state nationalism structured by the closed systems of club culture? What is the relevance of a reader's craft developed for an ability to recuperate by appropriation? How do the writer and reader bring a reflexive application of their skills and craft to a historical context so that they may enable critique? It is not the poetics that are a problem, for no device or structure is inherently enabling or disabling, but the way that poetics crosses the border into rhetoric.

What complicates the issue for Canadian women writers of language-focused work is partly a social context in which the audience is increasingly varied in terms of culture, education and political expectation; but partly also that they stand upon theory *and* the specific theoretical ground which they understand. Association with theory and philosophy should never disable poetics, for all are concerned with articulating the immediately pressing needs of life; but the association will hurt in the context of a philosophy that can be elaborated without attention to the contingencies of daily experience. That's the problem with the public perception of current theory.

However, and more serious, the theoretical ground that is understood from much of this language-centred writing, as *A Mazing Space* (1986) reiteratively points out, is the Freudian-Lacanian psychoanalytic discourse that has infused western feminist discussions about language. While it seems quite clear that the writing deals with women's oppression on the grounds of the world it inhabits, and that this discourse has been one of the most enabling, albeit authoritative, devices for articulating that oppression, the discourse also sets up conceptual barriers. Those who speak it have large authority because they speak the language of men and men listen to them, doors open to publication, distribution and dissemination, but at what cost? Being imprinted, impressed, put to bed and made public. Those who speak the discourse appear to be an anathema to the feminism of community activism, social policy and women's studies. The 'academic' or intellectual woman writer working in this discourse acquires a public persona that separates her radically from other communities of women.[19] It is not a rhetoric that encourages commitment from the reader, indeed it leads either to alienation or to a sense of collusion.

Cartesian Space: Fantasy, commodity/fetish, and reciprocity
To look at the kind of crossings between poetics and rhetoric that have been imagined in recent theory, can I first put forward a classical text, the *Phaedrus*, that offers metaphors for working on this problem. It is a text where Plato is concerned not with a 'true' but with the social, the body action of the 'good.' *Phaedrus* explicitly addresses the relationship between social conventions for communication in both oral and written media, and the need to negotiate these in response to immediate needs, by way of a metaphor of "love." To keep it brief, the text looks at love gained for money: i.e. acquisitive; love exchanged for the pleasure of regarding oneself: i.e. for power; and love which works by allowing oneself to be changed: i.e. by receiving the gift of the other, this third being the ground for a proper interaction between poetic and rhetoric.[20] This metaphorical tryptic insistently throbs through Western philosophy from Plato to Derrida. What is interesting here is what happens to it in Cartesian space—or to be more exact, in post-Cartesian space.

Cartesian dualism, conventionally read, splits the brain/body from the mind. Descartes proposes this as one way of explaining the limitations of language in its attempt to re-present the phenomenological actuality of the world. While Descartes recognizes this as unstable, the suggestion gains actual currency via for example Port-Royal logicians, and even the Royal Society.[21] The possibility of progress toward a stable representation of referential actuality, phenomena, occurs concurrent with and no doubt as part of the political necessity for the emerging nation states of Europe to present a coherent argumentative ethos to each other. It has withstood the tensions of the rational via Kant's relational twist to ideological representations, which (simply) throws into relief the elements of structure that need to be readjusted to keep the status quo static. The Cartesian split becomes an appropriate common ground, self-evident fact, and generates two interlinked spin-offs about the body and about language that in contemporary cultural theory are both linked to desire.

First the body: Of the many developments from the mind-body split, the most urgent for women has been its use in sexual and gender oppression. Currently laid out in Freudian-Lacanian theory,[22] the split allows for the suggestion that if you have a different body you must have a different mind—but technically this is illogical, for if there is a *split* there may be no connection between the two: just one of the enabling contradictions of this theory that Freud emphasized increasingly in his later writings. Lacan describes the system of stable representation of the state ethos as the symbolic: made by men for men because they control economic and governing power; they hold political office; they operate within and strengthen the ideological stability necessary to the nation state. Because women are somatically/physiologically different they cannot conceptualize in the same way and cannot fully enter the symbolic.

But also, Freud and Lacan work in Cartesian space because they need the split to cope with their fear. This fear is hydra-headed, but the one analogical example I shall pursue in the next section is the fear of inadequate language. To cope with fear, the concept of a split self found in abundant psychological metaphors throughout the nineteenth-century is formalized/scientized: the self is accompanied by the 'other' in different ways that generate the classic psychoanalytical terms of narcissism, neurosis and psychosis, and that indicate desire at work. The underwriting of stable ideology via an elaboration of the Cartesian split into the imaginary (body) and the symbolic (mind) tautologically sets the ground out to enable a justification of the self as a split subject. The search for any completion of the self becomes, by definition, a denial of the subject, a fantasy, something that drives desire. But fantasy doesn't search for the complete, it invents strategies to suppress awareness or knowledge of the other: Sometimes with the intention of realizing the other most acutely at the moment of suppression (the fantastic), yet most frequently leading to a dominating process that seeks to create ignorance/to repress—a repression which lies at the root of narcissism,[23] and at the centre of the fetish.[24]

This reworking of Cartesian dualism does interesting things to the Phaedrean tryptic. From money, power, and change/gift as metaphors for verbal communication describing different ways of interaction and engagement with the social, money is eliminated (cancelled by the professional exchange of psychoanalysis) and the remainder is inverted: The interaction of poetic and rhetoric in the metaphor of love as change/gift is found only in the semiotic, the imaginary, the chora; while the exchange of love for a version of oneself that describes the narcissistic and dominating gesture provides the necessary stability for the representation of ideology and becomes the central metaphor for the symbolic. The reversal allowed Lacan to gender the account of ideology via power: to provide a vocabulary for talking about the subordination and oppression of women; and to imply that there is a place pre-power, pre-symbolic.

Unfortunately, what Descartes remembered as unstable, and what Freud described as repression, Lacanianism sets into the possible as the ideal strategy for the power abuses of western state nationalism/doublethink: you accept that there is an 'other' and simultaneously repress it; you remember to forget the other. The psychoanalytic stance foregrounds ideological power as the determining characteristic for both gender and language, and then analyses how we ignore it. This dis-membering forgetfulness has emerged in the multinational state as ethnocentricity and can be read as a backlash, similar to the backlash against feminism in the 80s, against the moral intensity of theorists/philosophers such as Derrida and Brossard who use the Phaedrean tryptic in its fulness, as well as a backlash against the overwhelming needs of the disempowered 'other' as presented to the empowered by their own media/communications technology.

The shift of the Phaedrean tryptic to a hierarchical duality of an initial change/gift, and then more important, exchange/power, also has implications for the social understanding of poetics. Freudian/Lacanian theory is built on post-Cartesian thinkers and their conceptualizations of the self, and it achieves a flexible and popular discourse for these ideas. Just so, the implications of the theory for nationalism lie in the discourse field that opens up to the concepts already articulated in another domain; and the implications of the theory for poetics are most evident in the sophisticating of a vocabulary for contemporary practices. The dominating metaphor for poetics becomes individual sacrifice within and to a system of power,[25] that elaborates on the essential activity of fantasy, the role of commodification within fantasy, and the difficulties of reciprocal exchange that make the fetish both banal and constructive[26]: All of which is predicated on the concept of the inadequacy of language.

Now, language: If Descartes dreamed of a language that could fully re-present phenomena, he knew the limitations of language as a condition. But those working in Cartesian space took the dream as a possibility. This possibility held within it a multitude of utopias, including the hope that the new political systems of increasing state government could create a large and cohesive commonwealth to replace the feudal: no small dream. However, while the poets always knew differently, the politicians, scientists, philosophers, theologians (who had always had this tendency to forget) began, at least on the printed pages we still keep, to forget that representation is *necessarily* limited, and to think of the limitation as a problematic inadequacy. What Freud made accessible to everyone was a vocabulary for discussing this idea that representation is inadequate.

If Cartesian space splits the body from the mind, thought becomes articulable and separate from the body. Further, the mind cannot deal with the possibility of inarticulated knowledge: The history of psychology since the seventeenth-century is an attempt to deal with the detritus flung from this severance which makes the inarticu-lated/able (ie. not systematic/ideological) 'mad,' located in the body, deranged. Just as there are tensions in Freud's simultaneous and contradictory linkage and separation of the body/mind, so there are tensions in his contradictory separation and hope for linkage between the articulated and the inarticulable. At the centre of Freud's definition of psychosis, neurosis and narcissism, is the 'other' as inarticulable. The 'other' becomes allied with the inarticulable body, hence what *is* articulated is never complete, never adequate to reality because it doesn't deal with all phenomena. To articulate, to *think*, in Cartesian space is to enter a system of representation increasingly dominated by the need for stable representations of ideology. The more pervasive this ideological discourse becomes, the more stable the representation, the more inadequate the inarticulable. This is the strategy that invents desire.

When Lacan extends this inadequacy into the split between the imaginary and the symbolic, the symbolic, like the mind, becomes what is articulated, what can be said; and the imaginary becomes the 'body,' what cannot be articulated and is presymbolic. This is a necessary move if he is to make a case for the split subject and the structure of fantasy, and to prove his point he introduces the different bodies of women, using them with a casual curiosity. When you enter language you lose 'phenomenological plenitude.' This loss divides the self, leaving a desire for wholeness. The subject is always made up of the symbolic (necessarily masculine and phallic) and this inarticulable 'other,' which is constantly desired via Lacan's notion of reciprocity. 'Reciprocity' has been developed in terms of fantasy and resistance to commodification, and is of considerable interest to women, given that because women can't fully enter the symbolic they are 'other,' and because they are 'other' they can't enter the symbolic.[27] The movement between desire and knowledge as a movement between inarticulated and articulated is one that depends on a notion of linguistic adequacy underpinned by a profoundly post-Renaissance Christian ideology. A desirable object becomes known by being commodified, fully represented. The pleasure of such commodifying practice reinforces the sense that people live in an ordered, rational world of stable representation. Desire becomes something that leads to the satisfaction of repeating that order (repetition compulsion); or, it may lead to the terror felt at the edge of chaos (death), coincident with bliss or jouissance. Bliss is felt to be closer to the real because it's as if we make order out of chaos, risk ourselves in a metaphorical sacrifice. This also accords with a post-renaissance concept of 'beauty.'

But in effect it's impossible to distinguish between the two because you can never know whether 'risk' and 'chaos' are simply the result of not understanding the systematic order all around you. The one is fully-fledged narcissism, suppressing the absent term and projecting completions/commodities such as God or woman from the phallic symbolic: the economy of the same. The other is a fetishization of desire that locates the 'other,' displaces into commodity rather than completes the subject: an economy of displacement, the failure of which makes necessary sacrifices. Both operate within the structure of fantasy, and assume an inadequacy of language. The problem for women is that in either economy they are not only a central metaphor for desire, power and commodity, but also they are inarticulable and therefore unable to articulate.

The reciprocity that fantasy enables can devolve as just drawn, into commodity or banal fetish, but some readings offer reciprocity as a version of dialectical reasoning, constant movement of exchange between self and other, so that identity is internally alienated, and the subject is never complete. In this version, women cannot be offered linguistic adequacy, but neither are they commodified by others. The 'other' here is rooted in the body and the inarticulable, but can be written into the symbolic as the mystical, the religious. Of course in one sense this is Lacan (and others) simply re-discovering through poetics the limited rather than inadequate work of language, in a political world which has denied the instability of representation; but in another, it is a dangerous sidelining into experience marginal to ideological stability. In the face of theories that deal otherwise with the fear of chaos via concepts of total system (Althusser) and total inadequacy of representation (Baudrillard), Lacan has tried hard to deal with the sense of individual response, yet like them is still caught in the ambergris of Cartesian space.

Contacting Reality in Cartesian Space: Inadequacies and Practices
BUT, there are different approaches to the limitations of language made possible by reading Freud in alternative ways. To return to Descartes: By remembering the instability of language, part of the common ground for Descartes' thinking is that 'thought' is a way of working toward articulating the not-yet-articulated. Like 'theory,' which in many contemporary discourses tends to get separated from practice but which is in effect the same thing, his 'thought' is trying for appropriate representations of practice: but why? Articulating practice is understood variously as a way of contacting 'reality' and as a way of making individual practice social.[28] Freud described the in-articulable as the repressed, focusing on two different kinds of repression, into the unconscious (not possible to articulate) and the subconscious (possible to articulate). The 'unconscious' becomes a concept responding to the sense of a systematic stable ideology inaugurated by nation state governments that emerge in post-renaissance Europe. It is a way of providing an origin or raison d'être for the 'private,' and links the private with the body, particularly the body we cannot articulate.

If the unconscious is understood as a constructed political response to authoritarian politics, then there is a clear transition into a wide variety of social repressions under state governments which institutionalize community functions. If the state is authoritarian but also powerful and systematic, then the disempowered are not just partially repressed but completely repressed, eradicated from participation. The terms become: unconscious vs. system; private vs. state; isolated individual vs. nation. But what this also does, apart from providing a political rather than a biological reason for the unconscious, is ally the impossibility of articulation with disempowerment.

The alliance has a curious effect on people who are in effect empowered and should thereby be able to articulate because the system works for them. They hold the position they are in because a state system defines them as powerful in a particular way, so if people are empowered then their inability to articulate must be a result of the system. This seems to make sense because the system is presented as a symbolic mode of representation that is taken as necessarily (and hopelessly) inadequate. It is only those who are disempowered who understand that (in)articulation is work. The unconscious as the split self is the response of the powerful/empowered to their own sense of the hopeless inadequacy of the public representation of the symbolic to their individual and 'private' lives. And it is those who have been *relatively* empowered who have used the 'unconscious' as an analytical tool for articulating systems of authoritative power: for example Frantz Fanon on the colonial subject or Juliet Mitchell (among others)[29] on the repressed woman.

It is vitally important that authoritative systems of power are analyzed critically from within their own terms: They cannot 'hear' anything else because it is repressed, absent, dis-membered by forgetfulness. But those relatively empowered speakers are in a highly ambivalent position, dependent on the degree of their disempowered status. Within this powerful system of discourse, in order to talk about the disempowered, they have to talk about the unconscious, but in talking about the unconscious they accept the framework of authoritative state vs. private that creates disempowerment. If their aim is to interpellate a disempowered subject into the representative system (already taken to be inadequate) this is valuable because then that subject can be 'heard,' but simultaneously that subject is dismissable as inadequate. This inadequacy only diminishes as the representation moves closer to the sufficiently adequate and the subject is systematized.

In the eyes and ears and mouths of the powerful, the disempowered are dismembered, part of the unconscious, the body, the private. Like the unconscious/body/private, they are part of the 'natural,' the 'intuitive,' the 'primitive,' the 'not-civilized,' the not-articulated. For example, until recently the metaphors for women make no separation between gender and sexuality because the body defines their position outside the symbolic. Just so, the body defines the position of visibly 'different' people outside the system. This is one reason why class analysis was effective for so long: it was difficult to locate the 'poor' outside the system on body terms, so it was done in terms of the 'private'—although the spurious connecting of a working class with sexual 'perversion' or the cultural battle over fashion are indications of the way the media are used to transfer 'poor' into bodily 'difference.'

The relegation to the unconscious by state ideology, of women and other physically 'different' groups of people had been so effective a political strategy for stable representation that Freud's popularization of an emerging vocabulary for discussing this repression was of course profoundly unsettling. By definition the unconscious should have remained inarticulable. With psychological and psychoanalytic methodology, a discourse was formed both to enable people to talk about the language as inadequate and why representations are to be distrusted, and even ignored as in the forgetfulness of ethnocentricity; and to encourage people to attempt articulations of the 'different,' often using the body as the site for alternative articulations as in feminism's 'writing the body': re-membering and dismembering the individual in Cartesian space. But this version of language under-writes the sacrificial metaphor for poetics. Women, and others, can begin to talk and insert themselves into the dominant, but only at the cost of severance and mutilation. *The symbolic is powerful because it is defined by conditions of inadequacy materially realized by 'others': women are by definition inadequate.*

This is where it gets really difficult: This version of 'Writing the body,' re-membering the individual, within a system based on notions of linguistic inadequacy, is always going to run close to accepting the concept of the unconscious as biological and hence of a private, owned, and commodifiable sexuality and writing. Brossard speaks of writing as different from text, and "thought of as a machine capable of helping us resolve problems of sense, puts us in a position where we think we are able to produce truth, that is, reality,"[30] or that is, adequate representation. The urgency of Cixous' early writing, which reclaimed the body from metaphors in the symbolic system, is carried out by repetition—repetition that can never be exact and is therefore potentially various, yet repetition always under hideous constraints demanding that poetics becomes a heroic attempt at individual adequacy, challenging the *a priori* inadequacy of anything outwith ideology. Or: Kristeva's linguistic terror/ism. The violence of this enforced opposition describes precisely the system's brutality to all who are different, here women. At the same time it participates in the sacrificial metaphor, the writer undergoing mutilation and severance on behalf of a community.

Put in this abstract and rather dry manner, the sacrificial metaphor appears obvious in its futility. Yet it is not surprising that women writers exposed to a pervasive philosophical discourse field that defines poetics in this way should try to write back through it, as I am doing here, to other philosophical authorities in a search for another metaphor. For example, there is Daphne Marlatt's writing in *Musing with the Mothertongue*, through etymology and myth to the Kristevan chora. Or there is Erin Mouré's stab at Aristotle by way of a peculiarly Canadian emphasis that has been provided via the large number of writers who came into contact with the work of George Whalley: ie. Plato's Aristotle. Brossard speaks of this in *Picture theory*[31] saying,

No matter which cities, books repeat us, take the form of our emotions. The necessity for certain positions prior to feminist thought. Yes this body takes up a strategic stand in the streets of the Polis of men, yes, this body dis/places the horizon of thought, if it wants, this body is generic.(143)

Generic bodies, articulatable bodies, have to work through the sites of philosophical discourse to understand both how they come to be articulated and whether they can be articulated differently.

The see-saw between system and individual, authority and arbitrary, determined and relativist, nation state ideology and subject, this see-saw is predicated on a notion that there is an externally ordered world: a system. It is predicated on the concept that language should be able to represent that order. However, neither the order nor the representation is ever complete; and yet because it is 'supposed' to be, the incompletion is taken as an inadequacy, a failure, something to drive desire. In turn, individual people are reduced to subjects forever under a naturalized power-relation. Because many western societies accept a version of this implicitly in their structures of state government, it becomes an immediate reality that has to be dealt with on its own terms. And there are many writers in relatively empowered academic and intellectual communities who attempt to do so. But it can also be addressed as Brossard addresses the writing of Stein and Wittgenstein, working with the flexibility of a language never intended to be adequate. And it can be addressed on the other terms of writing the body suggested by the political gesture of the unconscious: of making practice social.

Making Practice Social
To 'Write the body' by writing from the practices of life must partly be in response to institutional systems, yet it is also to do with many areas of non-institutional daily life. I would like to argue that there are many sites where language is not considered a problem of inadequate representation with its penumbra of failure, power, desire and commodification. Rather there are places where we negotiate communications, work with other people to arrive at immediately appropriate uses; places where in effect we sometimes resent the sacrifice-at-a-distance made 'for' us by someone who has the apparent luxury of being *able* to choose to become 'other.' If representation is taken as necessarily limited rather than inadequate, all order is necessarily socially questionable and negotiable.[32] There is no mysteriously (or mystically) externally-ordered world. There is no need for the terror of chaos, and when things get commodified we know about it. Unarticulated knowledge can here be seen to resist commodification to the extent that it cannot be systematized. But the attempt at an articulation of it is helpful: We value the articulated particularly at the moment of its articulation because we know the context and the activity of discussion that made it possible. It becomes part of the way we assess common ground, take decisions and act.[33]

Poetics in western thought has always been a place to work on articulations that are difficult to make. It has provided a location for focusing on cultural tensions or knots and unpicking them, unravelling the weave of social texts and re-texturing, hammering out appropriate words, shifting the common grounds. Prior to the Renaissance other pressures bear upon the direction of poetics, but increasingly since the seventeenth century poetics has become contextualized within the pervasiveness of state ideology necessary to nation state ethos, and the context has shifted the emphasis to the heroic and sacrificial poet, also coincident with Christian humanism, that reinforces the primacy of power over change/gift interaction. Recent western writers have turned to craft and skilled practice, or the labour of care, in order to find articulations to value daily work outwith the success/failure criteria of symbolic power.[34] *Phaedrus* offers medicine, gardening, writing as textuality, as examples of the practices, the labour needed to maintain love as change/gift.

What emerges is a metaphor of labour, connotative with class struggle, physical work, birthing. There can be puritanical associations, but 'labour' here is not put forward as some grim duty; it need not be without a sense of Derridean 'play' but it is insistently communal in a way not easy to recognize in Derrida's own direct rejections of inadequacy in his concepts of fold, erasure, difference, supplementarity, etc: And while labour is work, it is not put forward as a mechanical or technical exercise in strategy, as in recent theories of communicative argumentation, but more as in L. Wittgenstein's own attack on the poverty of the case/silence duality, with his development of justificatory negotiation rather than judgements.[35] 'Labour' for me is also for the moment more enabling than 'sacrifice,' partly because sacrifice is cast as individual while labour is more frequently communal and I'm tired of being alone, and partly because I'm also tired of being a sacrifice and continually returning to heroic self-mutilation in face of the symbolic.

Poetics as Labour

The problem with poetics as labour is that it requires commitment to working on a communal agreement of some kind however context-dependent. Poetics asks the writer/audience to deal with the difficulties of articulations that untie cultural knots that bind us in particular ways, and reweave them into appropriate texturings. This is difficult work because it requires time and energy, so we need good reasons before we can commit ourselves to it. This is also vulnerable work because between the untying of the knot and the retying of the strands, our common grounds, which we both stand upon and understand, fall away. We need to trust to mutual support before we can do it. Again, Brossard describes such an "assemblage" or *contextus* of women working together at a film festival "Invigorated, we are women's creative energy gathered together" (*Aerial Letter*, 129); and later, context as "inspiration" that "restores to the community of women their energy. The energy of each captivating woman activates women's energy, and it is from this energy that a collective consciousness of who we are is born" (130).

The commitment to the labour of poetics has to come from the response of an audience that wants to attempt new common ground—But there are many difficulties surrounding both commitment and support. A common way of proceeding is via a small group thrashing things out and hoping by mediation (in print) that others will recognize the appropriateness, see the light. The structure is avant-garde, and runs uncomfortably close to ethnocentric club culture and to much modern science. Larger audiences/communities are more difficult to form unless one goes for less difficult shifts in common ground. My argument is not that the more difficult it is the fewer people will read the writing, or the more challenging it is. Rather, my argument is that the more dislocating the writing is to a *particular* common ground, the more or less committed people will be to responding to it, and that this commitment is affected by numerous conditions. For example, since dislocations to culturally foregrounded structures are easier than dislocations to more naturalized structures, generic and narrative grounds in which western education and mass culture specializes are the most likely to gain a large audience in the short term, but just because they are culturally foregrounded they are more constrained in the extent of their dislocation. It is more difficult to gain a commitment for a dislocation to a naturalized common ground because they are more difficult to see as grounds, but the effects are far-reaching.

Given this, dislocation can be an act of desperation, to loosen up the social and cultural restrictions no matter what: a gamesmanship of which language poetry has been accused. If language poetry addresses the frames of language itself—syntax, phonemes, morphemes—it will be more difficult simply because people take these grounds as natural. But it doesn't generate much commitment from the disempowered to say, as F. Jameson does, that since you can't disorganize the fetish of capitalist society the poet must work in the pre-symbolic of language; or to say as G. Hartley does, that poetics is meta-symbolic, and that you can't dislocate the symbolic system but you can comment upon and critique the structure. Both responses are from a position of relative empowerment, they both assume Freudian/Lacanian linguistic inadequacy and are rootedly anarchic acts which like all anarchy are contained within the system. Yet dislocation can also be a directed act, positioned toward a particular kind of work, with the problem being that the positioning may not be recognized because the grounds are so fundamentally shifted, or possibly being that this work may be of a kind people do not want to do on that position—they may not think it important enough or they may find it too frightening even with support.

Commitment will come from the perceived or enacted stance of the poetics, mediated by its cultural and social position (race, gender, ethnicity, sexuality...) and medium (magazine, book, newspaper, sheet). Commitment comes not from ethos, which is the relatively stable construction of the writing's voice whether generically specific or non-specific, but stance, which invites into shared work on articulation and appropriate significance. A stress on the labour of poetics as change/gift presumes that the individual is working with other people, doing work that is acted upon but not contained within state discourse, that power is a contingency. It also presumes that the individual is not alone because this would be an impossibility—there is after all no such thing as a private isolated individual. In effect we work with others all the time on a common ground of power relations which, with support, we are always able to attempt to reground by work on appropriateness for our communities.

Lola Lemire Tostevin opens her introduction to *Redrawing the Lines...*[36] by proclaiming variety, stating that the women contributing to this issue "never violate other women's theories, other women's freedom to express" (5), yet notes that not many women of colour responded to the invitation to contribute. Partly this may be to do with the status of *Open Letter* which is from the world of the relatively empowered, the marginal intellectual. Partly one suspects, in the absence of any information about how writers were invited to contribute, that it has to do with the penumbra of Lemire Tostevin = language-focused writing = white/male elite literary culture. However, among the contributors' accounts of their writing lives there is some awareness of this, particularly in the essay by Marchessault, cited in the opening to this discussion.

The accounts of women's writing lives consistently describe the importance of finding a textual community. Several do so through the vocabulary of Freudian/ Lacanian psychoanalysis as it is mediated by Cixous, Kristeva, Irigaray and others. Many do so through Brossard's theoretical writings. But all do so through lists of other women writers who form their communities and who are spoken of in terms of gift/change, embrace and love. Joanne Arnott says "The poem is the vehicle inside of which she and I meet, embrace, and give each other strength for the journey" (8). Anne Michaels says "not action instead of words, but rather, action and words, Writing is one kind of giving.

To become what you wish to give, quite another" (99). Or Nancy
Chater's political self-love which is love within a "collectivity ...
commitment/responsibility/accountability to a community or larger
social context" (32). Perhaps because these accounts are autobiographical they do occasionally construct a curious intersection
between genre-writing and language-focused writing, that moves
toward the kind of materiality of labour for writer and reader that
Brossard and Marlatt work within. This is the kind of stance that
engenders commitment. It offers recognizable common grounds and
provides a poetics to challenge, unpick and retextualize. In this it is
no different from genre-writing texts, Marchessault's "realism," where
working on materiality also goes on.

Coda
Work on materiality and common ground is often unexpected. It is not
to do with identity politics, solidarity or authentic voice, but with
being part of work with other people on the articulation of aspects of
life different to those defined by ideological representation. That
difference, and the perception of it, is important to our awareness of
the limitations of the ideological. But simply noting difference, in say
class, gender or race, is to note only the representation of it, not its
agency. To understand the agency you need to be part of the
communal work. Representations of difference are important but need
to be contextualized within their complex relationship with ideology,
for ideology is itself the strategy of a stable ruling system of permitted
representations that position the subject.

Psychoanalytic vocabularies offered by Freud and Lacan provided
a way of describing and analyzing this relationship between the
individual and the nation state, and their focus has been on ways that
sexuality had been constructed into a statement about the position of
the subject within ideology. Writers such as M. Foucault have of
course elaborated on sexuality not as the bodily erotic, but precisely
as permissable representations of the body within the state system.
Indeed, the erotic is rather a mode of agency: the eroticization of
desire occurs at the moment when the physical body fits the
sexual/sexuality; eroticization can be viewed as a way of bringing the
subject into the representations of ideology. Just so, beauty can be the
individual eroticizing actuality into representations of reality defined
by ideology. Power can be constructed similarly as an eroticization of
ruling.

But if the agency of eroticization brings individuals into representation, it also indicates that there are moments when individuals are not represented within ideology. The moment of instantiation into representation is at the same time the moment of commodification, and ideology simultaneously gives that sense of 'fit' to representation and necessitates the activity that leads to it. You could think of ideology as the source of contemporary western aesthetics, the bliss/jouissance of instantiation being dependent upon it. The simultaneity of bliss/jouissance with commodification in 'fit' is also the source of the attempts to maintain that moment, to extend recognition of beauty/desire/power beyond the moment of its occurence, which lead to the frustration of desire and yet also to the satisfactions of pleasure.

The possibility of 'fit' implies both notions of adequacy/adequate representation and of places outwith 'fit.' Those places outwith 'fit' may be preliminary unarticulated desires, or they may be quite different to the limited articulations of the ideology-subject axis. Within that axis all need becomes desire, and deprives the individual of further agency, leaving them overdetermined in commodified representations. Yet living together with other people alongside the operations of ruling state systems, as one set of events currently defined by the ideology-subject axis, need is not turned into desire but is held in the middle of many contingencies. Here, alongside, agency becomes the inability to turn need into desire.

Many language-focused writers, writing through the vocabularies of Freud and Lacan, write at the centre of the ideology-subject axis, because that vocabulary is located precisely there, between the individual and the nation state. Yet many also write through to the other side of representations, dealing in the middle of the difficulty of articulation with the agency of words that net together a material ground. This work is not representative; hence it can easily also be taken as undemocratic. But if we work with it, rather than merely note or observe its lack of representation, we may find unexpected commonality in the labour.

CHAPTER SIX

Critical Embarrassment with the *Bios* of Writing:

Autobiography and Social Violence

These readings come from a recognition that there is a growing body of a particular kind of work by women writers in cultures different to my own that I think is important to read if I and other women are to respond to the issues they discuss. Indeed we are specifically called upon to hear and respond by eloquent writers such as Emma LaRocque,[1] or the Native arts activist Viola Thomas who encourages readers to continue to empower women writers by,

raising the issue within the learning schools of whether or not their books are part of the schooling ... by seeking out their books and reading them ... by sharing what you learned ... with your beloved ones, because each of us in our way can help each other come to a better understanding by really sharing.[2]

But this kind of writing often causes embarrassment both to me personally when I read it for the first time, and in a rather more difficult way for me as a teacher, to my students when I attempt to include it on courses. Most worryingly, these works are often, possibly for reasons of similar embarrassment,[3] silenced by the world of literary criticism which at the least has a powerful means of disseminating them and extending the response.

My work as a teacher of English-language literature from a variety of literary cultures in Canada puts a focus on developing critical skills for cross-cultural work within an educational framework that is training readers in conventions acceptable to the tertiary institutions in Britain. Readers who have not learned how to read for difference as well as sameness find ways of rejecting or dismissing a text, and as they do so they dismiss the value of the person, and the life of the writer, and the potential for the conversation necessary to carry cross-cultural work with texts out into society. With the conventional expectations of realism that surround autobiography, conveying claims on truth and a congruency with 'reality,' there is even more difficulty in locating difference in the increasing number of texts written by people from groups until recently marginal to commercial literary production but central to social and political understanding and change. Addressing the ground of social violence and working by example from within a privileged institutional framework, these readings suggest that a reader's embarrassment with autobiographical texts, if approached positively can act as an indicator of difference and sameness. It can help readers to work out a vocabulary for new ways of reading, articulating differences in writing, talking about and acting from that work, which is part of the process of learning about and valuing other people's representations of reality.

In common with their contemporaries in many other countries, Canadian women writers new to publishing often write autobiographical or first person narratives.[4] The writers are taking hold of and making sense of their lives and inserting that life into a dominant social medium. As Nicole Brossard says with respect to all people who come to writing, "one must want, consciously or not, to make the world aware of one's existence."[5] It is markedly the case that people from groups in some way marginalized by the dominant social order, marginalized possibly by making access to literacy or to publication difficult and yielding writers new to a print public whether newly literate or literate of long-standing, frequently begin by writing autobiography. In order to remove from a position of marginality, the individual needs to communicate personal experience as significant social event. This may be done to engage others into the therapy of recognition and support which can then turn to common practice, or to authorize self in order to effect control within social and political structures.

In both cases the process of communication empowers and validates the individual and her community.[6] It starts a conversation with others who are invited to engage with and commit themselves to understanding that community because they too are at some point implicated in it. Yet in the institutional setting of literary criticism there are few skills taught for reading the conventions of autobiography, especially those of the often intimate mode of much women's autobiography, as a way of knowing that can contribute to understanding. As Bettina Aptheker says of an early reading of Adrienne Rich's autobiography, we did not know how to order women's experience as knowledge, because we had no method of 'thinking in common.'[7]

For both reader and writer it is important to develop such methods. Autobiography in both conventional and institutional literary culture in the Anglo-American west is intimately linked to devices of realism, foregrounding its effects with claims to authenticity. Yet autobiography differs from realism, or social biography, because it is about trying to articulate a vocabulary adequate to individual experience of 'reality.' There is here an issue I will not pursue about the writer's perception of what adequacy is and how far that representation interacts with learned constructions of reality. Instead, my focus is on the reader's perception and the politics of the reader's reading activity, particularly in terms of recognizing individual experience and the adequacy of its representation. Autobiography also has conventional rules guided by publishing pressures and pressures of the reader-writer agreement: Both text and reader are institutionally produced. Conventional autobiography is closely allied with realism precisely because realistic devices have carefully constructed and socially accepted and maintained truth claims, or claims on reality.

Both realism and autobiography stem from a moment in literary history, embedded in visual verisimilitude and in the tacit rather than overt use of assumptions about the representation of social reality. Conventional autobiography is conventional by definition when it finds the conventions recognized as adequate to expression. But autobiography, or writing about one's own life, has often been written outside of printed publication pressures yet still with readers and dissemination in mind: For example, religious autobiography, diaries, accounts of domestic lives, accounts of slavery. And while many of these writings are highly conventional, in others there are frequent differences from literary convention.[8]

Readers reading autobiographies, particularly those dealing with social abuse that cannot be evaded as a fictional construct because it is a social event continually being documented by the mass media, are dealing immediately with the politics of sameness and difference. Conventional autobiography, precisely because readers already know the conventions, can be contained in a tacit decorum of reading that usually denies the recognition of cultural difference. Readers have decorous strategies for repressing the actuality of the inadequate response our society makes to violence or abuse. Readers also have decorous strategies for appropriating this inadequacy and assuming that recognition of it is all that is necessary. The more different the events in the account of social reality from the reader's reality, the easier it is to elide into strategies for repression or appropriation. This is not to say that readers cannot engage actively with conventional realistic texts of autobiography, but that it is more difficult for them to locate the points of difference since realist texts are based on acceptance of common ground that denies the need for writer or reader or society to find more appropriate or adequate expression. When difference is located, it is often discussed entirely in terms of the institutional framework: critically and analytically but without attempting the theoretical exploration that can lead to a new vocabulary which articulates possibilities for social action.

Several of the first-person narratives discussed here are from socially marginalized women writers in Canada. By marginalized I understand those people who have difficulty of access to participating in the modes of communication that carry power and authority in their society. Canadians traditionally have available in writing/reading an identity-presenting process that enables a route into social participation.[9] They are educated in the habits and conventions of this process for a good ten years and sometimes more of their younger life. The specific intent of the Canadian education process is to impart skills in this process. Marginalized people in Canada frequently have a personal history that has been denied many of the routes for social participation, and in particular denied the route of access to education in their language of birth, literacy, writing, print, publication, dissemination and response. Yet it is through this route that social, political and legal power and authority is mediated.[10]

A new writer from a marginalized group can come with a far more self-conscious need to write self into social action. And as Brossard again suggests, the new writer has to be able to present a "positive image" for everything in their life; they need to deny nothing, even the things, or possibly particularly the things, that society would deny for them. This connection with the "bios" of the autograph[11] can be exacerbated by accounts that *appear* so technically unsophisticated that they must be actual; there is no other explanation. Yet the institutionally trained reader's and critic's anxiety about lack of decorum is not only with indecorous writing, but more unnervingly with indecorous reading.

Although readers often try to contain intrusions from other genres and strategies, in practice they find it difficult to do so. Embarrassment can result from the recognition that both the literary and the social conventions are broken. When reading from a privileged position readers can both repress embarrassment by claiming writerly failure or 'lack of control,' and can also control embarrassment by appropriating the strategies into an institutional framework. In either case the actuality of social abuse is evaded. There needs to be a recognition that other communities use genre in different ways, that there are different constructions of reality in other lives, that the implications of social violence are different for different communities. Embarrassment can be a help to this recognition because it locates points of difference.

Given the need to engage with texts concerned with important social issues, the readings here emphasize issues of sexual violence and abuse as a ground for beginning to discuss other social violence and abuse as well. The need is there because these texts are often dismissed by the institutions that teach literary criticism, for complicated reasons, as 'low-status.' Until we can begin to articulate a common ground, a vocabulary for such social abuse, which is more often subsumed into repression and appropriation, we cannot deal with it. The process of engaged reading is to locate the difficulties and differences, and find ways of discussing them that do not just repress or appropriate. Engaged reading, in this instance in a classroom, is about hammering out a way of talking about, articulating responses often for the first time, and dealing with immediate social and political events: Here, with social violence and abuse that we may not understand, that we may feel complicit in, and that will not change until the vocabulary and topical ground can begin more adequately to address it, engaged reading is social action and leads to social change.

*

In a British university classroom where I as a white middle-class woman deal in a formally accepted pedagogy for teaching English literature that does not acknowledge embarrassment, or indeed difference, as anything other than someone's failure, it becomes important to develop strategies that will encourage the positive use of these recognitions. The readings that follow of the six Canadian writers, are readings from a privileged position in my society of race, class, education and, increasingly problematic for my society, of stable family. In the readings there is an attempt to work through some of the uneasiness that a reader trained in the decorum of realism has with the culturally constructed status of realism as superior to genre fiction, and to address some of the difficulties this raises in reading first-person texts from different cultural communities. In the readings there is also an uncomfortable recognition of sameness and difference that comes from being a woman reading women's writing, which sameness provides a point of contact and a potential common ground for valuing and discussing, but is not sufficient to the differences of tribal community structure, colour, experience of incest and of social violence. If one of the axes of this discussion is the construction of appropriate representation in autobiography from a variety of different communities, the other is the politics of reading about social violence and abuse in different communities.

In Canada, the conventional generic area in which autobiography by women has been published is that of diaries, letters and journals which, because they have not been considered genres of formal published 'literature,' encourage us to read their autobiographical accounts as unselfconscious and intimate—although, as many other autobiographical genres indicate, there is no necessity for intimacy in personal accounts of life.[12] In western anglophone society, the formal decorum of writing in these earlier genres of diary, letter, and journal is now usually considered private, implying a confidential addressee and a story that is not to be revealed to others, and occasionally a measure of reader embarrassment results from the use of their intimate mode for the broad audience of printed products. More problematic is the transference of that intimacy into other generic forms, for once the date-line is taken off diaries, journals and letters, they generate a wide range of autobiographical models that carry with them some of the impetus to speak to an intimate audience, despite being aimed at printed publication and wide distribution.

For institutionally trained readers, an awareness of the private social role of these models often makes their personal accounts intensely embarrassing: But what exactly is there to be embarrassed about? The transgression of their conventionally unpublished status, along with their frequently unconventional—in other words non-literary/non-grammatical —narrative style, acts to authenticate them as documents from 'real' people somehow denoting informational content about socially private spheres. It is as if this type of writing reveals too much, does not employ the necessary deceptions of circulated, published, literature and leaves the writer unacceptably vulnerable, an actual person: as if instead of playing a game, the player leaves themself inadvertently defenceless through ignorance of the rules. Recognition of indecorous style or inappropriate social context becomes particularly embarrassing when the reader cannot distinguish between whether the account is autobiographical or fictional. We are taught that we can never hope to distinguish between the two. As critics we often ask whether it makes any difference. But in effect it does make a difference because awareness of claims to autobiography or to fictionality can help us to assess whether there is an exploitation of the intimate going on, or whether we have here new forms of social realism.

The focus of these readings is also on the way that all these first person narratives are traversed by genre-fiction devices. Some are overtly fictional, some have autobiographical elements, and some are overtly autobiographical. They may be grouped into texts that focus personal experience explicitly in terms of social realities and a community, and texts that focus personal experience only implicitly against a background of the social. In both cases the embarrassment indicates points at which we recognize the inequalities of social and political power. The first group of writings, by Maria Campbell, Beatrice Culleton, and Jeannette Armstrong addresses a number of specific marginalized communities but particularly the Métis and Aboriginal peoples of Canada and North America;[13] the second group of writings, by Elly Danica, Jacqueline Dumas, and Rose Doiron focuses on individuals living within variously marginalized communities in Canada.[14]

These texts are women reaching out to each other. They are published to initiate conversation about issues that are difficult to articulate, yet of pressing importance to discuss and to attempt to understand if anything is to be done about the violence, hatred and brutality in which that social abuse results. The narratives all have much in common stylistically and topically, particularly in their portrayal of events from personal struggle, despair, violence and abuse, and in their use of domestic tragedy and comedy, melodrama and genre-fiction devices. Unlike diaries, letters and journals, there is a great deal of embarrassment that emerges in critical responses to genre-fiction strategies in the intimate autobiographical mode. What is embarrassing at the outset is the sense that a cross-over between autobiography and genre-fiction is an exploitation of the intimate. Crossing over with conventional and obviously artificialized genre reading, this mixed autobiography can cease to be a commentary on the real and frequently becomes melodramatic, explicitly disrupting the expected strategies and topics of realism[15] precisely because realism depends on not foregrounding its artificiality. Occuring within the intensely realist traditions of autobiography and first person narrative, from which the realist stylistics of the post-renaissance novel may at least in part be said to derive, the exaggeration of melodrama will trigger disbelief, thereby losing an important element in the response to personal and first-person narrative.

Further, because genre-fiction writing is so involved in wish-fulfilment strategies, either exploitations of or challenges to social repression often concerning murder, rape, war, and sex, when its topics and devices are shifted into autobiographical writing it is difficult for the reader to read them without the habitual titillations and satisfactions of the consumerist expectations in pornographic sex and violence. Within the context of autobiography this response can implicate the reader in a more immediate way that often causes resentment. A similar effect is created in first-person narratives that claim familiarity by way of their immediate reference to social realities. Crudely put, the problem for someone educated in conventional literary reading is the tension between recognition of the writing as valuable social activity on behalf of women either communally or individually, and an anxiety about readerly decorum. Readers can become both embarrassed about the apparent naivety of the textual strategies that expose the writer's vulnerability and resentfully embarrassed about the vulnerability those strategies generate in the reader.

Embarrassment, unlike shame which is felt by those who live with knowledge of their disempowerment,[16] can be for the reader a humiliating recognition of being on the empowered side of an unequal struggle,[17] possibly a suppression of anger at the recognition that some-where the writer should have been educated into the rules, should have been empowered with choice. Lack of embarrassment may result from an inability to recognize that there is any struggle at all, or possibly from an arrogant assertion of necessary superiority as the reader denies or appropriates difference into the decorum of realism.

Yet embarrassment is of the reader's own making, partly resulting from an assumption that the rules are forgotten inadvertently, transgressed through ignorance, that only texts for conventional printed publication are literate. But of course the writers may have specifically set out to use these forms precisely because of their literary context: not following the rules permits them to challenge, which challenge is in itself is a potential embarrassment particularly if the reader perceives it as hopeless.

More complicated than this readerly perceived failure of written decorum is embarrassment that results from perceived failure in the reader's own decorum. Elements from the socially immediate world such as child abuse or violence or rape, are simultaneously significant social topics for wider power relations which in writing become literary topics for or icons of those pressures and deformations that instigate such social events. These writers may choose to throw forward the elements in order to draw upon social assumptions. Once more we find a tension between written accounts of what actually has happened, and accounts that implement such events as topics in literary writing. It is a tension that raises questions about whether the account is exploitation or there to initiate discussion about the social pressures around such events? In other words is it a challenge or a manipulation? Embarrassment arises when the critic or reader is not sure, because actuality is often the guarantee that an account constitutes necessary discussion rather than exploitation. On the other hand, not being sure can change the kind of necessary social action from being a response to an immediate abuse to being a more long-term response to broader social pressures.

It is within the readers' choice to empower the text for themselves and read it as a conscious product. The reader can conventionalize it and get rid of embarrassment, or can recognize through embarrassment the strength of the unconventional, the difficult to tell. Sky Lee speaks of the difficulty the 'Telling It' conference had in figuring out a workshop technique "to express anger safely,"[18] and she concludes, "By now, I know we can't express anger safely." But embarrassment is partly a condition of trying to do just that, and generates distinctly physical unease. Embarrassment that comes from an unconventional reading acts as a positive indication because it alerts the reader to a lack of socially negotiated and/or constructed controls, to hints of physicality and to need for work on articulation.[19]

With more publication of texts within the modes of autobiography and genre fiction, readers become and are becoming more aware of the different stylistic conventions employed within this mixed genre. Readers may even experience guilt for their embarrassment and suppress their anger—they may even forget it. But given that such a forgetting can naturalize positions of power and encourage the reader also to forget the social, I suspect that we should work on strategies that maintain the potential in embarrassment both as a guide to recognizing where there is a need for social change, and as a place to work through to ways of 'thinking in common' so that the need can be acted upon.

*

Each book in the first group of writings I am concerned with here has a different generic claim. One is autobiography, one is fiction with autobiographical elements, and one is fiction. Yet all three are linked by their common social and political purpose: to begin to articulate community experiences that have been repressed, and by the potential embarrassment felt as a result of melodrama and genre-fiction devices: their lack of formal decorum to the institutionally trained reader.

Few writers can import genre-fiction devices effectively, and those who do generate texts that cause considerable critical confusion, such as Maria Campbell's *Halfbreed*[20] whose intense control of realism contains the potential violence of the devices. Campbell's book is unusually difficult to engage with as autobiography because it has been edited down from over 2000 pages to less than 200. Campbell has stated in interview that in the process she succeeded in transforming her writing from a personal addiction into "a tool in my work to try to educate people and to make it easier for other women who were still in those kinds of circumstances."[21] Campbell chooses to present the voice of this 'autobiography' as that of a woman who as a young child read the 'classics' of her mother's library: Shakespeare, Dickens, Scott and Longfellow. However, she has to leave school early to help look after her sisters and brothers, and only turns to writing much later in life. The framework for the writing is the 'story of a life' set against a detailed realistic description of historical event and landscape that carries the burden of the broader social story of the Métis in prairie Canada.

The narrative moves from conventional novelistic presentation to a more disjointed, 'I'-centred story as it moves from description to personal recollection, but it never loses the control of realism. For example the story of having to tie the younger siblings on a leash of baling twine to trees at the edge of the schoolyard while Maria and the older children go to school is potentially the stuff of melodrama. The reader is told that for the first few days the older children run back and forth to the toilets during classes, to check on the younger, but one day the teacher tells them they must wait until recess. We know that something will happen because it always does in stories set up like this; and Maria knows it too although we are given no clue as to whether her irrational 'knowledge' is connected to guilt, responsibility or other emotivation. Sure enough, at recess she runs out to find Geordie all blue, with twine twisted around his neck. All in a rush, the narrative foregoes further suspense with, "I managed to get him untangled and pounded him on the back. I was sure he was dead but at last he came to, and while hugging him and trying to calm the others saw our teacher standing there" (105). Deflecting the potential tragedy with flat retrospective reporting, and any moral novelistic concern with 'character' by moving onto the teacher, Maria "told her [teacher] then about having no housekeeper; about our fear of losing the family allowance and maybe ending up in an orphanage" (105). The near-death is deflected by the repetitive detail of a list of fears; the fears themselves are made tenable and impossible to dismiss as overreactive melodrama by the event of near-death. Each narrative element controls the other's excess.

Narrative dislocation or excess is also controlled by the collocation of a number of different technical devices, each of which works against 'realism' but collectively builds a different kind of realistic account. At the point that Maria becomes a prostitute the sequence of events starts with a brief description of the desperate situation she is in, ending with "Then I remembered Lil" (133). Now for the reader, as far as we know, as much as for Maria, Lil could be a good samaritan. But the next paragraph changes gear. "I could say at this point that I was innocent and had no idea of what I was getting into. I have even tried to make myself believe this but that would be lying. I did know" (133). The continual repetition of 'I' which breaks the decorum of distanced narration, makes this account stand out as different, private and potentially discomfitting. What should the reader's reaction be? Certainly the character doesn't know how to react. The present narrator initially answers this with the comment that "I feel an overwhelming compassion and understanding for another human being caught in a situation where the way out is so obvious to others but not to him" (133). The text then comes up with, "Dreams are so important in one's life, yet when followed blindly they can lead to the disintegration of one's soul" (133): a broad general statement that on its own might seem, like most platitudes, to claim too great an importance for the private individual. But placed between the personal commentary and the following distanced narrative exemplum of the young girl in the past telling her dreams to her grandmother, the statement is both anchored to the mature narrator's voice and to the personal detail of the central character. It mediates between the intensely private self-questioning and the resultant story of Maria's prostitution, controlling any embarrassment that the reader might feel when the text appears to escape into cliché by yoking together the maturity of the present narrator's voice with the innocence of the dreams of the young girl.

The writer also has a way of speeding plot development on so quickly during sequences of horror and loss that the reader is left partly numbed but also incapable of taking in the full import. In two short paragraphs Campbell recounts Maria's departure from the drug pusher Ray; his profession of love; her move to Calgary with her young daughter; her inability to get a job; her resulting poverty and visit to the Welfare Office and of its rejection of her because she was ineligible. The detail is offered as an introduction to her subsequent unsuccessful plea for help that lands her back in Vancouver and on the streets. But the reader has little time or space for the conventional reactions of realism which might call for sympathy and end in sentiment, nor for dwelling on the emotional potential in the passions of loneliness, frustration and loss. A similar speed of narration carries along the account of the police entering Ray's apartment where Maria is staying several months later. In one paragraph, Maria contacts Ray after a long absence; he nurses her to health, picks up her daughter from the convent, gets them a job on a ranch in Alberta, but first arranges for them to wait in Vancouver until he gets back from Montreal.

Still in the same paragraph, two men arrive: "When you've been in the places I've been in you know cops when you see them"; they ransack the rooms, search the car; question her about Ray "where he was; who he was seeing; was I working for him; how long had I lived with him"; and then the paragraph abruptly ends with "one man grabbed my arm and pulled up the sleeve of my sweater. He pulled it down after seeing the marks were not recent ones" (145). In the next paragraph the action has already moved on to something else. What is particularly interesting, and a device Campbell uses frequently, is the interjection of the brief self-conscious comment "When you've been ..." against the tide of story detail that threatens to overwhelm. Another device here working in a manner similar to the tension generated in the story of Geordie and the twine is the way the reader's apprehension is raised by the action of pulling up the sweater sleeve, to be suddenly released in the following sentence. The device counts on our recognition of the topos of drug-busting, that the drug addict once recognized is usually arrested for pushing on circumstantial evidence. It does not matter that this may not actually be the case. What is important is that the topos is frequently presented this way in both fictional and informative accounts, creating certain expectations that are here disrupted.

The telescoping of realist narrative momentum may well be a pragmatic result of the severe editing the text has undergone. Yet the catalogue of disaster does not stop for the usual melodramatic response to domestic excess. Instead, in this passage the reader is swept along in the detail of the list, only arrested by a self-conscious cliché that alerts us to the writer's awareness of the potential for parody in that excess and by the introduction of another cliché that subverts the parody by not fulfilling our expectations.

Roughly breaking the expected narrative decorum is a strategy often used in this text, particularly in the construction of the 'I-centred' narrative which is built with simple syntax and very short sentences sometimes truncated into partial bits. The technique is found in many other similar 'autobiographical' accounts and indicates first of all an intense control over the events, a grammar that must be kept tightly ordered. But there are further elements indicated: it is difficult to write always referring the reader back to the first person without the continual repetition of 'I,' and while this emphasizes the self-questioning that is going on, it also focuses on an effect of orality, that many of the stories told by an I-narrator are conversational and colloquial. The brevity, truncation and formal ordering of the grammar are precisely not oral, but underline the oral by indicating the difficulty of transposing it onto the written page. Campbell also shifts narrative decorum in her repetition of identical names for different characters such as 'Ray' the pusher and 'Ray' the farm hand. Repetition is usually significant but the reader of *Halfbreed* is frequently left wondering whether or not it is because there appears only a haphazard, wilful twisting of convention in finding any significance. In this particular case the appearance of a second 'Ray' within only a few pages of the last is accompanied by a thrill of tension despite the knowledge that this one can't be the pusher.

The expectation of the reader is undercut in several other ways, but the narrator usually manages to take the reader through to a different set of conventions. One expectation derives from the structure of the endings of story strands. The central character moves on swiftly from event to event in the final third of the book, and the narrator usually tries to tie up one strand before moving on to the next. For example, when Maria leaves Grandpa Sing's restaurant, she is given a ritual gift (about which we hear nothing more—nothing like deferred gratification?) and the mature narrator's voice concludes with, "Many years later I saw Leonard and he told me that Grandpa had returned to China and had died there" (130). However, Campbell occasionally permits a strand to be tied off and then reopens it, which can leave the reader surprised or full of trepidation depending upon whether or not they want to return to that narrative. The effect is acutely felt in the final pages of the story when Maria, after several pages about her new political commitments, abruptly comments about the man she has been living with, "I'd never heard from David since the day we talked at the hospital, and had pushed him completely out of my mind. I didn't ever expect to see him again" (170). And that is it. The reader also expects never to see him again. Yet casually in the last chapter, in the midst of everything else "David and I were together again ... we were really happy" (178). On one reading there is inevitable irritation with a character who hasn't even told us that she's back with the one person she said she loved, and all this time we've been supporting her as if she were alone ... on another reading there is the gratification that true romance has won out after all, which is related to the narrative convention that romance is more fulfilling and trustworthy than political commitment. And on yet another reading we know that we are not supposed to take comfort: the narrative has focused from the moment things went wrong on Maria trying to achieve her dreams by attaching herself to a man; but here she has other attachments—these too disintegrate, but at the least other ways are possible. Further, it is precisely the response that because someone has a partner they no longer need the support of others, upon which this entire text is providing a critique.

Yet Campbell goes a long way to relieving the reader of any embarrassment about the social reality of the events in the text. She says that when she sat down to write the book it was at first all anger,[22] and one account of the editing process indicates that she was encouraged to cut out much of this material, particularly the account of her rape, because readers wouldn't be interested in it.[23] But it is precisely that kind of intimate detail that the reader is likely to remain embarrassed about: partly because of the difficulty of finding it an appropriate form, and partly because of the immediacy which resists any kind of elision into the broader ideological discussion.

Perhaps Campbell is wise to do so. The emphasis in *Halfbreed* is on the personal on behalf of the community, and the strength of the narrative comes from the control with which Campbell resists the private anger that drives the potentially melodramatic romance structure. Beatrice Culleton's attempt to include a considerable amount of this private anger tips the balance of her narrative, *In Search of April Raintree,*[24] away from the community issues that are also part of her structure. The book is a fictional account of a Métis woman and her sister growing up in prairie Canada. It tells through a realist narrative structure, yet without the controlled disruptive skill of Campbell, of two possible destinies for the Métis people in the form of two sisters April and Cheryl. Indeed it ends on a messianic note with the birth of a baby boy on whom future hopes are emblematically placed. Into this fictional context, there is massive eruption of private autobiographical event in the account of a rape, which overwhelms the community narrative and renders it ambivalent largely through a sudden shift into genre-fiction stylistics.

The stylistics of genre-fiction writing will be looked at further in the second part of this discussion, but a brief account of how they work here indicates the contrast with the writing in *Halfbreed*. Some men who have mistakenly picked up April instead of her sister Cheryl, who is a prostitute they want to victimize, are driving her out into the country. The man beside her says things like "'So, you're a real fighting squaw, huh? That's good 'cause I like my fucking rough'"

(140) or, to the driver, "'You're in this as much as us.'" When "his hand slid to the crotch of my jeans and I had to pull his hand away," he says "'Hey, you guys, we're going to have to teach this little Indian some manners. I'm trying to make her feel good and she pulls away. The ungrateful bitch'" (141). The speeches could be directly from a B-movie film script. The descriptions of violence are similarly familiar: a punch to the midriff,

knocked the wind out of me and sent me flying back against the left side of the car again. My head hit the window. The leader then grabbed the front of my blouse and ripped it open tearing the buttons off ... After his merciless onslaught, I was too weak to try to defend myself anymore. I felt him taking off the rest of my clothing and feebly I tried to put my arms across my breasts to cover myself. He shoved them aside. (142)

The following sequence documents a series of attacks on April's body that she keeps telling herself to leave passive and submissive, but which keeps struggling against the pain anyway. The sequence is a series of: rape, gang rape, fellatio, "And don't get any funny ideas about biting it or you'll be sorry" (144), and finally the "leader" urinates into her mouth. It is interspersed with more B-movie dialogue and the vocabulary of the victim's mind: "defeated" "listless" "rag-doll" "dismay" "sluggishly."

If the reader comes to this as a semi-autobiographical account a whole set of questions surfaces about why the writer is using genre-fiction devices from soft-porn romances, which underwrite the complicity of the victim in the abuse. Is it because this is the only available convention that currently describes in detail the events this writer wants to portray? Is it to focus on the way that April is faced with exactly that choice, of being a victim or refusing to be a victim, in the following narrative? Or is it an abuse of autobiography, simply using the claim to real life to exacerbate the titillation? If, in contrast, the reader reads this as an overt fiction, it is crude and unsophisticated. Do we recover it as parody? Are we more alerted to gender stereotypes? Either way the confusion is embarrassing because genre-fiction devices have been imported into a realist first-person narrative. Culleton herself says that she first wrote the book in the third person, but that her editor suggested the

first person, since writing in third person left a lot of places that sounded really 'Harlequin' ...Mostly the romantic parts, or so-called romantic parts. I'm not into a great deal of romance, so it was awkward'.[25]

I would suggest that the embarrassment the reader feels is profoundly ambivalent. On the one hand it diverts the text from the tribal narrative of a people for whom Culleton is attempting to articulate experience. On the other, it reminds us of the enormity, the social reality of rape. We can of course evade embarrassment by creating a neat critical frame such as: Culleton, who has said that this episode is autobiographical, is using the fictional ground of her novel where it is acceptable to recount a rape, to fill the gap left by Campbell's text, whose wholly autobiographical character makes it indecorous to include. Culleton says in interview,

> I didn't want to go through that part again. I had a problem with using what I felt was realistic language. Rapists would talk like that, of course, but I didn't like writing swear words and things like that so that was hard. I just went into it without giving myself time to think of a different way of putting it or anything like that.[26]

So we can have the authentication of the *bios*, the gratification of narrative completion or the sentimentality of wholeness, and we can structure the event away. The embarrassment insists on the rape not merely as an event, but as a social problem that gets too close for comfort.

Maria Campbell however has a different emphasis. She has said in interview, "I'm not really a writer, I'm not. I'm really a community worker. And my writing and all these things are what I need to heal my community with ... to heal myself."[27] The writing of *Halfbreed*, Campbell's first book, is autobiographical but with the aim not of defining private identity but of using the personal to address the political. Elsewhere the writer says that she "wanted to create political change through literature. ... I couldn't let myself get carried away romantically, because it's not my story I'm telling; it's the story of a people."[28] Indeed her writing is a catalogue of devices for constraining sentimental response. Yet the tension between the potential for private excess and the political description can unnerve a reader into reading the text as formally naive. This reading is encouraged by the overt presentation of the text as written in an intimate autobiographical mode by someone new to writing: a claim reinforced by the front and back cover of the paperback edition. Any embarrassment this may cause disappears when the reader becomes conscious of the strict formal control whose dislocations contain the melodrama and provide the book with much of its realist strength. It is a formal control that focuses on the social realism of its context and encourages us to address the immediate problems of the Métis community.

Jeannette Armstrong's *Slash*[29] engages in a rather different manner with the expectations of realism, because her writing moves the tension between individual recounting and descriptive historical account of political and social actuality, into a narrative of personalized history. The individual is very much present in the story, but it is structured to keep the individual subordinate to the history of the Native American Indian movement of the 1970s and 80s. This is not to say that the I-centred narrative is not still dominant, for it is. But the central character comes across as a generalized location for the experience of a lot of different people with similar life history.

The focus on tribal issues makes Armstrong's text, for me, one of the more difficult to read. As a white reader who is attempting to read from the potentially common ground of women's experience, particularly of repression, that common ground is made far more problematic.[30] It is significant that the book entered the public domain by way of the NAI press Theytus, rather than a commercial publisher, because it is not written primarily for traditionally educated white readers. But it is published/made public, and so becomes a ground on which necessarily alienated or different readers who want to make a commitment to engaging in the difficult learning about other cultures, may tortuously dance.

Many critics have read the book as well-meaning but naive, or simply as 'failed,' or dismissable because it cannot be understood—it's too different. None of these readings takes the risks of personal vulnerability necessary to committed engagement. No matter where it ends, if I am to work toward a positive construction of a reading, it necessarily has to begin just because of my difference, as a reading that comes from the fact that I am a traditionally educated white reader who is also a woman. In other words, although I cannot meet the text on the writer's ground, I am convinced that it is important to listen, to participate in the conversation and begin to discuss the issues even though my reading may be embarrassing.

Several devices underline an emphasis on the tribal rather than the personal. One is the initial displacement from the woman's voice of the the writer Jeannette Armstrong to the first person narrative voice of the male central character, which can be read as a sign of an awareness of gender politics within this aboriginal context. Another is the frequent and easy shift from 'I' to 'we' that occurs for example in the account about drugs and spirituality (50). On the occasions that the individual comes to the fore, genre fiction elements emerge. When Tommy describes his love for Mardi the words could come straight from Harlequin or Mills and Boon: "I wanted to put my arms around her and hold her and never let anything ever hurt her again" (62). On a first reading this is embarrassing. The cliché calls up all the pastel covers of wish-fulfillment fantasies. But read again, reminding ourselves of the woman writer for this male narrator, of the strong women characters in the story who do not depend upon men, the cliché becomes self-conscious device.

More problematic is the rendition of Aboriginal/Police violence which reads like a crossover between comic-strip and science fiction. To start the reader is given a retrospective account of the fighting, constructed in terms of a collective 'us' and 'them,' up to the point at which the police break down the barricades. Then the narrative becomes more immediate and focuses on the speaker.

I was right there in the thick of things. The police in their riot gear looked ugly up close. Like real aliens. One of them took a swing at me with his club. I grabbed it and twisted and at the same time brought my knee up into his crotch. Jesus, that must have hurt but he wouldn't go down alone and we fell to the ground rolling around. I tried to pull his mask off. I said to him between clenched teeth, "You son of a bitch, I want to see your eyes" . . . (156)

The narrative then moves back out to include the collective "we" of the other Aboriginals in the fight, describing the main character's actions fighting alongside others against the police. Interleaved with cliché and commonplace from "in the thick of things" to "clenched teeth" straight from an adventure story/comic, the underlying topos is of science fiction aliens, masked strangers who may be stripped of their power if revealed. But how are we to read the simplistic conventional stand-off between 'good' and 'evil,' and the valorization of individual violence that the constructions initiate? Sandwiched as it is between the opening utopian note of a "new feeling of determination" on the part of the Aboriginal peoples, and the later comments on manipulation by the newspaper press and its control by even more powerful organizations, there may be ways of reading that are signposted.

Utopias are often written in extreme terms of good *versus* evil. Much of science fiction *is* utopian in emphasis. And the adventure story/comicbook elements may be a response to the need to find some other way of describing this kind of violence than that found in newspapers. Newspapers report civil violence all the time, but frequently as here neutralize it into information or fail to print the 'telling' photograph. Violence in written fictional genres, at least violence that takes part in positive social action, is usually presented as group warfare. Individual or minority violence for social good is not commonly found in the realistic conventions of novelistic fiction, except in the elaborations of comicbook heroes and earlier in Boys Own adventurings. It should not be forgotten that both generic fields are concerned with would-be colonizers, and their use in the presentation of conflict between the institutional force of the police and the 'colonized' Aboriginal peoples is highly appropriate as a structural commonplace. But the analogy of the police as representatives of alien white colonizers, is made ambiguous both by the possibility that once unmasked they may lose their power and become human, and by the clear indication that it is the narrator's "You son of a bitch, I want to see your eye" that sets off the real violence. Crucial to the entire sequence is the pivot around these words. Beforehand the action is more distanced, still potent with the determination for change; afterwards the violence becomes intense, immediate and devastating. In this adventure story the hero does not win.

Most problematic of all for my own reading of *Slash* is the proto-Messianic ending. The birth of the character/narrator's son reads for a christian-culture person such as myself as a version of the Christ-in-the-stable story. The boy child "is going to be important to a lot of people" (233). In English he is named Marlon "for a man we both respected a lot" (233). Later in the depths of despair, the narrator hears "from somewhere from out there a little boy's voice that whispered, 'Papa, I'm a Little Chief'" (251) and is brought back to the necessity of day to day life. In one reading the child is important not because he is a human being but because he will be a future leader, a Little Chief blessed by the name of a movie star with the powers of a modern angel or saint. This is embarrassing.

There are markers to deflect the imposition of a Christian nativity myth in the importance of dreams to Aboriginal culture and in the background metaphors of the seasonal fertility of the cornplants which in early Aboriginal cultivations required intense nurturing by the community. The emphasis on Aboriginal culture may open up readings of the text to the possibility that just as the character/narrator has been subordinated to the overarching historical and political accounts of the community, so this 'leader' is representative of all newly born Aboriginal people. But it is not easy for me to follow this path. Easier, because although white I am also a woman, is the interesting reversal of roles this story tells. The mother goes out into the political world and engages with the institutional forces, while the father stays behind with the child and the community. The mother comes to realize that the particular political fight she's engaged on will not work but just before she re-enters the community she is killed. *She* is killed and the Child becomes a Little Chief. The reversal of the gender stereotypes of European society allows this white reading of the narrative to comment (albeit rather ambivalently) upon the dead-end that it is for women to conform to a man's world and upon the necessity for men to understand the domestic community; it allows the narrative to emphasize the connections rather than the separations between the generations of the sexes, as the boychild derives position from the death of his mother. In effect this kind of reading opens up the text to the ways in which it comments on my own European society. However the text itself has already provided enough dislocation of western society and gender construction to leave me profoundly uneasy with this appropriation. When I teach this text I am always left with at least some of my initial embarrassment.

The messianic reading is embarrassing for me to retell because the complexity of the text and the issues it addresses indicate either a wild lapse into sentiment by an otherwise tough political writer or a hopelessly inadequate reading on my own part. But this reading is only inadequate for someone who believes that a 'great leader' is a nostalgic concept. It is also embarrassing, and more importantly so, because for a non-Aboriginal reader the likelihood of the failure of any such leader is all too high, and all too obvious an indication of the underlying injustice about which we are doing little if not nothing.

Each of the writers here is primarily concerned with writing the personal explicitly into the social and political, specifically writing accounts of abuse into significance for the wide racism against Aboriginal peoples. They do so by frequently violating what a conventionally trained literate reader might think of as writerly decorum. The events of violence and abuse from social reality that they use can be helpfully embarrassing, locating points in the text where a reader, rather than repressing or appropriating, has to stop and engage with issues, try to voice the differences that separate people so they they can be addressed.

*

Differently difficult to engage with is another group of writers whose texts appear to claim the personal implicitly rather than explicitly against the social. Again the texts I want to read make various generic claims, to autobiography and to straight fiction. For these writings, without the overtly communal frame, it is far more difficult to come to a sense of readerly decorum. In order to do so we have to/are invited to supply a form of that society and engage with talk about its responsibility. These texts call on us to talk about the abuses by and of women within a familial structure current in the western capitalist world.

As traditional literary critics we are usually taught not to ask whether a narrative event actually happened, such questions are thought inappropriate. But take the case of child abuse which is a topic of such current interest: If we read an account of child abuse in book form there can be complicated responses. Why are we reading it? to inform, to titillate, to understand, to approach? Bound up in this is our sense of why the writer is writing. If they are exploitatively on a cultural bandwagon, this has completely different significance from an attempt to foreground an often hidden and evaded set of social abuses. If what is written has happened, we are often reassured about our own motives for reading, although that reassurance is questionable. Most difficult in traditional literacy is the text which does not claim authenticity but which uses the intimate to remind us of the horrors of abuse. The reader's embarrassment is frequently so acute we look for ways of displacing the indecorous back onto the writing. And this is one of the main issues raised by this other group of ostensibly more private texts.

One of the central elements of 'genre' writing is repetition of topics and of narrative structures. Critical consensus holds that the more significantly variable the repetition, the more interesting the writing becomes, and that this may even be a gauge of popularity—although other critical commentary suggests that popularity is an index of invariability, being able to depend on the stability of the narrative pattern.[31] But what often causes difficulty is both the period of time and the number of similar books between the introduction of a new topic, which may be shocking and is authorized as an 'original' event or 'true-to-life' or from the 'real,' and the acceptance of that event as a respectable fictional topos. This occurs in all writing but is particularly thrown forward in 'genre' writing. An insistent example might be that of the representation of the separation between parent, especially mother, and child.[32] The event/topos recurs in a significant number of texts from writers new to publishing, and on initial encounter can yield intensely painful readings because it is implicated into personal autobiography; but as the reader learns how to recognize and prepare for the event, that reaction often dulls, unless it comes to be re-read as fictional topos.

With the topos of parental separation there is a fair variety of rendition, possibly because there is a long history of a number of literary patterns in more flexible as well as 'genre' writings. But with the more recently acceptable topic of the experience of child abuse, physical, psychological and/or sexual, there is more consistency—particularly in depictions of rape.[33] Again, the traditionally literate readers' reaction to the event, as presented in much new writing, is frequently pain and shock. The event is recounted as autobiographical and is recognized as a social terror/fact. At the same time, while the shock of reading often overrides any possibility of generic distance, once the event is recognized however consciously or not as a generic element, it can be pornographically titillating and can implicate the reader into the individual guilt of sexual response or of inaction. This may not be particularly helpful since consciousness-raising through guilt normally causes resentment, and since it is engineered through an overt generic device it can easily lose contact with social reality. On repetition, from reading many other books into which it is incorporated, the terror of the response is often neutralized, which has certainly been the case with readings of autobiographical texts generated by British literacy programs.[34] The reader is left embarrassed partly I suspect because the events are so painfully intimate, partly because of the implications into guilt, but also because this is a relatively new topic to literate readership and criticisms emerge about 'copying': is the writer merely duplicating an event from another successful book? even that question: did this really happen?

There is here a similarity with response to the recognition of literary cliché. On first reading, before the reader sees its potential for cliché, the topos or phrase is often recognized as significant. If with repetition the topos fades in significance, it becomes cliché and often acquires the ability to embarrass. But what tunes in or tunes out the significance? One factor is that the reader may read the topos as a warning in fictional mode about a social problem which, having been alerted to, they sort out and find less problematic. It may be that increasing familiarity with the topos over time allows for a repression of the problem, which evasive activity permits the reader to experience boredom, which is itself an evasion of knowledge of repression.

Another factor may be the fictionality itself, that the reader comes to disdain a topos which simply alerts to a difficulty rather than does anything about it. Involved in the latter is a sense of choice: if the reader perceives the topos as autobiographical, or actual and unavoidably rendered, the repetition becomes necessary; but if the topos is perceived as merely a way of claiming some grafted authenticity, then it dilutes into cliché. Of course the readers are again capable of empowering the text for themselves, by remembering that autobiography is as rhetorical as 'genre' writing, but we do have to learn to read in a different way. In other words, we need to turn the event into literary topos and understand that its use indicates conscious literary choice, that whether or not it is repeated from elsewhere and whether or not it happened, the writer is aligning themself with a set of events and providing social and ideological commentary.[35]

But with a return to conscious literary choice we usually return to the possibility of titillation/ guilt/ implication which are linked to repression of elements in the reader's own life. Whether the reader is embarrassed because of a perceived lapse in the literary decorum of writing or because of a felt lapse in the decorum of their own reading, there is something here to do with the reader's own social structurings which are uneasy with or not permitting a literary awareness of certain elements and events of day-to-day life. This is a condition of much women's writing: that there are things we would like to say, but which we do not yet have ways of adequately articulating. We feel uneasy not only because we know that these things are not supposed to be said, but because when they are said they do not feel appropriately articulated. The textuality of the day-to-day has few literary renditions, and events from it portrayed in conventional forms are profoundly unsettling.

Take, for example Elly Danica's *Don't: A woman's word*.[36] This story is an autobiographical account by a 40 year old woman of her early child abuse at the hands of her father and his clientele. The writing tightens the I-narrative marks of short straightforward sentences even further under the restrictions of enumerated paragraphs or sections. Simultaneously the result is similar to a kind of tabloid-photograph comic book, a common format for recent pornography, in which each photograph has a one- or two-sentence caption, which sequence of captions tells some kind of story. The prose style of such captions is simple, deadpan and without metaphorical colouring, possibly mimicking 'neutral' reportage that commodifies people so efficiently in the mass media, but possibly the result of translation since in Britain at least much of this material is imported.[37]

Of course, context defines the similarity. The events and actions of this horrifying autobiography are obscene. As a reader I have little literary context to bring to the narrative. The only place I have ever seen these actions written about in such detail is in pornography, so the parallels emerge whether I like it or not. The point here is that this reading experience is not unusual. What becomes worrying[38] is precisely how readers make the distinction between a necessary presentation of obscene actions, and a gratuitous presentation there to excite and titillate. Let me make it clear: There is absolutely no way in which I find this book pornographic. The autobiography is a painful, courageous and shocking account. What interests me specifically is the cross-over between the actual life and the genre-fiction pornographic elements that occur in its representation, and the frequently embarrassed reading that generates. If the embarrassment leads to repression or appropriation, the shock of the account is distanced and displaced, but the embarrassment also acts to locate experience for which we have no adequate vocabulary, and to alert the reader to the need for engaged reading.

To give two examples: At nine years old the young girl is taken with her brother and sister to the races by her father:

He won't let me leave his side. He has something in mind. I am not here to see the races. He sends my brother and younger sister away while he discusses with his brother how they will proceed. His brother says he already has some customers. He beckons to a farmer who has been watching us. The three of them discuss a price and what I will do. I try not to listen. I know there is no escape. I don't believe what I hear. I think this is a dream. And I wanted to go out today. This is god's punishment for not staying home to help my mother. (11)

The reader is hooked into the sequence by the initial suspense of wondering what the father is up to. The preceding narrative has already shown us that he is a child abuser, so we are caught in a horrified attention partly I suspect because we await the information that this child is about to be raped. When the narrative says "I know there is no escape," it moves into a series of phrases that are closely related to pornographic prose: submission/victimization, which gratify the participants' wish for power; self-destruction because the victim has called this on herself, which deflects the guilt of the victimizer; the possibility of sacrilege, which allows for re-constructing the abuse as punishment for sin. These elements are not merely among the grounds and structures of pornographic writing, they are part of western cultural stereotypes for relations between the sexes. In pornographic writing such stereotypes satisfy wish-fulfillment fantasies and do not question their underlying assumptions. In this narrative the complicating factor is that the narrator here is a child. The child cannot see beyond the actions to question them, so the narrative runs on a thin line of presenting the actions as terrible without overtly commenting on them.

The writer constructs a narrative that is ambiguous about whether the child is raped. The reader may well think that she is, but the following detail focuses on the child's attempt to distance and isolate herself from what is going on and leaves it open to question. The device helps to underline the devastating effects of any abuse. The reader may connect ultimate abuse with the word 'rape,' but in effect any abuse can be as destructive and as appalling. Particularly in cases of child abuse where there are so many other difficulties/imponderables, it is important for the reader to recognize that just because the act of rape has not occurred, does not mitigate the actions that have.

Danica balances the narrative with humour—a quiet joke that foregrounds all the potential for rebellion that we often hear spoken about in terms of the anarchic bravado of comedy. Quite differently, on a minimal but distinctly resistant note, the girl-narrator tells us here that the father will not let a Chinese man go in with his daughter because the yellow of his skin "might rub off" (12). The next numbered section, which would usually have begun on a different frame of the story, instead makes a connection opening with "I turn yellow anyway. Strange, they say. How could she have got hepatitis?" (12). The humour is small but there, and introduces her determination to "learn to understand" (13) and to read as much as she can.

The other example I will discuss, and there are more, has the same generic problem of a younger narrator presented as one who doesn't understand the structures of power and manipulation in the actions or in their representation, and the example is similarly recovered through a dark humour. At the age of eleven, the girl's father invites in three prestigious members of the local community "A judge, a lawyer, a doctor" (46), for what she calls "the night of my death" (47). The girl describes being woken up and taken downstairs where the men, and her mother, are waiting. Her father, who has trained her to pose for pornographic stills, is taking photographs throughout these events:

Laughter. Move your head and shoulders so you face the door. Now turn your head back. Wet your lips. Again. Smile. Click. Tilt your head. Click. Open your mouth a little. Click. Wet your lips again. Hold it right there. Click. (48)

This combination of voyeurism and artificiality emphasizes the total and complete sexual control the viewers have over the poser's body. But then the action shifts into the next section:

7.9 Take your nightie off. I think he is joking. I look at him puzzled. In front of company? Take the damn thing off before I do it for you. Click. Laughter. Fear. (48)

The narrative then moves on to retell the instructions the father gives to the girl to display herself:

Put your hands under your breasts. Breasts? I don't have breasts. On your chest stupid, hold your hands under your nipples then. Lift your head. Look at me. Click. Click. The men sigh. The men laugh. Cute. ... He sets me up. Moves me like a doll. (49)

The ignorance of the girl, her lack of understanding about breasts and the potential resistant humour of that small exchange, can work to remind the reader of this girl's coerced and manipulated position. But at the same time that powerless position is one of the main elements in the sexual pleasure of the three invited men, as well as being a major part of pornographic gratification.

When the following section describes her taking off her "panties. Slowly. Like I showed you" (49) the mother has to leave to "make coffee," and the girl narrator says "Slowly, so slowly, the panties come off. He doesn't notice that my skin comes off with them. I peel myself out of my own skin. I am no longer myself.... A body sits here naked" (50). The "body" is then asked to perform other acts for the voyeurs, before it is forced to submit to rape by being held down, choked, suffocated and other threats of death. What is horrible about the violence is not only what is happening to the girl, but the knowledge that these actions bring pleasure to some people and further, the knowledge that reading descriptions or seeing representations such as 'snuff' movies, of precisely these actions also brings some people pleasure.

The silences that such objectifying and clipped prose introduce insist on a common ground of knowledge, that may be complicitous, being held between the reader and the text. Yet the writer recovers the narrative for the reader in the concluding and increasingly surreal account of this chapter which describes the father's attempts to sell the girl to the judge. The father makes the offer saying that the mother "has lots of girls, she wouldn't miss one" (57), and when the judge says that his wife wouldn't approve the father advises "You have to slap them good now and then, so they know who's boss" (57). Through this account, which flickers so carefully between the banal detail of commercial exchange and the absurd brutality of the action, the father drops his price from $400 to $200 to a gift in order to get rid of the girl, but the factor the reader notices as significant is the girl's repeated observation of the judge: "He looks at me again. The man continues to stare at me. He'd like to but he couldn't come up with that kind of money ... His wife wouldn't understand. He seems saddened by this fact" and finally he says, "I'd like to, but I know it would never work. I'm sorry" (58). Crucial here is not only that the girl would prefer to be sold than to stay with her father, but that she has the ability to convey some human characteristics onto the man who has just gang-raped her.

The carefully modulated detail of the bartering exchange allows the reader to surface into some kind of reality from the hell of the rape, but what an odd reality it is: A person is for sale, by her father to a community judge, who is only held back by fear of his wife's reaction. Such a wife is "not like your [the father's] wife." But the existence of women who might not accept these actions is virtually irrelevant; it only underlines the way that they are as isolated from the world of this kind of abuse as other women are complicit in it; it also raises the question of whether that isolation is a kind of complicity.

One of the many achievements of this autobiography is to say firmly that we do need to know in detail and to attempt to understand the horror of such abuse. From the outset, no one is prepared to believe that the abuses are taking place. Even the grandmother and mother rationalize that it cannot be so bad as to make it necessary to move the girl away from her father. Schoolteachers, priests, doctors, friends and sisters: none believe her. And one of the reasons they do not believe is that they simply cannot believe—they've never heard of anything like it before. Another reason, more difficult to assess, is that they know these things happen but repress that knowledge either because they feel powerless against it or because they know they are doing nothing about it.

The difficulty that the reader has with a child-narrator who cannot overtly comment or foreground the disgust of the events until she has understood the coercive structures they employ, means that the writing loses its explicit parallels with pornography only at the moment when self-conscious knowledge of her abuse allows the narrator to extricate herself from participation. But this writing goes on to describe how the young woman is passed from father to husband, who forces her to have a child through drug-induced submissiveness. Both the husband's actions and the collusion of the psychiatrist who cannot accept her story of abuse and prescribes drugs in order to help her become 'normal,' follow the pattern of the pornographic coercion of the girl. The reader comes to these abuses in a sense of relief that the child abuse has been left behind, an almost welcome embrace of accepted social practices: after all it is a cliché of our society that women often need drugs to be prescribed in order 'to cope.' In the retrospective glance, an awareness of the similar pattern of abuse throws forward the casual brutality of such practices and the ease with which we fall into accepting them in the absence of an alerting social or cultural framework.

Another danger of the parallels with pornographic style, imagery and event, is that the reader will be embarrassed because they are not able to distinguish between the terror of the actual and the sexual pleasure of the expectations aroused by literary representation.

However, the availability and use of these parallels is a sharp reminder of power abuse. In other words the genre-fiction elements from pornography may embarrass the reader, but the reader is left in no doubt about the implications of the events. The embarrassment results from a confusion between the actuality of the events and the implications of the style of their literary representation. That embarrassment can lead to a self-conscious engagement with the narrative. The later events of this woman's life do not use the embarrassment of genre elements to insist on this engaged critique. However, perhaps, once the reader has begun an engagement, the cliché of the doped suburban housewife should fall under similar scrutiny. It is certainly the case that Elly Danica, by making such a critique possible, has started a conversation about experience that is painfully difficult to articulate yet which would otherwise be left in silence. Although explicitly personal, the writing engages the social both pragmatically in its means of production which has generated a lot of discussion,[39] and in its self-conscious use of literary convention which requires extensive reassessment on the part of the traditional reader.

A text that can provide a helpful contrast to *Don't* is Jacqueline Dumas's *Madeleine and the Angel*. This writing presents an account of child abuse that uses the crossover between genre-fiction, here fairy story and religious fable, and autobiography quite differently. The signal contrast is that *Madeleine and the Angel* is not autobiography even though it uses a first-person narrator. The writer is perceived to be overtly writing not to re-present part of her own life but to build a representation of the familial complexities of domestic abuse, and this simultaneously distances the actual and leads the writing toward an explicit focus on social and cultural issues.

One of the most startling contrasts between *Don't* and *Madeleine and the Angel* is the contrast between the controlled even denotative prose of the former in which a quiet joke stands out like a flag, and the firmly metaphorical language of the latter where emotions tug and flow. The contrast speaks for the difference between the isolated victim and the family of victims that the two books present. But further, because this is a first-person novel not an autobiography, it may be that the writer feels that she cannot appropriate the specific details of abuse, and so her writing task is different. The highly controlled flat prose is less needed precisely because the details of sexual abuse are implied rather than explicitly illustrated.

For example, Pauline's first sexual experience with her father is introduced by a scene in which she is just beginning to think about her emerging sexuality by remembering a boy out kite-flying. She undresses in gleeful enjoyment and is going to try on her older sister's clothes, but then she realizes her father has been watching. But he smiles. She asks retrospectively "Does he really step into the room?" (28). She follows the question with a series of other questions that deflect the scene into "When he entered my mother, did she grit her teeth in triumph, in acquiescence, or did she long for more? ..." (28), and concludes the scene with "I remember the eyes of my mother watching from an open doorway" (29). Sometimes the sexual threat is suggested by the father's verbal seduction of Pauline to "see" the Devil, after which she tells us of dreams that the Devil has taken her over. Sometimes the abuse of sex is described through Pauline's account of her sister Marie Jeanne/Maria Goretti's being called into his room during the night by their father: The loss of warmth and comfort as the sister leaves the bed shared by the two girls; the account of her washing herself on her return, her retching and her cleaning her teeth; and her final cold isolation curled up in a separate space back in the bed. As with *Don't* it is misleading to describe the scenes out of their context, because their implicative style conveys great horror and disgust. But this writer is more concerned with a different kind of control, which emerges through a concern with story-telling and story-writing itself.

As the title suggests *Madeleine and the Angel* works a religious obsession into the metaphorical pattern of a religious fable of the Angel and Devil, that allows the mother of the family to justify the actions of the father. At first despite and then because of the many 'stories' the mother and father tell themselves and the children to accommodate his actions, we are left wondering whether he may not be clinically schizoid. The possibility is simultaneously a neat device for naturalizing the gothic features of a Jekyll and Hyde story, and a consoling strategy for the writer and reader who can then displace the cruelty of the actions of the father into mental illness. Certainly there are moments almost of wild celebration, of intense personal caring, that the father brings about and which lure the reader into searching for explanations. It is curious how the genre device of psychiatric metaphor, because it claims some kind of non-fictional authority or status, is not embarrassing. It takes the responsibility of the individual to address the issues a little further out of the reader's hands by indicating a deterministic ground that will 'explain the problem'.

Underwriting this deflection away from the father's actions is the accumulation of material about the mother. We are shown the letter she writes to her future husband at the point when he clearly wants to call off the union saying that he realizes that he shouldn't get married to anyone. She claims that "God had brought us together," "God threw us together because He meant it to be so" (173); but she is also pressuring him into marriage saying "It is too late now," and the reader has to keep open the possibility that Madeleine was pregnant. Yet if the mother, Madeleine, is responsible for bringing the father into a family unit, she also seems to be the main builder of the Angel/Devil metaphor. The one time that she gets drunk she tells the two girls Maria Goretti and the narrator Pauline, about the special role that their father has in acting out God's will and the terrible fights with the Devil that God has in the father's body. She is the mediator and realizer of the metaphor that enjoins the sisters to silence about the abuse of their bodies.

Madeleine is not just using a fictional device to represent the reality, but has come to take the reality conveyed by that fiction as actual. She comes to believe that the reality of abuse is the only construction in which she can take part, so she positions herself within it to maintain it and extend it to her daughters. Madeleine is the mediator and realizer of that abuse, as well as in the end the destroyer. The narrator tells the story ostensibly during the time that her mother is being held in hospital subsequent to killing her husband with an axe. But the mother, we are told briefly and early on, "used to catch us for him" (64). It is for this that Maria Goretti can never forgive her:

> He was chasing me once, remember mom, Madeleine? Remember? And you opened your arms just like that, to hug me. I went to you, you squeezed me so hard it took my breath away. I love you! I love you! you said. And then you called him. Michel! you called, Michel! I've got her! I've got her!
> I'm not going to fall for that again, said Marie Jeanne . . . (185)

It is the mother's behaviour for which Pauline seems to be searching for an explanation, and through the interwoven narrative of her own motherhood and growing relationship with her daughter Elise, she goes some way to examine her own potential for this behaviour. One of many explanations that the narrative signifies by repetition is that of the accommodation that people make to such abuse by telling themselves stories. The power of stories to transform is seen at the beginning when the narrator reads her daughter the story of "Elise and The Wild Swans" in which the fairytale Elise must make her eleven brothers nettle-jackets in order to transform them from swan into human being. After the reading, the narrator asks "Do you make up stories in the schoolyard, invent a heterogenous world in hopes that the word spoken will like magic bring about the desired transformation?" (8). Her mother's metaphor of Angel and Devil becomes the heterogenous world that always offers the hope of transformation, but in the meantime keeps her locked into accommodation of actual events. In the end, for Madeleine the metaphor becomes real, and it is at that moment that she is liberated into thinking that if she kills the Devil the Angel will triumph. When the dead body of her husband does not transform into Angel, she asks "But where's the Angel?" (169).

The invention of a heterogenous world that retains the hope of transformation is the structure of utopian fiction. But unlike realism, which is the only literary structure that institutional readers of English-language writing usually take for granted, it depends for its action on self-conscious recognition of its own impossibility. If it is taken as magic, taken to have effective power to control, the inventor is thought of as self-deceived, a fantasizer. We accept the process in children because it is part of the way that they learn about the relationships of power that surround them; but we usually do not accept the process in adults because it is perceived to be a demand for individual power over society, excluding any contact with that society, refusing community. The reason we appear not to worry about the ability of realism to construct a self-enclosed and hemetically naturalized world is that it is so congruent with ideological demands that it inexorably brings the individual in line with the institutional structure.

Freudian psychoanalysis is based on the premise that psychosis and neurosis are versions of belief in the magic of story-telling, and that we all need to retain self-consciousness about their fictionality. There is a signal omission to the story of "The Wild Swans": the anchoring detail in most versions is that the last, eleventh jacket is not finished; the youngest brother always has a swan's wing instead of a human arm. This failure of complete control is a constant reminder of the inadequacy of human inventions/stories. It is also a guarantee of their helpfulness, because it is the indicator of self-conscious awareness. The moment that the invention is taken to be magic, to be effective in the real world and therefore making contact with the social, it is always exposed as inadequate: There is no Angel to be released.

The question asked by the narrator after reading "The Wild Swans" has a second part:

Elise, do you keep your truths concealed between the four walls of this house, hoping to thus hide the threads which so inextricably tie us together?

The woman Elise in the fairytale has to keep silent until she has woven the nettle-jackets for her eleven swan brothers. Her silence ensures the effectiveness of the magic in the jackets that will transform them back into human beings. The silence of the family; the silence of Madeleine, Maria Goretti and Pauline, ensures that the possibility for transformation in the Angel/Devil story may just work. Exclusion of society is necessary in the structure of fantasy, for the moment it impinges on the private world that world fails. But this points us to the inadequacy of society itself: If there were social practices that allowed us to talk about such abuse then the silent protection of the possibility for its transformation would not be necessary. This family may keep silent, but neither does society want to hear. And Dumas self-consciously reminds us that society is also happier with the transformative powers of story.

The collusion of this society with domestic abuse is reinforced by the affair Maria Goretti has with a woman writer. This writer finally cannot cope with the actuality of Maria Goretti's pain and breaks off the relationship, "In her work she feeds off such experiences, appropriates the details and transforms them into something which goes beyond both of us. But she doesn't want to pay for them" (184). Through this kind of intensely literary intertextual play which self-consciously controls the intrusions from the already high-status generic devices of fairy tale and religious fable, the novel builds the analogy between silent collusion necessary to domestic abuse, and the abuse by society implicit in its own silent collusion with the fact of that abuse. It opens up the debate to social, political and ideological discussion, carefully outlining the hatred between the sexes and within families that will increase if nothing is done. Maria Goretti, after a failed lesbian affair, isolates herself. Pauline, after a season as a sexual predator on both men and women, removes herself to looking after her child.

Discussion here is opened up with a different emphasis not only because the writing directs us away from the personal to the social in the use of fiction and intertext, but also because fiction and intertext allow the reader to agree and disagree, make assessments and criticisms about the kind of articulation the writing offers. The moments of embarrassment have already been recognized and turned into possibly appropriate words, that the reader engages with on a common ground of literary practice that diminishes the differences of status and privilege that so often lead to embarrassment. This is a story not a life, a story about silence which attempts to break the silence. People in literary cultures know the rules for reading stories, and these rules have limitations as well as positive contributions.

The narrative of life is far more difficult to negotiate, particularly as I have tried to discuss, in writings from people who do not come with such intensely literary traditions as readers and critics like myself. However, it is precisely this kind of writer who is beginning to write about events ideologically repressed not only by society but also by a lack of literary conventions for doing so. The use of what are frequently dismissed as naive and crude genre-fiction devices in some contemporary autobiography is embarrassing to the institutional reader not only because of the apparent banality of the device or even because of the material which we have a tacit agreement to avoid, but also because the lives it gives us are lives that many readers in privileged positions are not used to seeing or recognizing or accepting as possible. The intent of this essay is not just to legitimate genre-device or reactivate cliché or to explore their skilful development in the hands of these writers, but to ask for a recognition of the need to discuss how these lives come to be possible.

This tension between the social reality and the literary mediation of the ideological or social, is duplicated in the tenuous line followed by publishers who recognize that the maximum seduction is achieved by a book which professes fictionality but which can be marketed as overtly hidden autobiography. We cannot say that it does not matter what has happened, because it does. The recounted events are part of the validation of the individual, part of the common ground of the community they are creating. The sense of the personal carried by autobiography has important social activity. If this moves into the traditionally literary it moves into the ideological: It does not cease to have an activity but it shifts the ground of action into the more general world of politics, knowledge, psychology and philosophy. Jacqueline Dumas' *Madeleine and the Angel*[40] is a highly sophisticated literary product whose sympathetic understanding of the complexities of the issue leaves the reader at a loss about what to do in the immediate, but with much to think about in the long term.

The text of *My Name is Rose*, by Rose Doiron who is described at the start of an abridged version of her text in *Women and Literacy* as "an adult learner at the [Toronto] East End Literacy Project,"[41] is bald, immediate and potentially shocking. It is also written with precisely the aim of getting people to "talk more about what it is like to get beat up" so that "Maybe, someday, it will stop," as she says on the back cover of the book itself.[42] This book explicitly uses the comicbook format, and its 66 pages are roughly half-filled by photographs and half by attendant one- to three-sentence captions. Yet in this account of probably not much more than a thousand words there is a story of the narrative scope of Campbell's *Halfbreed*.

The structure of the narrative in the book is to open with a summary introduction which dwells on the character Rose's current happiness yet persistent bad dreams about her abuse in the past. The reader is then taken through the detail of her abuse as a child, her entry into a home for children where she makes a (first?) good friend and the (appalling) inadequacy of the schooling that she gets there, her (desolation at) leaving the home at the statutory age of 16, and then her brief (comforting) stay with her mother before the landlady (cruelly) kicks her out into (rough) life on the streets, and her (despairing) return to her father. He once again beats her, abuses her and this time also has her sterilized, but she leaves him for another (uncaring) man who also beats her. Somehow she (courageously) leaves and goes to work, where she meets Paul. The rest of the narrative is about her growing relationship with Paul, her final leaving of her father, and her marriage to Paul followed by a honeymoon under a rainbow at Niagara Falls.

The significant response in retelling this story is that it is peculiarly difficult to leave out the qualifiers that I have placed in brackets. They are certainly not there in the text. Indeed despite the tight focus on the life of the central character, there is rarely any element of private, self-conscious narration. The prose resembles reportage rather than either the deadpan tense control of *Don't* or the metaphoric weavings of *Madeleine and the Angel*. But it is a reportage that takes away any colouring or emphasis, so that the most unexpected elements are conveyed with the status of a neutral fact that makes necessary our assessment because it offers none of its own. For example, one of the first sequences reads:

Aunt Carol said,
"Come into the bedroom, Rose."
She took off my clothes.
There were bruises
all over my body
and cigarette burns
on my back. (p.17)

This continues on the following page with:

Aunt Carol called a social worker.
The social worker took me
to a home for children.

The home had a gate.
The gate was locked. (p.18)

The neutrality of the narration is emphasised by the parallel narrative events, both instigated by "Aunt Carol," and conveyed by a direct and simple prose that particularly in the second section works by making the objects of one sentence the subjects of the next, as if they all have the same value, as if they are arbitrary signifiers in an externally determined chain of cause and effect. Yet the gate is locked, and this is where the sequence ends. Are we to think that Rose is threatened or caged by this locked gate? The reader doesn't know, but has found it necessary to think of both possibilities and to move on to the implications that the locked gate raises in actual experience for both Rose and social worker: the possible fear, the need for reassurance.

The overall story structure may be one of romance but it is told with few of the conventional elements of the genre fiction style. Much of the reader's assessment also engages with the page layout and with the photographs. Although the prose tends to present issues evenly, the layout is frequently used with minimalist but significant effect. The first section of the text reads:

My name is Rose
I live with my husband, Paul.
We have been happy
for many years.

But I still have bad dreams. (4)

The isolation of the final line, similar to the isolation of the final two lines about the locked gate, alerts us to an emphasis and possibility of significance. Just so, where there are full-page photographs with captions opposite, the reader slows down. This is partly to take in the relationship of a double-page spread, and partly because we are taught that in books a small number of words should get greater attention (like poetry), but partly because elsewhere the narrative movement is *effected* by having more pictures and captions on each page: One photograph with a caption opposite is an indication of a need to pause rather than a need to move on. Pages where the photographs dominate and the captions at the foot are short, such as those showing Rose on the street, focus on the emptiness of that experience—that there is no story for it, merely a number of isolated moments. The effect is to move the narrative along quite quickly where there are half-page or smaller photographs with longer accompanying captions. From the moment when Rose meets Paul the words accumulate and begin to fill up the pages, so that the concluding account of her marriage to Paul builds up through pages 62-63, which unusually have three photographs and a lot of text, to the final four pages which are made up of two full-page spreads with one photograph each that slow the momentum right down.

Also taken into the reader's assessment of the events are the contents of the photographs. These are rather more problematic than the prose because they are posed and highly stylized representations of events and emotions which suggest the possibility that the elements that go to make them up are semiotically sophisticated. For example, what do we make of the visual similarity between Paul and Rose's father? More straightforward are the faceless social worker, the father dressed up in his respectable jacket when he takes Rose to be sterilized, the many empty bottles of beer on the table as her father beats her up, or Rose's changing hairstyles.

Of course the text asks the reader to respond to layout, photographs and words as a whole. The genre fiction elements of romance are couched, by way of the introductory ten pages, in a traditional dream framework within which the reader knows that the ending will be consolatory. The book offers a potentially utopian ending, but the introduction has already reminded us that this utopia is marred by the bad dreams of the past. In contrast, the abridged version in *Women and Literacy* ends with the last section of the book's introduction, explicitly enclosing the utopia. This may be necessary for the context of that abridgement, but it changes the emphasis of forward-looking courage that the structure of the book implicitly indicates.

The text tells us that this woman is taken advantage of partly because of her inability to speak, which obscures her abuse from other people and allows her father to pass her off as retarded. Apart from Paul, the only person she is pictured talking to in the book is "Chubby," the man she meets who treats her like her father does. And it is her ability finally to say to him "No more. I am not a slut. I am not a slave" (46) that gives her the impetus to go out and get the job where she meets Paul. This finding of voice in the story is analogous to the writer's finding of voice when she acquires literacy and writes in order to speak about and enable an ending to abuse. Both Rose, and Rose Doiron, effect a practical change in their lives that moves them to engage with, criticize, and with hope change their social world.

Important for this discussion is that there is immense potential in the text for the embarrassing sentimentalisms of romance fiction. It is awareness of this embarrassment that has engaged this reading into trying to articulate the forward-looking courage of the text. Rose's society takes her in but does not help her adequately; it then casts her out, as a "young adult," with no support. The society allows other adults, here the landlady, to define Rose as a "kid" and cast her out again for that reason. The society allows her to be taken in by men who label her retarded for their own convenience. And then this society treats her in the inhuman way that such people are treated within its terms of reference. This society is of course one of our own. The book provides a sense of an enclosed community in which people need to start to talk about the problems not just walk away from them, because there is nowhere different to walk to. In this sense the writing is the autobiography of a community not just an individual, and how each can try to engage with society, which is also presumably why Rose Doiron chooses to write and publish her story. As such it is in some ways an autobiography of all those who live in such societies, and Rose's bad dreams are also our own.

*

All communication leaves out more than it puts in, and writing makes available a large number of ways of temporarily filling in the gaps through shared recognition of the significance of real events. Mary

DiMichele addresses the reality of child abuse in the poem "The Primer,"[43] on just these issues of the autobiographical and the fictional, the actual and how we can talk about it. Of the child subject of the poem she says:

They think we're the same
but we're *not*, the writer
and the text. You see she called me in
to interpret. They're immigrants
and that's *not* the whole
story as you may suspect.
If I could tell it to you!
No, it's just what she remembers
perhaps just what she *wants*
to remember

   that's all I've got to work with.
But what she forgets is just as important.
What she forgets is more
important.

When we write or when we read we cannot hand over a person. We engage; we interpret, translate, transpose through the common life of written language to ways of articulating difference, and hope to make possible some ground for social change as we do so. The complicated tensions in the various responses to autobiographical accounts have a lot to do with whether or not they are treated as autobiographies or as first person narrative fictions, as texts of realism or texts of self-conscious generic marking. What does emerge is that those who use the written word to communicate and manage to get access to the printed medium to participate in those words, do so in order to deal with their day to day lives. These women open the conversation and ask for supportive response. In that response readers have an opportunity to find ways to 'think in common,' and from that common ground move toward action.

Part Three

CHAPTER SEVEN

Personal and Public Negotiations

Personal and Public Negotiations

If the relationship of power between the individual in the nation state, which underlies much current political philosophy, is shifting as effective power is put in the hands of the multinationals to which nations then become subject, then the strategies of individuals responding to nation states become an important source of analogous action for the nation state itself. Further, strategies of individuals devising new relationships to public action become vital initial steps in the inevitably different interchanges among the powerful, empowered, and disempowered. Newly structured nations wishing to enter global politics have to construct a national ethos, an ideology by which they may be socially and culturally recognized. They cannot afford not to do so, or they will disappear. Yet these nations have a central problem: how to avoid reduplicating the repressions of previous powers. The issues are directly parallel with feminist work on strategies from which political theorizing about nationalism can learn much, ones that avoid the duplication of patriarchical power which overlays the family onto the state as a transparency that filters all public action.

To focus the following three-chapter study, the readings concentrate on the topos of memory and writing as a significant conjunction for both the individual and the nation; a conjunction which is enacted at times as oppositional power games or personal memory vs. public history, and at times as a process of constructing new common grounds where personal memory *is* public history. Memory and writing provide ways for the individual to engage in public activity and to define concepts of self. Memory, when articulated in writing, makes possible communication between individuals and their larger communities: specifically within the nation-state structure defined by nineteenth and twentieth-century western politics.

For the western, post-Renaissance world, official history from a variety of institutional contexts has been the public memory of the formation and activity of nation states.[1] I would define a postcolonial country as one emerging from domination by a nation-state power. Countries formerly colonized by a nation-state power have the problem of legitimating their postcolonial status by attempting a different national structure that may resist the duplication of power-dominance over other countries.[2] However, no matter how different their specific historical conditions, they come up flat against the monolithic ideology or ethos of the multi-national extension of the nation state,[3] toward which the discussion will move in the second and third parts of this section. The Canadian writers who will be discussed here write about individuals caught in the same problem on a personal scale, and offer through their activity, explicit and implicit analogous commentaries on postcolonial strategies.

The negotiations and agreements between personal memory and history form the primary means by which people engage in public activity in nation states. This poses particular problems for people who have no valid national 'history' and no necessarily consistent access to validated identity-forming processes in that society, such as publishing or disseminated writing. Many postcolonial writers, including many Canadian writers, examine the position of the individual in contemporary nation-states, and from an outsider's perspective are concerned with the failure of successive attempts by romanticism, marxism, anarchy, freudianism, modernism and postmodernism to deal with the enclosed structure of the ideology of nation-states.

The position of individuals within nation states is determined partly by the quite specific ways that the ideology or ethos of the state is constructed. The rhetorical strategy for nation-state ethos is technically fantasy with a suppressed term: a structure within which power is maintained by a veil of ideology based on the acceptance of stable representations, which is anchored by a suppression of the necessary inadequacy of representation. Ideology works by requiring individuals to remember to forget its artificiality. Within this ethos the individual as 'private' is also a veiled or obscured entity/self. Nationalism is predicated on establishing grounds as stable and then working from them. The acceptance of stability can be a collective agreement, a corporate expediency, or a totalizing system with overt or covert coercion.[4] The more the construction of the grounds becomes suppressed, the more potential there is for coercion; and the more the state functions become assimilated by nationalism, the more obscured the grounds become. Furthermore the drive to assimilate state functions which began in the Renaissance and Restoration has an economic impetus that gets transferred into questions of power and ideology.

Virtually all ways that people accept grounds for argument are initially based on agreements about the articulation of grounds and how they work. Acceptance asks for a public memory, a history: it takes different modes, has different implications, dependent upon the structure of the public. The structures of the nation state that control part of public memory depend upon the fixity of the representative modes of ideology. And while there are many narratives carrying public memory, those of the nation state carried and to some extent still carry economic and ideological power. However, increasingly the narrative of the nation state is becoming a cultural artefact, a commodity displaced by the ideological and economic power of multinationals[5] and global aid agencies.[6]

Because the ideology of the modern nation state has been predicated on the stable representation of agreed-upon grounds for contradiction, contest and debate, and because its representation is usually assumed to be unquestionable, it has often been taken to be monolithic. One of the few ways open to change by individuals, apart from the anarchy that is complicit with authoritarian political structures, was to shift the processes of representation, thereby infinitesimally shifting the grounds of ideology. The action doesn't change ideology itself, but works on destabilizing its assumed representations. This is presumably one of the several reasons that the emerging nation-states in Europe of the seventeenth-century were so concerned with controlling potentially disruptive and deceptive representations and finding stable representative systems in science and philosophy—centring on Descartes for whom all philosophy is representation[7] And this is also possibly one of the reasons that in this period the artist is perceived as 'hero,' in an intensely contradictory welding of an ideologically-approved topos with anti-ideological action.

One of the most consistent elements in many of the challenges to nation-state ideology is the reaffirmation of the individual as a fixed essential identity. (Post)modern techniques of analysis allow that fixity to be fragmented, but this often leads either to a complete enervation of social and political activity into games[8] or to the formation of small groups of people cohering around fragments held in common and working in the local hyperliberal position that excludes a larger national or international view.[9] This problem of how to validate social decisions besets postmodernist political theory. However, the impetus in either of these pluralist activities begins from a concern with the way we choose the appropriate context for fact, event, interpretation or memory, and with the way we establish the common grounds upon which individuals act and do things. The word 'individual' in this discussion has no connotations of either fixed identity or pluralist fragmentation; it is used to talk about a body caught into necessary social action. The work will focus on the way that the following selection from two canons of Canadian writing tries to deal with the dilemma of individual identity. Its articulation from the individual, of the postmodern dilemma that the fixed identity, when fragmented, becomes politically enervated or eviscerated, along with that impetus to the construction of a self within and for the needs of a material community both local and global, has many parallels with the working of figuration, strategy, and stance in texts. This study will weave through text, individual, and state looking for inter-locking commentary.

*

Empowered people, people with access to the conventional routes of communication and publication in a society, are more likely than those with difficulty of access to be taken up into the canonical literature of publication/education. And, since the postmodern is a dilemma primarily for the empowered, it is not surprising that many Canadian writers within the larger and more popular canons are concerned with issues of postmodernism.

The postmodern dilemma, of how to make a basis for decision and action in an artificially constructed system, results from the strategy of obscuring and hiding, on which the ideology of the nation state insists. All social action derives from agreements that have chosen limitations. It is only when an ethos such as ideology suggests that these are 'natural,' that the artificiality or constructed aspects of social behaviour become problematic.[10] I suggested in chapter one that 'ideology' as a strategy for national government worked relatively well for the small, socially class-coherent groups of people in power.

Disagreement in the post-renaissance period was funnelled through representative 'party' political fronts. However, with growing enfranchisement the voices of the potentially empowered people within society become much more diverse. To control them the strategies of ideology have often used the life or death imperative of war, they have manipulated economics, and in a few idealist cases they have extended ideology's claims on natural reality by instituting highly authoritarian attempts at totalitarian political systems.

One of the striking aspects of postmodernism is the degree to which it provides strategies for making people aware of the limitations of ideological structures: the artificiality that ideology tries to obscure. Another aspect is the degree to which postmodernism provides strategies for making people agree to the extent of the artificiality. These two directions were studied in the work of George Bowering and Frank Davey, in chapter four. However, there is a distinct difference between the postmodern moves toward ideology of a nation state such as Canada, empowered but working always under the pressure of an awareness of external economic control, and the postmodern moves of colonizing, imperial nation states. More generally, there are many differences among the ideological moves of postcolonial nations, differences that depend upon the coincidence with or separation from the ideological moves of the specific nations involved with their colonization. In common with Latin American postmodernism, Canadian postmodernism since the 1950s and 60s,[11] has used the artificializing of national ideology to warn about the growing strength of multinational power, for these countries, at this earlier time, predominantly from the United States.

The postmodern works rhetorically through the stance of fantasy: It foregrounds artificial structures within the ideological conventions of realism, and uses them to build alternative worlds which remain stable by becoming as isolated and systematic as ideology. Fantasy and realism are the twin structurings of private and public desire, and they use similar techniques and strategies. As I suggested earlier, in Freudian terms, if fantasy is the fetish of the private individual, realism could be defined as the fetish of the collective public audience of private individuals. Just so postmodernism and popular culture are infused with the double movement of the fantasy stance: both being implicated into the ideological (banal fetish) and yet potentially critical of it (constructive or reciprocal fetish). The nation state ethos which constructs the individual as private creates an isolation that problematizes all social discourse. As a result other strategies which articulate or theorize themselves in terms of realism/fantasy, such as authenticity or autobiography, also partake of the double movement of remembering to forget. However there is an impulse in many of the restructurings effected by writers with difficulty of access to education/ publishing/audience, that could be theorized differently as work which is not attempting to respond to the desires of the private individual, but which treat the individual as a socially-bound person. Only by anchoring articulation in the socially immediate context can the potentially incessant recursiveness of fantasy, which ideological artifice merely suppresses, be maintained and made overt.

For the empowered, and particularly acute for the relatively empowered, the postmodern dilemma takes the form of remembering to forget the artifical structure of ideology. Which returns the discussion to canonical writers. Writers in the contemporary English-language canons of literature in Canada were, for many years, crudely separated into thematic and structural groups. There were and are still writers who are taken to form a canon that critiques ideology by taking on its immediate issues and by addressing the genre conventions for conveying these issues instilled by educational training. Among these are Margaret Atwood, Alice Munro and I would argue Michael Ondaatje. Their writing squarely and courageously faces the dilemma of social action, and deals both with foregrounding the artificiality of ideology as well as the way individuals naturalize the artifice. At the same time there are Canadian writers whose writing can be taken to form a canon that critiques ideology by destabilizing its representative conventions of language and structure. The writers discussed here are bpNichol, Robert Kroetsch and Daphne Marlatt. Taking the artificiality of ideology as a 'given,' a necessary obscurity to be broken down, the burden of their work is the building of social action on different common ground.

From both canons there is work which moves out of the postmodern at the point where the private subject/nation state dichotomy collapses, at the point where the 'artificiality' of ideology becomes less important than the individual coming together in the labour of a group.

*

Memory: Personal Memory and History
Fundamental to what this section will talk about is the action of

memory and in particular its relationships with writing. However, a problem that has emerged is that there is little critical or theoretical vocabulary for explicitly discussing the procedures of those relationships.[12] So some attempt has been made to lay out the ground of approach that is used here.

Memory may be described both as the means to fix or to fictionalize and narrativize the past (the present as it goes by), which holds a curious ambivalence since fiction is also the key to unfixing. It is almost as if we store up events and images of potential unfixing for restructuring into patterns, that we then call identity and/or self, or social and/or historical validation for self. Freud suggests that the ability to make narrative is precisely the activity that halts the continual repetition compulsion arising from an event that we need to remember.[13] This happens in both personal and public locations, which are tightly interconnected with each other. For the purposes of this discussion history, or historical and national memory, is the place where personal memory engages a public activity.

Conventionally, history is a set of events from which we interpret and restructure with devices of ordering that derive validation from tacitly agreed-upon procedures. For example, there are narrative patterns which accord with what we culturally accept as a mimic for chronological time, or interpretations of public events about which many people have rememberings because there are grand narrative patterns for their reproduction.[14] Without the narrative we often do not know how to remember, and so we do not re-member, re-call or re-present.[15] These ideologically bound narrative strategies produce a sense of tradition and continuity. In the diverse, enfranchised modern nation state, they also form the basis for what we call factual knowledge which is another necessary set of cultural common grounds for a broad public. But memory is also a way in which an historical event is socially recalled and made relevant or appropriate to the present. Memory allows the present individual to engage with the construction of a past event or 'fact,' which is recognized as the social response of a past time. Yet memory also engages with the past necessarily on the material ground of the present, and is therefore part of our own immediate social response. Personal memory doesn't enter the public arena only in terms of testing history's facts and the way they duplicate and/or fit the grid of habit, but also in terms of searching for possible contexts that made those 'facts' appropriate, and locating which current contexts would continue to make them appropriate.[16]

The necessity of searching from a position of current context directs the memory into negotiations, between the individual and the social, that construct the self: which is, for the purposes of this discussion, the activity of personal memory. Selves may differ depending upon how the memory is used: they can be private, personal, communal, public, material—in other words various. But no matter how private and isolated the personal memory, that privacy is a result of an agreement between the society and the individual. Often the self when defined largely by historical memory is simply an act of forgetting, neglecting the structures of society, taking national conventions as a system of rights and becoming a private individual. This produces a concept of fixed identity, a stable self-figure like the 'heroic' or the 'ego,' that dissipates on any close look. We can't fix an event or topic or figure and still have it remain socially active and relevant. But neither can we have the figure constantly sliding and/or deferring: Both are selfish and narcissistic, avoiding action.[17]

As we approach a memory its surface slips; we fall beneath and we could then continue falling or we could choose where to stop. We can construct new surfaces which may also give way, or which may materialize as appropriate to the immediate need. Memory always coheres around the engagement with a need; sometimes it's a satisfaction or resolution, sometimes a temporary pragmatic arrangement, and sometimes a practical structure for work. Personal memory, analogously with public memory, is a place for asserting both similarities and differences with the members of the community around us. A personal memory, whether fixed or briefly cohering, is a memory or set of memories that provides stability, and we often resist any challenge to this set. When others do challenge a personal memory we get upset, like two people arguing violently over the way an apparently trivial event, commonly experienced, is re-presented. It is not an argument over factual events, but over the construction of their appropriate context; the disagreement is an indication of the different needs of the individuals not being recognized. Memory is curious: it does seem to ask for validation by agreement, from the grand narratives of public history to the personal coincidence of just one other person, for this validation is part of the negotiating process between the individual and the community.

Memory and Writing: Genre and Language.
Most representative and communicative activity is negotiation between personal memory and history. Written representation or communication, because of its status in many contemporary societies, has a particular relationship with memory and can do a wide variety of things for it. We, that is people in print societies, arrange past and passing events through figurations: associations, organizations, topics, etc—all devices of ordering and structure that derive their validation from a number of sources in sensory satisfaction, repetition, social use. Writing offers memory differing ways to order or to structure, and in doing so changes some of the ways that memory works.[18] The written, by an unfortunate confluence of ideas occurring at the moment of its access to a broader popular audience via print in the Renaissance, gained authority by implying a stability of representation, even of fixed truth ("it's written there in black and white") which were precisely the aspects that had worried earlier classical and medieval commentators on the graphic medium.[19] At the same time, from the Renaissance period to our own, the written has developed genres and languages, often with low ideological authority, that permit discussion of other memory objects than 'fact,' that provide a site for the study of actual phenomena in their instability (eg. the novel), in their ambivalence (eg. in fantasy/allegory), and that attempt to articulate things not in conventional vocabulary (eg. the gothic).

The concept of 'genre' is used here to indicate conventions of figuration in, for example, structure, narrative, metre, character, that are consciously taught, often foregrounded as constructed, and which help build a critical distance for the writer and reader. They are certainly an overt part of the process of cultural consumption and fundamentally caught in the dilemma of popular culture: They can be challenged and dismantled in order to oppose by analogous work the stability of commodified objects in social life. But to reach an audience as wide as that influenced by the commodities, they have to play upon their own cultural accessibility to consumption. 'Language' on the other hand is used here as a term to indicate conventions of communicative interaction learned so early on as often to be considered innate, such as grammar. A central critical and philosophical dilemma over the constructed/innate working of language has led it to be metaphorically linked to the 'body' about which we have similar worries: we cannot precisely locate the boundaries of either determinacy, yet both can create intimacy, elide critical distance.[20] The separation between the learned and the innate is of course one peculiar to western state science and society, and it raises a central question about memory: is memory innate? or do we learn how it works? do we learn to work it?

Memory is both what is there from which we remember: as in the past event that triggers off remembering; and the process of that remembering itself. Remembering: re-membering, recalling/calling, making a present, making present, probably with change and responding to the present need.

Public memory of history engages the past in a social present for the group. Personal memory of self engages the past in present process or in present fixity for the individual. Public or historical memory uses structures most appropriate to the politics of the place; it is responsible for the construction of private identity in nation states, just as it is responsible for the construction of fragmented identity in the postmodern world where the power of nation states is effaced by that of multinationals. Personal memory is often a structure or action that we are not used to articulating. It is a delicate weaving of not necessarily consciously constructed memories which filters one's life, orders it, leaves us beaten when it sets itself up against the flow, and which we need to attend to but usually take for granted, which plays tricks on us.

Writing uses devices both generic and linguistic that yield a set of agreements or conventions about what we are prepared to recognize as a representation (an act of memory), and which may satisfy that recognition for different reasons or may radically destabilize it. We do not know whether the satisfaction occurs because the re-presentation seems to mimic what we think we do when we remember, or whether the re-presentation provides generic strategies communally accepted that enable us to participate in that community, or whether the re-presentation describes patterns that underwrite the ideologically bound. In each case it is difficult to determine whether or not the satisfaction is related to a neurophysiological satisfaction of biological need, in other words both our social construction of the neurophysiological actions of memory as well as the actual determinant body.

In each case writing is concerned not only with the re-presentation but with the limitations of remembering the past, re-membering the body; and with the processes of dis-membering, taking the body apart, and with forgetting, foregoing the getting together of the body.

If dream is how the body makes sense of its location, and assesses the appropriate, then memory is what connects dream to action or writing. Memory becomes the recognition of appropriateness for action, and writing becomes a physical articulation of discussing that connection and its implications. In one sense the generic is what we educate our society's members to recognize as a memory structure, while language of all kinds of media is what we teach our society's members to do to survive, to be able to connect dream and action. In another sense generic strategies encourage us to question, with the potential for both satisfaction and criticism, the ideologies that surround us, while language strategies ask us to question the representations of those ideologies, radically destabilizing them and therefore needing much greater commitment to the effort of the work, yet at the same time offering the possibility of different collective common grounds.

It is fairly simple to deconstruct both ideology and the stability of representation needed for ideology. But while this is an important activity for contemporary individuals in postcolonial societies whose politics are often predicated on the assumption of inherited ideologies based on stable representations, it merely re-states what most people actually experience with communication: that it is unstable and never exact, often inadequate and difficult. However, deconstruction undertaken, ideologies questioned and the representations destabilized, there is a need to sort out other grounds for action: both for postcolonial society to continue and for broad reasons of communication and survival, and to enable further destabilizing that can resist the imposition of inappropriate representations. The processes of memory provide a way to assess value, decide on appropriate grounds and take action. Much writing is precisely about memory doing this, but is also implicated into the memory processes that do it.

Certainly much recent Canadian writing foregrounds memory and forgetting as topics that makes it possible to discuss the problems of 'self' and 'appropriate action' that complicate postcolonial writing. Canadian writers are often concerned with the definition of 'individual' or 'self' within their society and are left with the question: how to recognize the appropriateness of the individual within society; as well as: how to choose the appropriate context for fact/event/interpretation/ memory, and thereby establish the common grounds upon which we do things.

What the following chapters go on to attempt is, first, a study of the use of generic devices in three Canadian writers, and second, a study of the use of graphological language devices in a further three Canadian writers, as explicitly commenting on memory processes as a way of appropriately locating the individual in society. It should be said that this group of writers, who have produced a substantial body of work throughout the 70s and 80s, is a small handful from the large and growing number of writers in Canada working in English. It is hardly representative even of the second or third generation Canadians, and/or of the immigrants, that its writers comprise. And the group is certainly even less representative of the writers who have gained access to publication from the recent migrations of Caribbean, South American and Asian peoples, or of the renascence of Native American Indian culture over the last 25 years. However there is a discourse about self-validation that the members of this group have in common with many others both in Canada and without, particularly with those people whose primary media for communication, representation and articulation, are the same as or only minimally different from those in the recently dominating colonial national culture. To put this more crudely, a writer from a conventional Western European background fixated on print culture will face the predominantly print-governed society of a country like Canada with a different set of questions and problems than the writer from a partially oral cultural background.

CHAPTER EIGHT

Genre Strategies

Personal Memory and Official History: Survival of Self

The appropriate location for the individual and how it may be determined by memory is an issue taken up throughout the works of Margaret Atwood, Michael Ondaatje and Alice Munro. Their writings are to varying degrees concerned with the historical framework for the individual that emerges in the generic definition of their texts, and the writings run between the positions of a liberal humanist identity and the ideologically defined subject called into being by social pressures. Each writer re-presents the problem of the 'self' in terms of contesting memories and their relationship to communication, usually story-telling, in effect negotiating a position of stance related to the immediate needs of the story rather than any determinist source either biological or social.

Often unspoken but present in the background of the stories, and a central concern of Margaret Atwood's *The Handmaid's Tale,* is the rhetorical structure of the history in which the individual finds itself. For Atwood in *The Handmaid's Tale,* history is explicitly that of the nation-state where all state functions of education, religion, etc. are at one with and controlled by the government. National history is portrayed in a manner similar to Orwell's *Nineteen Eighty-Four,* with which the book has many resonances, as a procedure technically structured on fantasy: you define a limited set of grounds and then behave as if these grounds are the only ones. The procedure generates tautological, self-referential processes. This strategy of forgetting is also a strategy necessary to the commodification fundamental to capitalism,[1] and it is interesting that capitalism happily exacerbated nationalism into nation states which depend on the same structure.[2] Literary fantasies in the realist genre use an explicit set of devices to achieve these ends, and Atwood ensures that we become conscious of those devices and make them analogous to strategies of political power. *The Handmaid's Tale* foregrounds the way that many political strategies for definition are put in place by men, and that women are often in the anomalous position either of behaving as men want them to or of not knowing how to act since the permitted grounds disallow their action. This structure is immediately analogous to Freudian and Lacanian constructions of power and gender,[3] which are of course contemporaneous with the political structures of authoritarian governments emerging in the twentieth-century, and it may be due to these corollaries that so many of the writings that have come from Canadian writers are openly concerned with the politics of gender.

The fiction, and to some extent the poetry, of Margaret Atwood may often be read as critical commentary on literary device and structure. From her early poetry that reenacts Northrop Frye's *Anatomy of Criticism,* and *The Edible Woman* that parodies structural anthropology, through to the more sophisticated analyses of gothic romance and of science fiction utopias in *Lady Oracle* and *The Handmaid's Tale,* Atwood handles literary criticism as a fictional genre. It can also be said that her criticism, for example the contentious *Survival,* which lays out much of the bone structure for a theory of the postcolonial 'other' in Sadeian terms of victim and victimizer that others such as Fanon, Foucault and Bhabha elaborated before and since with rather more care, is at the same time best read as a farcical categorizing of Can Lit that has acute satiric accuracy for Canadian criticism.

The novels are also satiric in the classical tradition of simultaneously advocating and criticizing their topics. They present literary structures such as romance, travel, utopia, realism and ask why the structures are satisfying: how do readers recognize their generic expectations when they read? In *The Handmaid's Tale* and *Cat's Eye* in particular, the writer explicitly lays these questions parallel to those about memory and how memory can satisfy and fulfil expectation. In *The Handmaid's Tale* Atwood provides a critical exegesis on the problems of memory as necessary both for a definition of self and for participation in the public or in history. The story of the Handmaid Offred can be retold as: A woman is living in a futuristic fantasy-world-made real, into which she has entered only with the loss of her personal memory. The narrative tells of her attempts to continue to exist in this world-where-she-has-no-memory, at the same time as she attempts to recuperate her past self and construct some sense of herself as a personal individual. A final twist is put on the story when the reader discovers that the text is an edited version of events Offred spoke into a set of tapes, that has been reconstructed into an historical account by someone else two hundred years later.

From the opening paragraph of *The Handmaid's Tale* Atwood's central character-narrative is shot through with attempts at memory that depend almost entirely on sensory events to trigger them off: the smell of the dancehall (13) of the turned earth (22) of lemon oil (90); the feel of the weather (53) (173) or of actions like not stepping on the lines in the pavement (34) or holding a baby (73) (136); the hearing of song and sound (64) (113); the taste of food (173-4) (219); and most of all *sight,* for seeing is believing. There is a plethora of visual experience tied to memory that accumulates through the narrative although nearly every example is about the deceptiveness of the visual. Offred talks about a television program she saw as a child, in which Serena Joy, her current mistress, sang as part of a gospel choir. The memory of the past is rendered in precise detail to present a television scene with which many contemporary readers will be familiar and about which possibly sceptical. But it is juxtaposed with the actuality of the present in which Serena Joy's acted out desires have been realized, and the reality is horrific. Or there is the red smile of the tulips which becomes terribly superimposed upon the red smile of a hanged man. Or there is the memory of nineteenth-century paintings of women in harems which Offred in her earlier life was taught to read as erotic indolence, and which she now re-reads, knowing more of how enforced idleness feels, as "about suspended animation; about writing, about objects not in use" (79). Or the Commander posing in front of his fireplace like "some old come-on from a glossy men's mag" (147) where the memory of the deceptiveness coincides precisely with the present experience.

Many of the triggered memories develop into sequences that are like patches of colour that Offred is uncovering on the obscured canvas of her earlier self. To start, the sequences are brief. For example the memory of not stepping on lines in the sidewalk develops into a sequence of memories both about women's past control over their own lives and yet the continual threat to their lives from men, of both of which the current society relieves them. The memory of Serena Joy on television develops later (55-6) into a sequence about her change from a gospel-singer to an advocate for a new social order by way of a series of memories from newspapers and other television shots. The memory of touching her daughter in the bath (73-4) turns into a sequence where Offred recalls someone stealing her daughter from a pram in a supermarket, and then of the new state stealing her daughter from her. Yet each sequence is halted by the memory of a cliché from the current society usually mediated by "Aunt Lydia," the woman responsible for inculcating the new values: Freedom from, not freedom to (34), Look out for the Wives (56), Don't get too attached to the material world (74) and so on.

As the narrative proceeds the sequences not only get longer but start to refer to things *after* Offred loses her memory. One set of visual memory triggers is related to television and film, which by the effect of their own sequential movement set up inner narratives. While these work in a manner similar to the other visual stimuli, usually to highlight change, deception, re-reading, as for example in the sequence remembering a television interview with Hitler's mistress (154), they also tell stories. At one point in her indoctrination Offred is shown a film of the "Unwomen" or feminists. By chance (?) it contains footage of her own mother "very young, very serious, even pretty" (129), and on its conclusion she moves on to narrate the memory of her mother coming over to visit her and her partner Luke, when she is much older "wiry, spunky, the kind of old woman who won't let anyone butt in front of her in a supermarket line" (130).

These different versions of her mother are extended near the end of the account when Offred tells about her friend Moira who had seen her mother in a film clip about the "Colonies" to which the present state has sent all undesirables. The extension is significant not only because it completes another part of the sub-plot, the background picture to the devastation being wrought by the current political state, but also because it presents Offred much more in control of her memory and using it to construct significance. This later sequence shows her remembering something Moira tells her, and then carefully switching into a conscious memory action "I can't remember the last time I saw her..." which develops a sequence from her past where she finds her mother's house turned upside down by the police. Offred then returns to something Moira has said about her mother when they were both at college, but explicitly concludes the sequence with "I bring myself back, to the here, to the hotel. This is where I need to be" (265). Offred here not only controls her memory with far more skill, but has also internalized the significance of Aunt Lydia's haltings of earlier brief memories: She now does this for herself.

Superficially it appears as though Offred is using the memories to build a past for herself, but in effect she is using the past to assimilate into the present as an individual. There are many reflections on the activity and process of memory in constructing a self throughout the narrative, and indeed at several points these become one with comments on writing or telling stories. One of the first observations the narrator explicitly makes on remembering/re-presenting the past immediately follows a sequence where she tries to remember her daughter. This sequence is also important because it is the only place where we get some clue as to how she might have lost her memory: she says "I know I lost time" (49). But whether it was "needles, pills, something like that" (the only 'device' Atwood uses) or the shock of severance from her daughter, neither she nor we can know. Offred goes on to say "I would like to believe this is a story I'm telling" (49) not a reality, for if it's a story she will be able to control the ending. Yet "It isn't a story I'm telling./It's also a story I'm telling, in my head, as I go along" (49). All memories are apparently of actual past events, but are constructed into specific present ones. Further, "I must be telling it to someone. You don't tell a story only to yourself ... A story is like a letter. *Dear You,* I'll say..." (49-50).

For most of the first twenty chapters, Offred struggles with memories and sequences, trying to order and understand them. One of the greatest hindrances is the lack of communication. As Offred notes of Aunt Lydia's insistence on the acceptance of sacrifice and duty, it can only come about for future generations "Because they will have no memories, of any other way" (127). When the Commander of Offred's house begins to seek her out for his own illicit desires, the fact of their illicit status begins to provide Offred with the example of an "other way." It is from this point that she also begins to take some control over her memories. The exercise begins with her attempt to "reconstruct" her first meeting with the Commander when he asks her to play Scrabble with him (144), to go over what she said, what he said, and so on. She even adds obviously fictional details, such as the knifing of the Commander, into this reconstruction. Immediately following she comments "what I need is perspective ... Otherwise you live in the moment, which is not where I want to be" (153): or the comment flowing directly into her memory of the filmed interview with Hitler's mistress. Just as spelling for the Scrabble games was difficult, "like using a language I'd once known but had nearly forgotten, a language having to do with customs that had long before passed out of the world" (164) just so memory and story telling have to be learned and relearned if forgotten.

As if the earlier chapters are there to give an idea of the difficulty of dislocation, by chapter 26 we move to a narrative impulse where Offred can give us a retrospective account of events in the "present," as if memory has almost caught up with her. Part of the process of telling her story, re-presenting the memories, is to structure her way through the morass of the past to the thing she finds significant. One of the acutely painful experiences is that of forgetting. Early on she says of a memory of her daughter that it "fades," becomes a ghost. Later on, more skilled at reconstructing, she tries "to conjure, to raise my own spirits," the people from her past, but she no longer can (203). Slowly Luke fades as well (281). Although crossed with the pain of a bereavement, the fading is also presented as positive, as an indication that she cannot remake those particular memories into a self that can deal with the present. In stark contrast is Janine who collapses into the past and has to be re-called by Moira who says "Get right back here! You can't stay *there*, you aren't *there* any more" (228). Of herself Offred says: "I don't have to tell it: I don't have to tell anything, to myself or to anyone else ... It's possible to go so far in, so far down and back, they could never get you out" (237), but "That will never do."

Memory and its structuring begins to get conflated with explanations of place and time and appropriateness. A clear instance of this sophistication occurs near the end of Offred's narrative when she goes up to the room of the Commander's guard, Nick, to have sex. We are offered three different reconstructions in the form of fictional genres: one romantic, one realist and one lyric. What is important is that Offred is consciously detailed about the events being offered: she is constructing reasons about the validity or appropriateness of the links between memory and action. By the end she has created not only a self but a "you" to listen—both of course part of herself—and here she also recounts the appalling event of "salvaging" and hooks her narrative into historical importance by suggesting that it may in fact be important to exchange the account of events with someone at a later time: it is a record of barbarism that needs to be known. Early on she says that although she and Luke had heard the newspaper stories about mutilations, killings etc., they had worked hard to remain ignorant of their value: "The newspaper stories were like dreams to us, bad dreams dreamt by others" (66) that they refused to connect to action.

Significantly, she connects their laborious ignorance with their refusal to participate in writing "We were the people who were not in the papers. We lived in the blank white spaces at the edges of print. It gave no more freedom. /We lived in the gaps between the stories" (66-67). Just before the account of the salvaging she notes "I would like to be without shame. I would like to be shameless. I would like to be ignorant. Then I would not know how ignorant I was" (275): without memory, without the possibility of connecting dream to action, without being able to tell others. But she opts to do all those things and write herself into an individual position that can communicate and represent significance. If she doesn't they will "erase" her as they erase the memory of her from her daughter's mind, leaving her "blank ... between parentheses" (240). At the end she is left with having translated herself into a present individual who has the memory skills, the skills of re-presenting, to assess and act on needs. The alternating sections of Night/Day/Night/Day/Nap/Day/Night/Day etc. that structure her entire text take Offred between dream and action in chunks that gradually weld together through the action of memory, so that the final "Night" section is invaded by the realities, demands, immediacies of action: but at least she is prepared.

What Atwood achieves with chilling clarity in the final futuristic section is a repositioning of individual action within the historical memory of 2195 AD. Despite the horror of the Gileadean regime, little has changed at the university history conference. More to the point, despite the tale of individual struggle and courage, the historians are interested in Offred's account mainly for what it can tell them about the structure of the Gileadean state and the men who set it up and controlled it. The construction of the grand narrative is focused on a better comprehension of the political map of the western hemisphere (312). Its intention is "not to censure but to understand" (315) the actions of Gilead: a laudable, tolerant, humanist approach that we are asked to weigh against the nearly-in-the-present-of-1990 actions that we would have no difficulty condemning. The historians want to "establish an identity" (315) for Offred, yet she has established one for herself in the text. They want an identity that will become involved in the grand national narrative, that requires a stable sense of individuality. She has produced one that is in response to immediate need.

History is a way of establishing community but also a way of fixing and manipulating society. Histories may use texts of personal memory for the needs of their own time, but they also underline the impossibility of retrieving personal life: what is missing from this kind of national history is the sense of the individual. An individual cannot insert itself into national memory or its historical writing. It can only present the future with the ambivalence of its contradictions, through a different kind of writing. In *The Handmaid's Tale* history makes a 'fact' of Offred; and since we have the past context we can assess the extent to which the fact is inappropriate realizing that the reappropriation by this "history" is inadequate to her context. Yet as we discover retrospectively, the future historians have access to exactly the same materials. Is it because these historian-editors have reconstructed the narrative themselves that they are left blind to the personal memory? Or is it something to do with the kind of public memory they are recounting, with its emphasis on national identity, that must subordinate the way personal memory challenges the stability of the representations that mediate its ideology?

What Atwood provides for the contemporary reader is an example of a text in two genres. The last section is in the form of a quasi-documentary; it provides a satire on fact, on historical observation, on national grand narratives. The much longer chunk of the text that makes up Offred's tale is an imaginative rendering of the simultaneous doublethink of all post-Renaissance dys/u/topias, which present the social and political controls necessary to maintain the fantasy world, at the same time as the individuals who know that the fantasy world is not real. Here that doubleness is figured forth in the alternating sections of Night and Day, of lyric dream and realism. Initially, neither one can admit the other, but gradually as the personal negotiates the public and puts itself under self-constraints, the two come together in the simultaneous admission and ignoring of certain events.

Although Atwood may delicately prise apart the double-strand of the fantasy stance that has allowed nation states to control their subjects and allowed to individuals a kind of private self, she cannot get rid of it. This distance on genre that criticizes and satirizes yet does not radically shift has advantages and disadvantages: it holds the structures that the society uses for shaping representation up to scrutiny; it does not directly challenge them but neither does it alienate the reader. It speaks to the reader about what s/he knows, not about what is unknown or rather unarticulated.[6] Similarly, Atwood's approach to women and feminism is immensely critical but never immediately challenging.[7] Atwood's female heroes from Susanna Moodie onward continually write a version of history that is communal but never impinges on state politics in a direct way. Although she has been criticized for this, because the position can underwrite women's disempowerment, it is also a structure that permits her to emphasize women's continuing exclusion from power, and to offer both possible and fantastic alternatives in the name of women. If people are not so much concerned to insert themselves into the grand narrative of national history then they may present other ways to write a public memory.

*

Legitimate Memory: Fame and the Commodification of Self
The seductions of fame offered by the grand narratives of history are a dominant element in the work of Michael Ondaatje. Ondaatje, also, focuses on the generic and conscious literary devices that we are taught by our culture to recognize and use in an attempt to define a self. He is an acute observer of cliché, classical allusion, contemporary intertextual reference, into all of which he explodes rapidly flowering images taken from the central cultural metaphors of North American obsession: cowboys, stars in space, jazz, sex. All of his narratives, whether prose or poetry, tell about the terrible destructive search for a fixed personal identity that will challenge the way that the state/public history forgets and erases individuals. Yet at the same time as the search for a reconstruction of history that will validate that image of self-identity, there is hovering around all the narratives the central person elusive, carrying a history that responds only to the immediate.

From *The Collected Works of Billy the Kid* to *Coming through Slaughter,* to *Running in the Family* and *In the Skin of a Lion,* the writer concerns himself with the negotiations between personal memory and historical memory, and with the commodification of self necessary to fame and to all public heroes. Billy the Kid is a public icon, a cultural cliché with so fixed an image that it can proliferate wildly through North American media. So the question forms: is there a person initiating that? if so what is it? how has it managed to commodify itself? But this is also the cultural icon as outlaw, and links directly into the idea of the artist as hero: both maintaining and destroying the representations necessary to society. *Coming through Slaughter* shifts the focus onto the personal and the interactions that the artist as person has with the artist as historical figure. The artist can become a hero by commodifying self, but may also have self commodified by the public and then need to engage with that other version. The concern with the artist is also a concern with how we make figurations, not only how we enter history but how we can make history part of ourselves. It is a process of inculturation that is an im/emigrant habit showing up in the fascination of much Canadian writing with cliché and social convention.[8]

Ondaatje's figures are Classic neo-Romantic figures whose image of the lone artist against the system is part of the economy of the vicious circle inscribed by nation-state and private individual. Just so, in conventional romantic style they all hover on the borders of madness and criminality, and end either as insane or dead. But Ondaatje controls the myth in order to examine it. Most of the narratives have the structure of a detective story foregrounded as a conscious device. In common with many other twentieth-century writers interested in structure, the detective story genre is used here to allow for a critique of 'truth' and of 'fixity.'[9] Answers are only posited to indicate their inadequacy. And increasingly, these narratives turn from questions about truth to pursuing the tensions between the historical fixity of identity and personal ambivalence.

The most radical use of the detective genre is *Running in the Family,* which is a different search into personal memory rather than public history. There are no answers expected; this is an autobiographical construction and the writer knows too much to expect answers. Further, this first lengthy prose fiction work loosens the tensions of Ondaatje's poetic control. Rather than riding out to the manic edge where the individual challenges ideology by evading its representations and jumping into chaos, the writer here turns away from the drive to commodify self, insert it into historical memory, and turns toward personal memory. The account of this family in Sri Lanka is however an ambivalent text. The writer is accounting for people who may be displaced but who are also relatively empowered: they can to an unusual extent define personal memory *as* public memory even though that public memory may not be the one they want. One of the conditions of an individual within a nation state is the need to simultaneously acknowledge and deny the constructed status of history.[10] At the same time the writer-narrator is writing a history, yet trying to create it not from national memory but from personal memory. The ambivalence lies in our knowledge that these personal memories are of people who mediated the rule of the colonizing nation state.

In a sense these relatively empowered people are the best placed to understand how history works and to suggest ways of withstanding its need for fixity. The result is a catalogue, an encyclopedia of outcasts, anarchists, eccentrics, all those who sit complicit on the other side of state authority, in many ways parallel to the heroes of Ondaatje's earlier books, but resisting single identities and therefore resisting commodification into an easy grand narrative. What is different here is that the writer-narrator does not get swept up into that heroism. There is little sense of the writer-as-character, more of the writer-as-storyteller who starts with "the bright bone of a dream" (21) and ends saying that he is no detective but can only "move among the scattered acts and memories with no more clues" (201), and more important: "My body must remember everything" (202).

All of these narratives present the detective story framework of the seeker and the sought, moving from the oppositions of Billy the Kid and Pat Garrett, to the more intimate pursuit by Watts of Buddy Bolden and the running among the memories of the family. As the search becomes more intimate, the hero figure loses its cultural iconicity and fragments into anarchic eccentricity. At the same time the personal memories from the observer of the hero take on more and more significance. Ondaatje's *In the Skin of a Lion* (1987) may be read as an elaborated account of the detective story, in which the observer casts the criminal, anarchist, artist, thief *against* the hero, as figures without an historical memory against the commodified individual who has acquired fame.

The narrative, which is enclosed in the framework of a remembering of the central character's lover, begins with his childhood as a lone child living with a father who is by turns silent and explosive, for he is a dynamiter. The boy too learns how to explode and uses this talent later on both for work and for political purposes. But first he becomes a "searcher," trying to win an enormous reward by finding a rich man,

Ambrose Small, who has run off. Small is the hero, from whom if you find him, you gain a heroism—literally in this case you commodify yourself. In Patrick's case love intervenes, and by the time he finds Small, the man has become a recluse, the hero who evades fame. If Patrick "was a hero he could come down on Small like an arrow"—but he has been told by his lover Clara who would lead him to Small, "never to follow her" (83) and so initially he does not. Why? Because:

All his life Patrick Lewis has lived beside novels and their clear stories. Authors accompanying their heroes clarified motives. World events raised characters from destitution. The books would conclude with all wills rectified and all romances solvent. Even the spurned lover accepted the fact that the conflict had ended. (82)

Soon his sexual memory tells him differently and he goes off in pursuit of Clara, only to find Small back in Patrick's own childhood home town when Patrick doesn't want him any more.

Interwoven into this first section of the narrative is a tale of the building of the Danforth Bridge in Toronto, during which we are introduced to the immigrants Caravaggio and Nicholas Temelcoff and the man Harris who employs them. The immigrants have the problem of being people without history—indeed people without the language of the society who then learn it from films, actors or records. Temelcoff, without a public language, "became a vault of secrets and memories. Privacy was the only weight he carried....This man ... would walk off and leave strange clues about himself" (47-8). Both Temelcoff, and as we later learn, Caravaggio, stop working for the city, one to become a baker and the other a thief. Harris though goes on to other public works, like the water filtration plant, which is where Patrick begins to work.

The second section of the book is both a story of Patrick's third pursuit, that of another lover Alice, and of the emerging narrative of class economics. Harris is a public servant, employing thousands of workers, at the same time as building these public works "for himself. For a strong dream" (110). He is an artist, a choreographer of space, architecture and natural geography, whose tools are "Ash-grey faces" (111). Against this employer but distant from him because of utter economic dependence, are the workers. At first isolated from this community, although working on the filtration plant tunnel as a dynamiter, Patrick becomes involved with them and goes to a social-political-artistic event at which he becomes fascinated by the dancer.

This performer turns out to be Alice Gull, a friend of Clara's whom he has already met, and with whom he now goes to live along with her daughter.

The following development of Patrick's politicization by Alice is a reversal of the usual gendered narrative portraying the sexual romance of politics, in which women follow powerful men into class analysis/action because of their bodies. In a sense, Patrick's politicization is a way for him to begin to insert himself into historical narrative; his skill with explosions can help him take on the role of anarchist and challenge the powerful. And he will do this, although he feels "nothing but a prism that refracted their lives ... when not aligned with another—whether it was Ambrose, Clara or Alice—he could hear the rattle within that suggested a space between him and community. A gap of love" (157). Alice dies, exploded by mistake. In avengeance, possibly, Patrick goes north and explodes a leisure area for the rich.

On release from prison in the third and last section of the book, Patrick ties up with the escaped prisoner Caravaggio, the immigrant turned thief. Together they plan the grand anarchic act of blowing up the water filtration plant, which involves Patrick swimming down the tunnel he has made from Lake Ontario and into the building, planting explosives as he goes. Bruised and wounded by a small escape blast, he succeeds, and walks up to Harris's office where the man is working. There in the penultimate chapter of the book the political discussion lines up. Harris attempts to calm Patrick by telling him of his working-class background, how "he hated the officials of the city but now he loved City Hall" (235), now he wanted "excess, something to live up to" in the city. To this anxious mixture of class lullaby and seductions of power, Patrick poses only his memory of Alice.

Alice, Patrick, Cato (Alice's earlier lover), Caravaggio—all of these anarchists are acting from commitment to and memory of another person, because there is no tangible community out there; it is their only way of writing themselves into history, by spinning faster and faster around to suddenly crash into the monolithic system of power and explode. This is an image that Ondaatje gives the reader throughout his writing from the stress of machines with "the one altered move that will make them maniac" (*Collected Works of Billy the Kid* 41), to Patrick's literal blindfolded physical explosion around his small room detonated by Clara's small change of position (*In the*

Skin of a Lion 80). Alice's political words are not her own though: Caravaggio echoes them exactly, Harris recognizes lines from Diogenes—Ondaatje is presenting us with a story of constant repression, almost futile public action if you resist the grand narratives. Harris himself is part of the great narrative of class history that has permitted him to 'move up,' but only by forgetting the others, his earlier community, and only by "sell[ing] himself every time" (242), turning himself into commodity.

In a completely different generic stance from the detective story quest for answers, it is possible to read *In the Skin of a Lion* as a vast physiodrama peopled by an allegory of types. Caravaggio, Temelcoff, Alice, Small, Clara, Cato, Harris: all become wild figures stamping and dancing on the periphery of Patrick's vision: all these possibilities for personal action that are in effect refractions of Patrick, rather than he the prism refracting them. Each of them acquires at times the extraordinary metaphoric density that Ondaatje's poetics can confer. Caravaggio disappears literally "into the blue," and appears "out of the blue," as the blue-painted man camouflaged against the blue-painted ceiling of the penitentiary hall. Ondaatje's writing has a deep trust in the literal base for language, as his thematics have a deep trust in the possibility for communication in love. Yet this physical body of the text is refocused quite clearly on the necessary interaction with history.

There are hints of other ways to engage memory: when Patrick presents Temelcoff with a photograph to remind him of the time he saved a nun from falling, he remembers "the exact date which his memory had lost—and pleasure and wonder fill him" (148):

Nicholas is aware of himself standing there within the pleasure of recall. It is something new to him. This is what history means...Patrick's gift, that arrow into the past, shows him the wealth in himself, how he has been sewn into history. Now he will begin to tell stories. (149)

Patrick's searches, researches, are not simply to find answers. They become part of a process by which individuals can connect themselves to their communities; construct common histories appropriate to their needs. This analogically directs the reader back to the structure of the book, which is a memory of Clara that Patrick is recounting to Alice's daughter, after all these events are over and on their way to meet Clara. His willingness to talk is in contrast to his attempts to remember Alice while in prison, where he "protected himself with silence ... as if saying even one word would begin a release of Alice out of his body. Secrecy kept him powerful. By refusing communication he could hold her within himself..." (212). Only once, when his friend Caravaggio is attacked does he break his silence because "his father's neutral song slid out as warning" (212). Silence, refusal to communicate, may be generated by a fear that we will discover there to be nothing appropriate to today if we articulate our memory. Yet silence about the personal, a peculiarly male trait in western culture, also leads to explosion and destruction. His willingness to share his memories of Clara is partly because she is still there to help him reconstruct her back into his life.

The elusive centre of the book is the construction of the self of the teller, which we can only read by way of the series of his stories: a series of contexts where the personal and public memories meet. For many Canadians, the history in which Ondaatje places Patrick is as unknown to them as it was to him. Ondaatje makes Patrick the alien insider who "knows nothing of the place" (157), but who, when attached to a community, can assume "responsibility for the story" (157). Having read *In the Skin of a Lion,* what becomes insistent is the question of facticity: did any of this happen? in any version? does Cato's list of repression exist on paper in some archive? or is it simply part of a mythical landscape? The 'simply' underscores the need to connect oneself consciously to community and to history but, like Temelcoff and his photograph, there seems to be a need for communal validation of that connection. Personal memory enters the public arena by negotiating with the facts of history. Ondaatje is concerned to demonstrate that the facts alone do not help but the contexts that make those facts appropriate to personal need are vital. Storytelling becomes not a way of commodifying self into heroism, but of inserting oneself into a dialogue with a larger community.

*

Private Memory: Stories we tell ourselves
Personal memory in each of *The Handmaid's Tale* and *In the Skin of a Lion* is firmly in the context of a particular public need. With both texts it is as if historical necessities demand a certain response, insist on a negotiation. If the writer chooses to take on a socially topical narrative about repression of an individual who in *The Handmaid's Tale* a woman, or about the disempowered position of individuals such as impoverished immigrants or the working class, then the

presence of public 'need' will be highly directive. The stance of the writing, which is underwritten by the genres of the two texts, is either to present the individual as being put into a necessary negotiation with the public demands, or as putting itself into that position. While incorporating both positions, the focus of *The Handmaid's Tale* is to the former and of *In the Skin of a Lion* to the latter, probably providing an analogue for the positions of power in which the writers place the gender of their central characters.

More difficult is the work of personal memory in a position where the historical is obscured by convention. It is hard to remember the habitual unless it is passed through a foregrounding lens. This is one reason that realism, or the writing of place and/or social immediacy, is important to the reader: for exactly that foregrounding of the mundane so that we can remember the constructions of our present and have a door to the evaluation of needs. One Canadian writer who captures that sense of evaluation, and combines it with a trust in the possibility of personal identity inserting itself into conventional history, is Alice Munro. Munro has written a large number of short stories which have been collected into books since *The Dance of the Happy Shades* (1968), some contributing to the genre of serial short stories also used by Margaret Laurence and others in which the collection forms a coherent "whole book."[11] Although Munro has consistently been fascinated by memory, the discussion here will focus on just the title short story of the collection *The Progress of Love* (1985), and on another story from that collection, "Miles City, Montana."

In Munro's early writing, for example the story "The Peace of Utrecht," there are a few brave essays into loosening the knot of figures that our memory is, and following the tensions that tie them up and get released upon the loosening. Yet many of the collections from the 1970s such as *Something I've Been Meaning to Tell You* or *The Moons of Jupiter* focus more on rearranging the images. With *The Progress of Love* there is a relaxation, a shift of gear into memory as a group of voices focused around the moment that calls them, and distils them through slow time into a study of what the present needs. "The Progress of Love" has a highly complex chronological structure that eludes easy ordering into a timescale of events. One way of re-telling it would be to say that it opens with the narrator, Fame, talking about her mother and father in a series of apparently unconnected memories that only acquire significance from several re-readings.

After this introduction the narrator proceeds to tell us about her memories of her childhood with her mother, her mother's memories of Fame's grandmother, and Fame's memories of visiting her old house on the farm with a lover from a few years back, all clustered around her several memories of the visit to the farm by her mother's sister, Beryl.

Quite apart from the unique detail of social observation at which Munro is highly skilled, the short story works by setting up conflicting memories, contradictory constructions of an event that addresses the needs of the individuals involved. Aunt Beryl's visit to the farm makes it possible for Fame to hear an alternative version of one of her mother's stories in which she recounts first finding *her* mother hanging by a rope and then running in her nightgown to fetch her father from his place of work in the town. Fame's mother, Marietta, has been introduced to the reader as a "serious" person, but only later on does this characterization seem to be significant for her telling of this horrific story. The alternative version offered by Beryl, who has been shown to be humorous, self-consciously ironic about herself and others, is that this "hanging" was a joke. Further, it was she as a little girl who was the first to notice that the rope wasn't tied to the beam. Fame says that she didn't "have a problem right away with Beryl's story" (23), but it "didn't vanish; it stayed sealed off for years, but it wasn't gone" (23). And that is all that is said.

The narrative then moves into an elusive section that starts in the "present-time of telling" and shifts to a memory in which she revisits the farm with a current lover, Bob Marks, and tells him that her mother burned three thousand dollars in the wood-stove while "My father stood and watched her" (26). Rather abruptly unconnected in the chronology, Fame's memory then casts back to another point of Beryl's visit where her mother tells, apparently for the first time, that she burned the money, and she remembers her father saying "'What money are you talking about?'" (28). The account jars on initial reading for it is difficult to understand why Fame told Bob Marks one version of the memory, when her own recollection is different. However, what has happened is that the present-time narrator has been moved by the memory of the conflicting memories of Beryl and Marietta to remember conflicting memories of her own. The contradiction in the story of the "hanging," has released a buried memory that contradicts one of her own current memories: "Why, then, can I see the scene so clearly?... How hard it is for me to believe that I made that up" (29-30).

What her current memory made up was not a factual event but a necessary context where her father "protects" her mother, "one of them is doing what seems natural and necessary, and the other believes that the important thing is for that person to be free, to go ahead" (30). In the opening sequence of the story we are told of Fame's mother saying "One drop of hatred in your soul will spread and discolour everything like a drop of black ink in white milk" (6), and we are also told of her father in old age mistaking her for her mother and speaking to her in a "voice like spitting" (6). From this point, the reader can re-tell the story as a story of hatred that permeated the mother's life, hatred for *her* father, that spread out to Fame and to Fame's father. The image of the two together burning the money that would have enabled her to be educated allows Fame to contain the hatred so that it will spread no further—to re-present it as a kind of devotion or freedom.

But where Munro most helpfully places the action of personal memory is within the story-telling time. At the end Fame says that she no longer tells the story of her mother burning the money, not because "it wasn't, strictly speaking, true" (30), but because she could no longer longer expect people to approve of the action. Further, she herself has realized through the process of contradictory memory that she cannot approve it, not because it deprived her of many opportunities, but because it represented a complicity with repression, a refusal to recast the memory of a hated person into something constructive. And this is precisely what Fame is doing: reconstructing past memories to make a self that is appropriate to her current needs. Her mother told her stories, but they were "the stories and griefs, the old puzzles you can't resist or solve" (14) what women tell women when there seems no alternative. Fame notes that when she "just had the two boys" she felt that these stories could now stop. Another kind of story-telling replaces it, which assumes that we can take action about ourselves, we can to some extent control the identity that emerges into the public community.

Memory is a way of controlling desire, but it can control desire by closing it down or by providing a site for the release of its possibilities. Marietta lived in a silent world, separate from her husband, where self was enclosed and unchanging. Fame lives in a world where expectations about relationships between men and women had begun to change. But greater communication, broader control over the structurings of self in a communal context, means that one must respond to other people's needs not only one's own, and so we must be willing to change our own memories.

The underlying figure of re-membering in the story is of the house on the farm. Early in the short story we are told of Fame and her mother wallpapering the room for Beryl with blue cornflowers, and when she returns to the house with Bob Marks, the edge of the blue cornflower wallpaper that she uncovers raises all kinds of emotions in her that lead to a brief outburst between the two of them, because what he wants to recall is not what she wants. In the conclusion to the story, Fame remembers Bob then trying "with imagination" to recall something more appropriate to herself, and recognizing this, although his is not an appropriate memory at all, she accepts his attempt. In the present story-telling time, the narrator observes that:

Moments of kindness and reconciliation are worth having...I wonder if those moments aren't more valued, and deliberately gone after, in the setups some people like myself have now, than they were in those old marriages, where love and grudges could be growing underground, so confused and stubborn, it must have seemed they had forever. (30-31)

The trust in the possibility of personal identity that much of Munro's writing shows is carried toward the reader by her sophisticated control of devices of realism. The unsettling chronology of memory in this and other stories, never leaves the reader alienated because the precision of realist observation within each small section provides an overwhelming sense of coherence and stability. The story is bound up with a traditional notion of "progress" that is conveyed by the various depictions of relationships between men and women, to which are given a distinct sense of change and improvement. However, Munro masks any involvement with ideology, often indeed linking a character directly with the representation of a commodity such as Beryl's "écru" underwear. There is self-consciousness in these strategies, but criticism is reserved for individuals not for history. The conflicts in the structure of memory are nearly all within the personal, although frequently set off by an intrusion from the historical, and the personal memory usually works by accommodating itself to that intrusion.

A more clear-cut involvement with the social and cultural stereotypes of ideology emerges in a number of other short stories both in *The Progress of Love* and *Friend of My Youth*. One writing from the earlier collection, "Miles City, Montana," is a subtle exposure of the impossibility of controlling personal identity. It works precisely against the trust that momentarily coalesces in "The Progress of Love," by framing the moment of mistrust as the child's first loss of trust in a parent.

The narrator of the story places an event in the nearer past, next to an event remembered from childhood. The inexplicable elements of the traumatic near-drowning of her own child are set alongside the recalled drowning of one of her childhood acquaintances, which had left her baffled and angry for very different reasons. The memories that gather around the present need are to do with the way parents expect a child to trust them, but also expect to be forgiven when that trust fails. of course, there is no reason why the child should forgive. It is only those parents who do not insist on trust, whose children are "self-possessed," who are "let off the hook."

However, what is interesting about the presentation of social reality is that there are pressures upon individuals that inexorably complicate their attempts to define their own sense of self. I argued earlier that realism was a tacitly agreed-upon construction for conveying stable representations, yet it is also particularly open to deconstruction by way of historical readings. Contemporary realist texts are made more elusive by being in the present time of the reader, but cultural and social analyses can briefly take the place of history. "Miles City, Montana" not only provides a series of cultural stereotypes for its own deconstruction, but also discusses the way in which this re-reading takes place.

The overriding metaphor for such a re-reading is the interaction of memories and the way that they get transliterated not only through personal needs but through social expectation. The drowned body of the childhood friend is remembered personally with gruesome detail that cannot have been the case; and the event of his returning body, supposedly worse according to "people" because it was to a house that had no mother to grieve for him, in fact is to a house which has a father who to all appearances is sensible and caring.

The discrepancy between memory and actuality caused by social expectation and convention is more apparent to the present narrator, and carries over into the narration of the nearer-present event about her own child. This opens as if triggered by a photograph of herself, her husband Andrew, and her two children Cynthia and Meg, just before they set off on a long trip from Vancouver to Ontario to visit the grandparents. The detail available to the reader is extensive. First, the car is described: it is brand new, and their first brand-new car. It is oyster-coloured, although the dealer had a fancier name for the colour, yet surely the reader asks, "oyster" is fancy enough. It is a "big small car," it has prestige but is appropriate to their lives (we find out only later that it is a self-consciously chosen European car). The description is loaded with words expressing the status that the car conveys onto the family, which is also perfectly nuclear with two parents and two children.

And then she describes herself,

standing beside the car. I was wearing white pants, a black turtleneck, and sunglasses. I lounged against the car door, canting my hips to make myself look slim (87)

in the conventional pose of the woman who sells the car in advertisements all over North America, the woman as commodity, slightly worried about her weight, hoping that she gives back to the camera the image that it demands. And she does. The husband says, "Wonderful .... Great. You look like Jackie Kennedy." The narrator comments that all over the continent women who gave back the appropriate image were probably told that "they looked like Jackie Kennedy." The attentive reader is picking up on the signals that will explicitly be given later on, that the husband appropriates the wife's image, like a tourist he captures it on film and multiply copies it to send around to all the relatives, sharing out these commodities of car, family, and wife, that speak to his success. It is an attitude that also presumably contributes to their divorce.

Readers could pick up this metacommentary by themselves, but it is not clear that the woman at the time of the picture was able to do so. The rest of the short story is at least partly about how those images get constructed, and how difficult it is for the individual to be aware of that process, and indeed what we do when we become aware through memory. In the car, Andrew begins to discuss the "image" of the new car, and draws in the six-year-old Cynthia. When he describes it as "sensible, but it has class ... like my image," Cynthia replies, "That means like you think you want to be, Daddy?" It is clear that he has a concept about what he would like to be, but it is not at all clear that the social perception of the stereotype is the same as his own.

That individuals assume that they can control the images that they project and the lives that they lead is focused through the control that parents apparently exercise over the lives of their children. The present narrator, in thinking of this trip, says "It seems to me now that we invented characters for our children, ... enjoying the contradictions as well as the confirmations of them" (89-90). And implicitly she describes the way that she confirms and contradicts what her own parents had in mind for her, when she talks about the happiness of working with her father during a flood on his turkey farm although she was about to leave all that life behind. More clearly she discusses the expectations that Andrew's mother and uncle have of him, and of his willingness or not to reflect those images back to them. Yet both of them turned out as "strenuous children, ... relentless seekers of approbation"(97).

One set of images over which she has little control at the time concerns Andrew. She is at a loss to bring together her confused feelings about him, but from a distance they replicate the combination of authority and care found in parents. At times his body stands "between me and whatever joy or lightness I could get in life," and then suddenly he is "my good friend and most essential companion" (91). The narrator shifts ambivalently from warmth to scorn at the alacrity with which he takes on the "ready-made role of husband, father, breadwinner," while she is self-perceived as selfish and untrustworthy, for which qualities he loves her.

But what the story addresses directly is the image the narrator has self-consciously chosen for herself as the confident and indomitable mother, not the kind that sagged into trivial burdens (90), whose foolish promise of a swimming pool materializes like an answer to magic wish. Technically, the central event of the story is the near drowning of her younger daughter, but the significance of the event is released into the preceding and following pages asking for re-readings. The event loops her memory back to the death and funeral of her childhood friend, raising all those questions about parents' relationships with their children: how far are they responsible for their children's well-being, lives, or futures; is it an individual or social responsibility; is it a responsibility or a delusion arising from adult claims on authority; and if people can't even control their own lives, how can they claim authority over other people's?

The linked commentary on images, characters, and roles, and how these are shot through with social and cultural pressures and with familial tensions that replicate social authority, all of which the narrator has chosen to stand against in her self-defined approach to motherhood, suddenly become pertinent to herself. Like Andrew, the image that she thinks she is has little protection against reality, and is thrown forward as the construct it is as a result of moments of extreme stress. In the moment of noticing something different, something that alerts her to possible danger, she reacts to preserve life, and certainly not as the indomitable mother who will leave her child to independence. it is almost as if she is trying to overlay the earlier experience of a dead body with a saved body, just as Cynthia momentarily overlays the dead body of a deer with the apparently dead body of a girl. The reconstruction of what happened that follows, and the projection into what could have happened, are rebuildings of her image. She calls the latter projection "shameful," yet in effect it's no different from the former, just more obviously about the pleasure we get in trying to control our realities.

Unlike "The Progress of Love," "Miles City, Montana" looks at the way personal memory gets fused with social expectation, and at the way that individual identity, which we derive so intimately from personal memory, is continually shot through with and moulded by cultural and community pressures. The social reality of history in this story is not one of definition and change but of replication, and of the difficulty of refusing that replication. At the end of the narrative she understands that he childhood anger was a confused mixture of realizing that parents cannot prevent accident or death, at the same time as recognizing for the first time that they should not pretend an authority that claims that it can. That pretence lays the wrong ground for trust. Trust cannot be in the absolute authority of a fixed identity. It has to be in and by way of understanding the complex limitations and constructions that surround the personal, that deny heroic action, and allow for the "natural and particular" mistakes the older narrator and reader can position as social and individual, and for forgiveness. The social reality of history, which the genre of realism conventionally mediates, is everpresent in these texts as detail with which personal memory must engage and renegotiate.

*

Personal Memory and Public History: Responding to need
Similarly concerned with personal memory responding to the need of
a moment, a place and a context, but less accommodating about the
defining features of the context, is Margaret Atwood's *Cat's Eye*. The
narrative here is also about women and women, women and men, hatred
and self-destruction; yet Atwood asks us to focus on the dangerous
ambivalence that simply accommodating to someone else's version of
oneself can generate. The novel has to do with the way memory makes
us: that if we have no way of relating out to a community, then the self
becomes privately constructed within a circle of victim and victimizer
that Atwood tautly reproduced in her early poem "The Circle Game,"
and satirized in *Survival*. But what is a 'community'? how do we find
or define one? or do they simply define us?
     Cat's Eye looks at the communities of family, school and work, and
crosses them all with issues of gender as it questions the making of
self. In the process, this wok offers an overt response to the
complacency of recent hyper-liberal thought which evades the
problems of general human issues (universals) by focusing on
community. The bourgeois-liberal community can indeed function in
a 'civilized' manner,[12] but the moment the inequity of imbalance of
power arises, its stance works merely as the isolated particular world
of private individuals on which the state depends. Here, by crossing
such a bourgeois-liberal position with the striations of gender,
Atwood eloquently shows up the abuses of which it is capable.
     Structurally, the novel splits each section between the present and
the remembering of the past. The memory of the past is represented
as part of the present, for in a sense the past is our future. The memory
foci are on two main characters in a group, Stephen who is the
narrator's brother, and Cordelia her early friend and tormentor.
Explicitly, the present recounts Elaine Risley on a visit to Toronto to
open a showing of her paintings: a retrospective exhibition with all the
implied connections of 'retrospective' both with finality and with a
kind of autobiography. But also, painting as a medium is one
communally sanctioned way for the individual to make contact with
others. On one hand the pictures re-present personal memory for a
public place, and on the other hand the pictures allow the public to
commodify the artist, agree about fame. As Elaine notes she has "real
life" and her career (15). When the personal memory is re-presented
in a way perceived to be wholly appropriate for a society the

commodification is total; there is no negotiation or contest in a grand historical context made possible by the fantasy of nation state ideology.

From the early memory of making friends with girls at school, where they all cut out pictures from the Eaton's catalogue, paste them in a scrapbook and say, "'Oh, yours is so good. Mine's no good. Mine's awful'" (53), the construction of gender as a trap is set. As a child Elaine thinks it easy to enter the world of girls where most of life is to do with presenting yourself as a consumer of material objects and saying you've done it badly. This kind of insistent internalizing of an oppressed position is something the girls do to each other. Atwood documents in a precise and clinical manner the victimization by fear and abuse that leads to self-abuse, self-hatred and psychological disruption. There is nothing world-shakingly excessive about their behaviour, but there is instead the sense of inevitability and isolation that unchecked bullying and teasing constructs and depends upon. From thinking that it is easy to be part of the world of girls, Elaine turns back to her brother Stephen and to boys as her "secret allies" (163), but she only achieves a separation from the bullying girls, particularly Cordelia, after they leave her to die in an icy river and she is saved by a vision of the Virgin Mary.

This event is the focal memory of the story. It is the memory she immediately forgets in order to break the circle of victimization; it is the figure of memory that keeps battering its way into the periphery of her consciousness, whose absence leaves her sometimes with a response she can't "quite make sense of" (248). It is the event that teaches her that she is "nothing" (199), a feeling that is part of herself and that surfaces even more unpredictably than memory throughout the rest of her life and is there as an emphatic response to her present 'retrospective' at the start of the novel (41). At the same time that the event leaves her the feeling as if she were nothing, it gives her the strength to leave Cordelia and the other girls but only at a price: that of becoming a victimizer rather than victim. She learns how to enjoy verbal savaging of her enemies; she joins Cordelia, about whose own abuse the reader now gets a glimpse (248-52), in rewriting the memory of a friend as heavy, charmless and ridiculous (230-1). Although to the reader Elaine never becomes as cruel as Cordelia, she continues to hear the voice of hatred in her head for many many years; it even lures her to a suicide attempt when other people later in her life make her feel as "nothing." Only at the very end of the story does she invert the structure and momentarily become her own saviour, taking on the position of the Virgin Mary in her childhood vision and "releasing" Cordelia from her head.

At the same time as all this forgetting and this "missing" time that is a disease of the memory (201), her dreams and then her pictures carry Elaine's memory on. Memories of the dreams of her young days begin to surface just at the point that the girls begin their intensive abuse before they leave her to die in the river. It is as if the memory of the whole experience of abuse backs up into dream until it can find other mediation. Chronologically the memories of dreams stop when Elaine starts to paint, indeed the memories of dreams become increasingly more painterly, transforming the written figurations into visual images. But structurally in the novel the descriptions of paintings are interleaved by the present-time story into the memories of past time. In the middle of the sequence about bullying and abuse, Elaine wonders what her mother knew about it. Immediately following is a description of the painting "Pressure Cooker" which depicts her mother dissolving from suburban housewife to backwoods cook, by way of magazine sketches of women's fashion and then white textured spaces (150). Elaine dismisses the critical responses to her painting, saying that it is simply a picture of two places in which her mother cooks. Yet of course once in the public, the mediation releases other social and historical contexts.

When Elaine is changing places with Cordelia in terms of the power in their relationship, the present-time Elaine tells us of a picture of Cordelia she painted called "Half a Face," as if she herself might be the other half. When she begins to study art, she starts by painting out of the Eaton's Catalogue and paints through to "things that aren't there" (337), saying:

I know that these things must be memories, but they do not have the quality of memories. They are not hazy around the edges, but sharp and clear. They arrive detached from any context; they are simply there, in isolation... (337)

Quite explicitly she turns from the dream of deadly nightshade that has contained the threats of poisoning from Cordelia (145), to painting "a glass jar, with a bouquet of nightshade rising out of it like smoke" (337). In moments of self-disgust she paints Mrs Smeath, the mother of one of her early tormentors and encourager of the abuse, as the incarnation of Eaton's Catalogue womanhood. Yet Elaine is incapable at the time of understanding why she hates this woman (352).

The penultimate section of the novel takes the reader firmly into the present and Elaine's visit to the opening of her retrospective. Here she describes the paintings, in some cases redescribes them in the light of having recovered her memory about the near-death in the river—for example, she now understands her hatred of Mrs Smeath as vengeance. In the process, the paintings lay out a chronology of her life: there is Mrs Smeath, her mother and father, the people from other cultures with whom she has identified, her brother, herself, and the Virgin of Lost Things who presides over space and time. Seeing them all there Elaine realizes she can no longer control the meanings they release: "whatever energy they have came out of me. I'm what's left over" (409). They are not extensions of herself but products. They are also past.

While the narrator, Elaine, shuttles back and forth between memory and present-time, providing a series of contexts for the paintings so that they become the "transparencies," the figurations through which we look at her life, she also shuttles back and forth between men and women. As a child she is devoted to her one friend, her brother Stephen, who becomes Cordelia's alternative, until overwritten by other men such as her lovers and then her husband. Although she has her mother, this figure is displaced by the dominant image of a woman constructed from Mrs Smeath/Cordelia: the female split into smug conventional catalogue woman, with "defeated eyes ... heavy with unloved duty" (405), and the psychotic resister/colluder, figuration of every western disorder of middle class womanhood from food abuser to self-destroyer.

Atwood is an acute, and sometimes savage, observer. This novel also documents Elaine Risley's anxious and fearful relationships with other women in the context of the recent history of feminism, as well as the subtle, pervasive brutality to woman that reduces them not only to hating themselves but also to hating each other because they become icons of what is not wanted or valued in the society. Elaine's tormentor is a woman, yet this woman Cordelia is from a family that has colluded in permitting her father to abuse her psychologically—the whole family structure aids and abets the self-hatred that emerges. Elaine herself, in entering into an unequal sexual contest over the male art teacher, colludes in the abuse by attempted abortion on the abortion on the part of her rival. And so on.

Just as in her painting "Falling Women," where "There were women—but it was about men" (268), the novel is implicitly about the way men turn women into objects of hate simply by remaining still—but it is no use "blaming the rocks" if you get cut. In the iconography of the novel, "Falling Women" is a transparency overlaid on Elaine's near-death in the ravine river, on the recurrent motif of male rapists lurking in ravines (241, 344) and more appalling, overlaid on the imagery of the rocks as a graveyard of ghosts: men become the ghosts of women's present as well as their graveyard. It is not surprising then, that the Virgin Mary to whom Elaine turns in rebellion against Mrs Smeath's male "God," is the one who saves her. This is not to say that men need overtly turn women into objects, but that their silence is collusive.

Acting differently or constructing personal memory in the face of massive ideological coherence, no matter how desperate, is extremely difficult. Atwood portrays Elaine going to a feminist meeting and feeling nervous "awkward and uncertain ... Sisterhood is a difficult concept for me, I tell myself, because I never had a sister. Brotherhood is not" (345), which could be a slogan for part of the feminist movement. Nevertheless she finds through these meetings a vocabulary of resistance that allows her to leave her first husband. It is made clear later on that he is not hated, but simply obstructive. The older Elaine still sexually desires him, yet is not confused by romance.

Because the support she gets from feminism is necessarily overt and different from conventional behaviour, Elaine can be overtly critical of its ideology, particularly of the pressure she feels to hate men and deny her heterosexual desire, when she at several points has talked about her visual and sexual hunger for their bodies. What she resists is the structure of any ideology, a structure that defines your thought for you, although repeatedly Atwood shows Elaine benefitting from the pragmatic solidarity of sisterhood: It is her woman friends in Toronto who include her in an exhibition that legitimates her pictures which her husband thinks are "irrelevant." It is through support from a group of women in Vancouver that she climbs back from post-suicidal depression. Left to herself she is quite capable of saying that "Young women need unfairness [to men], it's one of their few defences" against being "in thrall, in harness" (365).

What Atwood presents in Elaine is a woman who cannot trust women—not only women who can vocalize their concerns, worries, pains, but also those others "hopelessly heterosexual, a mother, quisling and secret wimp" (379) who all "avoid each other's deeper wounds." Cordelia has taught Elaine not only to hate herself, something that her dream/ painting/ memory has to some extent rescued, but also to hate other women. The narrative is quite clear that the structure of middle-class, white, English Canadian society has made Cordelia do both these things too, and that while responsibility for that society is both men's and women's the men have had the open power to do something about it—but they remain silent and still. Or like Elaine's brother Stephen, they turn to science, that other outlet for dream, more legitimate for men than painting "pictures" because its impingement on the real world seems to give it power, and of course it is used to manufacture and control power by the state construction of science funding.

In the final section of the story Elaine watches two elderly women gossiping and fooling around on the plane back to Vancouver. Seeing them she says that what she will miss, what Cordelia's actions and disappearance have destroyed, is such friendship with another woman which becomes possible only when they are older and beyond fitting in to someone else's world. The retrospective exhibition provided in its pictures a series of memories. This story is only about a few of them, for each picture could become another set of memories; and in a sense, since all the chapters but two are titled with the picture titles, they do. Yet there are no pictures, and no memories, of Elaine with another woman other than Cordelia. Neither is there a picture titled as the last section is "Bridge," again iconographically important to this novel yet ambivalent. The perception of the need for female friendship, a version of self-trust, may be a bridge that she can now cross; it may be the bridge that disintegrates beneath her dreaming feet and leaves her falling, skirts belled out, onto the rocks below. But it is significant that this story gives no dream or memory for it as a picture. This may be Elaine's "real life."

Whereas with both Ondaatje and Munro, there is a sense of trust in language and genre, Atwood's continual foregrounding commentaries on genre whether satirical, parodic or ironic, indicate a double awareness that reverses the movement of fantasy rhetoric: she wants to define the grounds for action, but also to indicate constantly their limitations and extensions. Atwood is a grand structuralist, who understands precisely how structures order reality, convey significance and self-validate, and that they are made by people. In *Cat's Eye* she uses realism as another system of ideological representation with particularly strong claims on 'truth' that are rarely examined. She offers the process of dream, memory and the visual allegories of Elaine's pictures to indicate not the falsity of realism, but its inadequacy: a procedure that Atwood's own poetry engages with much of the time. It is as if dream is the way we cope with bodily experience we cannot articulate because the body is not here presented as part of the public or communal structure. Memory becomes the way we recall the experience into a structured form, and writing or painting or science become the media for re-presenting that structured form and making communal the personal. Certainly, it is the story-maker or story-teller in all of these works who makes communication for the individual possible.

What is interesting about *The Handmaid's Tale* and *In the Skin of a Lion* is that the historical framework they provide for their individuals has no effective way for the self to participate in the public arena, and this may be a dominant reason for Munro's erasure of the public. The ineffectiveness is underlined by the position of women in these stories, but is analogous for all people. The nation-state structure builds in a masculine fantasy for women that deprives them of alternative ways of being. Marxism recognizes the oppression as a reduplication of class oppression but cannot deal with it, neither can Romanticism or heroic anarchy, and all relegate the women of Ondaatje's text to the inheritance of free art and elusive mystery. Atwood's *Cat's Eye* slyly presents the male, particularly the brother Stephen, as the mysterious and elusive. But the mystery is profoundly complicated by the implication not only that the mysterious is something you have forgotten yet which your body remembers, but also that while the mystery of an other self may be sustained by their personal fantasy, their isolated common grounds, those common grounds may eventually intrude on your reality—the father's fantasy of environmental destruction, becomes Elaine's reality. What this underlines is the determinant materialism of our lives and the difficulty of recognizing the appropriate personal and public action relevant to it.

What the complication of Atwood's writing also underlines is the problem of reduplicated power structures from the oppressor to the oppressed. In the overt ideology of feminism and the covert ideology of the historical nation-state largely defined by and for men, Atwood poses the question of how colonized peoples can resist legitimating themselves by way of the same authoritative strategies that they have experienced under colonizing powers. The story of *Cat's Eye* is in many ways a study of the necessity for that legitimation for the individual, and the individual's difficulty in achieving it, at the same time as it warns that groups of individuals often behave differently, responding not to the needs of the material but to easier expediency. The writer knows that the former action is often despairingly difficult; she has no illusions about that. But she suggests that if individuals can attend to the material so must the group. The logical implication is that national history can be written differently only if it adopts a story-telling procedure that takes its audience as something outwith its own reality, leaves the enclosed grounds of self-reflexive and self-validating fantasy, and deals with communicating national memory to a larger public. If national memory no longer assumes that its audience operates on the same grounds, then the stable representations that underwrite the fixity of ideology necessary for state control will be loosened. It is an interesting idea because it addresses the problems raised by postmodernist pluralism directly: it asks for self-definition rather than continually sliding surfaces, but it also insists on a negotiation between national memory and the larger political histories that are being written in the contemporary world.

*

Multinational ideology, national culture and personal memory
These writers persistently question the ideological by foregrounding its sanctioned artefacts through the generic devices that it conventionally uses as literary aide-memoires. Atwood works with an array of generic modes and kinds including satire, parody, irony, burlesque, dys/utopia; Ondaatje focuses on quest structures, detective stories, the cliches of romantic heroism; and Munro teases apart the tissues and sinews of realism. In different texts these writers behave as outsiders perceiving difference and asking of culture and ideology 'how do I get in?' or 'do I want to get in?', and as insiders pressing at the structures of their lives and locating the parts where it breaks down.

The generic devices are used for indicating both the artificiality not only of ideology, the ethos of the nation state, but also of personal identity. For the private individual in a nation state, retaining stable versions of history requires the double process of forgetting and remembering. The individual knows that the grounds are constructed but then has to remember to forget that structuring. While a primary narrative prompt for public memory in the post-renaissance western world has been nationalism, both mediated by and obscuring various economic realities of class conflict and the capitalism/socialism lock, a primary narrative prompt for personal memory has been family structure in all the various emphases that have culminated in twentieth-century psychoanalysis. The texts by the three writers discussed here all question these 'aides memoires': they tell how these narrative prompts become ideological common grounds that by asking us to remember in one particular way, encourage us to forget in another. And they remind us that nationalism need not be tied to the state, nor the family to patriarchy.

It is significant that the writers are *able* to perceive the genres as signs of artificial culture rather than as ideological *a priori*. Canadian society, in common with a growing number of other societies, is culturally mixed. The state policy has been to encourage a wide cultural diversity and difference which builds an environment in which writers, whether born in Canada or not, are surrounded by different cultural and social standards and could be expected to ask questions about the value of the dominant culture. What the reader can find are particularly noticeable effects of the way culture works in a nation state. Those parts of the ideology that the nation state does not depend upon forgetting emerge as 'culture': Precisely at the moment of shift they are highly volatile since they are still partially within the obscured and naturalized ideological structure, and awareness of their construction can act as a destabilizing factor on the rest of ideology. But also, when aspects of ideology are *perceived* as constructed and brought into culture, it is a sign that the ideology is losing stability and power.

Culture may surface from ideology but it may also be wrested from ideology in a conscious attempt to dismantle the stability of the nation state or the power that structures the private lives of individuals. Nations will remain, with their cultures, but the power of the nation state, which depends on the obscuring of artificial representations necessary to maintain its grounds, will be lessened. At the end of the twentieth century, when in effect ideological stability is found more and more only in multi-national, global power structures constructed by contemporary economics, national ideologies are more and more apparent as 'cultures,' as artificial modes of representing grounds upon which we form our current agreements about society.[13] Indeed nationalism today, with the severance of nation from state structures of power controlled by economic forces may now be a way of legitimat- ing multinational ideology by obscuring its activities. But national culture may also move toward a destabilizing and foregrounding of multinational ideology, just as mixed ethnic and racial cultures have questioned the nation state.

For these writers foregrounding culture as artificial public memory is not only a way of insisting on personal memory but also a way of dealing with national power, indicating its limits, insisting on its contingent legitimacy. But to replace national power with personal identity can begin to reduplicate the fixities and concealments of the ethos of the nation state, and it is particularly easy to fall into reduplication if the writer is criticizing specific ideological artefacts or representations that are merely objects of cultural consumption. This is one reason why Munro's writing is so robust. It works within the framework of a naturalized ideology which offers no analysis of how things change publically, at the same time as it is totally concerned with the way individuals need to use memory to locate ambivalence and make appropriate decisions. A central topic for many of her short stories is the fact of changed memory, which is offered in finely structured repeated detail from within the individual's personal experience of familial and sexual relationships. The writer is concerned to indicate *that* individuals remember differently, not *how*, and this allows her to move her characters to new points of stable identity while never allowing the reader to depend upon these as fixed.

Both Michael Ondaatje and Margaret Atwood deal with 'how,' but in different ways. Ondaatje's writing works *as if* ideological narratives exist separately from the personal. You can participate in them but you cannot change them. If you participate in them you commodify yourself, just as other cultural artefacts are commodified: you enter the processes of fame. However, personal memory permits change, even enables change; constructing it allows you to construct a self. The way that individuals remember differently and make ambivalent their identities is here specifically through the body memory of sexuality and dream, released and potentially stabilized by the experience of 'love' which Ondaatje does not analyze. Atwood analyses everything, at the same time showing characters who consciously sit back and avoid analysis. Her writing has become more and more concerned with the way ideological narratives limit and coerce the individual: She proposes instead the personal memory working from dream to articulation and focuses on the individual's constant negotiation for self-definition. The move to ambivalence in *The Handmaid's Tale* is underlined by the textual structure of the 'editing,' whereas in *Cat's Eye* it is more immediately personal with the resistance to coercion and fixed identity foregrounded by Elaine's imminent fame as an artist.

The individual is perceived through the characters of these texts as unable radically to destabilize national ideology—Ondaatje offers this as a failure while Atwood suggests it is addressing the wrong narratives. The answer is to move constantly toward a position of unfixing/ambivalence/moral decision responding to need. However, it should be recalled that with each writer the movement is articulated and made public in the publication of the books. In parallel with Elaine's painting or Alice's dance, there is an offering of the position of unfixity to a broader audience, the reader. It is this gesture that invites a collective assessment of appropriateness. It is not a populist gesture because populism tells you what to do and why; it feeds off ideological certainties. Rather this gesture enacts a position, and is made possible by the use of generic conventions that simultaneously collude in cultural common ground and ask the readers to distance themselves from it and find the points of contradiction and ambivalence.

CHAPTER NINE

Language Strategies

The three writers to whom I now turn are different because they focus on language rather than genre, although in no way exclusively. Robert Kroetsch, Daphne Marlatt and bpNichol are each concerned with a radical destabilizing of the representative media for ideology that encourages notions of a fixed identity and the private individual. At the same time they are also concerned with the construction of closeness that builds communication or communicative groups made up of interacting individuals with different grounds for action.

Devices of genre foreground the commodities of culture, particularly of national culture, only at the point where they lose their power. Indeed challenging the significance of those commodities may contribute to the loss of power. Differently, devices that throw into relief the media of representation, the process of the production of the commodity, make significance out of structure itself and watch the result. Dislocation and relocation of the *production* of ideology is contradictory work. It moves toward the closeness of newly held common ground at precisely the same time as it resists and alienates from the ideological grounds holding people together. The contradiction in the work also results more intimately from way it brings people into a community at the same time that it articulates difference.[1]

Although the closeness focuses on the construction of new common ground while the resistance and alienation focus on the destabilizing of habitual common ground, distinguishing between the two is not easy.[2] Even within the construction of new common ground it is not easy to distinguish between a response to present need and an evasion of it: between the construction of a common ground which has a temporary solidity that can make possible necessary social action, and the building of a new alternative space with a coherence that permits escape from social action and the repetition of habitual patterns. Sometimes the two sets of grounds, for action and for withdrawal, are structurally the same but used differently. More often, the devices used to structure the ground or space *themselves* have certain ideological weight or emphasis that encourages one response rather than the other. For example the genre of utopia has carried different cultural valuations in different historical periods, ranging from intellectual discourse to fantasy to the marvellous.

Another example of the ideological weighting but also affecting the destabilizing of habitual common ground might be the use of neologism which is frequently necessary to articulate concepts or precepts that we want to distinguish from the conventional: the literary critic's shifts between meaning and significance, or subject and topic, are but two instances. However, this careful and painstaking attention to the ideological loading of a word can also become a jargon. Nearly all groups of people have corporately-agreed languages which are both generative and exclusive, generative because habitual language often has to be resisted and changed if it is to be adequate to the articulation of new experience, but becoming exclusive and alienating itself when it is used as a private code either when its articulation is so difficult to understand that it obscures or when it is used purposively to create a private group.[3] The privacy of club culture language, when exacerbated into fantasy by national ideology, is one of the problems for this group of writers which is so centred on linguistic detail and frequently criticized for elite isolationism.

Authoritarian political systems exploiting a national ideology have become highly effective with the sophistication of economic control over technology, particularly the control over information technology and communications[4] (Gifford 1980), which has allowed for extensive manipulation of the media conveying that ideology.[5] As the state nationalisms of Germany in the 1930s or of the USSR in the 1950s or some Latin American countries in the 1960s and 70s can underline, small group megalomania or oligarchy becomes successful when it can turn its desires into populist issues acceded to and implemented by large numbers of people.[6]

There is an extensive literature on such political rhetoric that lies parallel to the literature on strategies for postcolonial domination.[7] Essential to the success of the rhetoric is that the making of power, or the construction of the ideological assumptions, be obscured. The less complete the obscuring, the more violent must be the coercion. [8] The more complete the obscuring, the more the strategy can be seen to start with some conventional common grounds and build them into a systematic structure of seemingly unquestionable ideological representation: Or, the more the strategy can be seen to start with a conventional public memory and build an acceptable group history. There is nothing inherent in state nationalism that should ally it with this structure, but the coincidence with economic controls of capitalism and technological controls of information management allow it to exploit the rhetoric.[9] Those controlling power are precisely those who must be capable of the 'doublethink' process—knowing the ideology is constructed yet simultaneously forgetting.[10] What is interesting is precisely that a group acceptance of a particular public memory or national history constructed in this way allows for the acceptance of a set of 'self-evident' grounds that can provide justification for group action. Justification of individual action is more difficult.

Postmodern strategies for challenging such systematic and mapped control over public memory derive from the coincident emergence of structuralism, poststructuralism and deconstruction, each of which aims to indicate exactly that 'making' or 'construction' that state nationalism needs to obscure.[11] But the economic structure has not changed. The postmodern world is faced either with the crisis of recognizing the 'doublethink' process as a necessary to live within, a problematic that has drawn heavily on the psychoanalytic tradition for psychoses and split 'identity,' or with the politics of 'small communities' where the construction of the grounds for agreement and social action can be handled by individuals (oligarchy without the populism) but only at the expense of ignoring global and multi-national power structures[13] and always with the imminent possibility of consensual agreement eliding into the corporate basis for new state control.[14]

These options within postmodernism have quite different implications for groups within first, second and third-world countries. Postcolonial parallels for writers concerned with the issues of (what used to be called) third-world countries,[15] have gone a long way toward using the issues emerging from 'split identity.' They have provided strategies that continually assess, particularly via personal memory and the public memory of history, the appropriateness of any ground for the present needs of a country or a people.[16] But the second set of issues around 'small community' politics have proved less amenable to shift. This set forms the basis of one of the increasingly frequent uses of the term 'solidarity,' but it does not deal with the problem of 'ghettoization' which denies the simultaneity of different voices.[17] It may be that these political issues are more difficult to shift despite their drawbacks for addressing nation state problems at a time when state control is passing inexorably to multinationals, because state control is still largely in place as the dominant ideology of most first-world countries, like English Canada. Yet unlike the U.S., Canada has always lived with the presence of a more-powerful state: Britain or the United States itself.

Canadian postmodernism, as Canadian postcolonialism, has since the late 1950s been in the position of recognizing that its nation state is always subject to a greater economic power.[18] The English-Canadian literature being discussed here is alienated from itself not in terms of national identity as with the locus of much third-world literature and classic post-colonial theory, but in terms of economic identity which affects not national ideology so much as as its modes of representing itself in for example publishing. There can be little impetus to write 'the great Canadian Novel,' which would give the 'novel' a distinctive Canadian difference, when the genre of the novel itself and the inexorable web of commodification, publication, and distribution in which it is caught, is perceived as the problem. This recognition of the problem as allied with economic identity is an indication of the extent to which Canada sees its national culture in a global rather than national power structure.

Some postcolonial literatures have used postmodern strategies to question and assess self and history, often through the working of memory. Many are now beginning to act upon the appropriate grounds of these assessments, sometimes using them consciously to build different national identities—an essential strategy for negotiating with much of global politics which still functions, at least culturally and diplomatically, through national identities. Postmodern literature, from countries such as the United States, which has little effective history of postcolonialism although much of immigrant exploitation and imperialism, has done much to dismantle historical memory and tear down ideological structures; yet the utopian impulse of the disempowered, even the self-disempowered, still lurks behind the conspiracy theories of the self-alienated powerful:[19] there is no one taking responsibility for any building that will need continual restructuring.

In contrast, this restructuring appears to be the condition of post-modernism in English-speaking Canada, to build continually structures for future and on-going undermining. This can also be seen as a condition of English-Canadian postcolonialism: it functions within the same ideology as the economically colonizing power(s), yet it has no control over that ideology except to foreground its assumptions. There is an apocryphal story about Robert Kroetsch being asked to attend a conference on the 'western' at which most of the participants are from the United States. He goes and gives a talk about cowboy heroes who question themselves in the quest for the impossible, about great good and immense evil and how difficult it is to recognize the two, about moral dilemma and the way men need guns or horses or women—and everyone else at the conference thinks he's being straight....

History and Memory: Desire for significance
Texts by Robert Kroetsch can be read as lying at the centre of the postmodern dilemma for some forms of postcolonial theory. In contrast bpNichol's writing openly works with modernist tools refined to extraordinary precision in the search for ways of building new common ground, ways that will allow many different voices to speak. And Daphne Marlatt's work engages in a rather different project: an attempt to deal with the practical difficulties in the articulation of one of those voices.

bpNichol's *The Martyrology* is a text that can be reconstructed as focusing on precisely the issue of distinguishing between engagement and evasion of present needs. Roughly speaking, Books 1 and 2 create the possibility of a fantasy world, while Books 3 and 4 split it apart in a very modernist way by juxtaposing that world with the ruins of past worlds. Books 5 and 6 look more at the sources, structural and otherwise, for the ways in which we make coherence/coherent worlds, and they increasingly send the reader out, give the reader the gift of an ability to make their own worlds that is the focus for *Gifts: The Martyrology Book[s] 7 &*.

Nichol, who died tragically before time in 1988, is one of the most compelling figures in Canada's recent cultural history. An experimentalist in sound poetry, performance, and group work, in concrete poetry and graphics in many media, he cultivated, tended, and attended to the English language not only in his own work but also in his editing of other people's. And, unusually, he rarely alienates the careful reader. Most critical approaches to what has been called 'language poetry' tend to eschew narrative; yet many of Nichol's commentator's find themselves returning to story.[20] What Nichol moved toward in the writing from the 70s and 80s is a medium for enabling the reader to construct their own coherences.

Book 1 of the *Martyrology* is a curious mixture of melancholy and desire, although it calls itself a 'history.' The reader begins with Gertrude Stein's line "Let me recite what history teaches. History teaches," which recites both the impossibility of exact repetition at the same time as materializing the irony that graphic words provide the illusion of exact repetition. As Nichol points out in Book 2, the repetition/impossibility of repetition is parallel to the problem of the self as identity/entity, again from Stein, and is intrinsically connected with concepts of memory and history. In a generic reading, Book 1 is a quasi-science fiction text, with many of the trappings of mapped place, hierarchies of families, documents from the past, coded names, that underwrite traditional Sf. This generic structure of fixing the "saints" into legend is a self-conscious device to underline the story of their passing away, their fading.

Nichol has spokenly frequently of his discovery of "St. orm" and the sudden flowering of significance form the words' combination of letters.[21] The early *Martyrology* is partly an elaboration upon desire for significance, the way we invest the arbitrary with personal meaning and then try to maintain it. But it is also an elegy for the certainties of language and for the certainty of human control over both its arbitrariness and its potential for meaning that cloudland comes to present. The process of telling the stories of the saints in cloudland is referred to as "dismembering the heart's history" with its private constellation of "too many" saints and heroes. This conscious deconstruction lies in tension with the bitterness and rage of knowing that "nothing remembers // except we write in terms of past moments / instances of unperceived truth / ruthless working of the mind's ignorance / against us." The saints are part of the self, "created / ripped whole from our lived long day" yet there are "no legends that could not be lies." The poet/ muse St. reat exemplifies the danger that people who use words can get into when they believe they can control language. They, like him, can be driven into the illusion of cloudland. As if to counteract the illusion, the writing inserts a parallel (hi)story of friends of the ordinary, people like "dave and barb," all of whose interventions increase in number as Book 1 moves into Book 2.

Absent from these story lines is that of the speaking voice, yet a contemporary reader can recover this. This early text sets up the personal as private individual control, radically separated from the real life of a public community. But, at the time, Nichol was writing in a present voice that could connect the two worlds. As noted in the "Afterword" to *Gifts: The Martyrology Book[s] 7 &,* Nichol always felt that the sequence *Monotones* should have somehow been built into Books 1 and 2, or to have preceded them.[22] From this angle or line the sequence can be read as a voice of 'self,' obsessed with memory and actuality, a voice combining the saints and the ordinary in a series of questions about language, meaning, and self. The absence of that ambiguating voice leaves the worlds of Books 1 and 2 closer to the possibility of enclosure than they might have been and closer to the postmodern dilemma of cynicism, paranoia, and melancholy; the lack of that voice makes it more difficult to enter Nichol's linguistic terrain and all too easy once inside to attempt to pattern it.

Book 2 opens with a series of comments on the inadequacy of the saints' control over significance, the failure of language to be true or sufficient: "there is nothing which is allegory," that dark secret of language's significance which defines the articulation of the real; instead, all is "expliation," at least a step away from articulation. The speaker exhorts "let us forget them [the saints]," yet he recognizes the necessity of the attempt at language and turns to prayer. What he is left with is breath, and the weight of finding breath, telling the breath that is life/living. The relationship between memory and history, and the way that dream is connected with words that can tell life's breath, becomes insistent thoughout the text. St. reat, on migrating to earth and the world of the mind, forgets cloudland within a year. Despite dream and the brush of memory it releases, his mind fills up with "library daze," and history, fixing him down, "history being in me is my story." More explicitly, we find memory allied to the body, and history, on the ground of the rational mind, to forgetting. When it loves history, memory "forgets does not remember."

As Book 2 moves along, history, as well as being the fixity of a public record, accretes a broader sense of language of the history of human beings. The story of "saint rike & the lady of the past" recounts an attempt to remember where "all speech becomes a reaching over distances," and the text begins a commentary on the alliance of speech and poetry with the articulation of memory: "all poetry a function of history / breathing now // referenceless world / i do take refuge in / surrounded by memory." Once written, poetry becomes history but is precisely a "breathing now," the immediacy of this public articulation of a present which is itself referenceless—something that the speaking "i" takes refuge in while constantly surrounded by memory.

The flow from the personal, negotiating memory into the public articulation of history is reversed by St. orm, who through language returns history to the individual in the form of memory. Language internalizes public story into the individual. While memory facilitates articulation of the actual, the language always changes the actual when it articulates it. In contrast dream appears as an illusion of stable articulation. Curiously, dream becomes an articulation of the past as passed, and memory becomes an articulation of the present: "form then is what the present takes / seen as the past moment bursts forth / takes shape amid the air you freeze in / trapped by a history you cannot acknowledge / the poem become the life work." Remembering is here an impossible fixing that lies and deceives, "never remember was it the mahayana's said / true buddhahood lies in turning back / taking what you've found & turning it outward   into the world." Memory is both "entity," defining self in the moment which "establishes flow," and "identity" for "it is so much more soothing to live with memory."

There is by the end of Book 2 a searing contradiction between the recognition of the separation of the individual and public community, and the knowledge that they cannot be separate. It is a contradiction between the insistence that memory puts on present process, on making the present continuous, on an avoidance of illusion and continual shift out of ideology, AND an awareness that memory connects "i" with "we" of history, and also insists on a common public terrain of some kind that lets us construct values for how we act socially. The voice moves, in contradiction and ambivalence, from a brave gesture of "we spend too much time comforting each other" to the tension of arbitrarily clustered individuals silent and alone, "thinking that way i did riding the bus out this evening / people none of whom i knew / we sat beside each other / wrapped in our separate silences." Book 2 concludes with a similar ambivalent moment where "everything is present and tense," for "nothing's free of presence / others pressing in / your friends assert themselves as loving you are tortured with / gradually you learn to enjoy // thus you write history /...."

These last comments come from the concluding pages of Book 2 and are rewritten from the original publication of 1972. So it is slightly less surprising than it might have been that Book 3 opens with a consideration of precisely these points. Book 3 talks about a growing awareness of the need for a community in order to understand language and life: that language is part of breath and the body, but it is also communicating and has to have a context, a communal sense of "we." Where Nichol's contribution to contemporary political philosophy is most profound is in his elaboration of "community." In light of the obscene use by recent hyperliberal commentators of the vocabulary of care and community, built so painstakingly by feminists articulating the value of domestic work during the 1970s and 80s, Nichol's work here is invaluable if contradictory.

Perceiving that the transcendental/universalist traditions of western philosophy that recognize an order or power external to human beings lie at the root of much hatred, racism, and other abuse, several commentators have attempted to focus on the local community. This has been moved away from the 'community' articulated by Gadamer, which can still be heard in much postmodernist discourse, and works by refusing a larger social context. In contrast, the hyperliberal position acknowledges the larger context, but claims that the leisure and culture of the bourgeois liberal permits 'us' to 'evade' the entire concept of 'universal.' It proclaims 'our' ethnocentricity, and supposes that because it so proclaims it is immune from criticism. It operates in a 'club culture'[23] but no one will be prevented from having their own club around the global bazaar.[24]

As a religious believer, Nichol does not deny the external order or power, but neither does he ascribe to it the transcendent or universal. The 'we' of community in Nichol is gradually articulated by Book 5 as 'family.' Again, this family is not structured on explicit psychoanalytical master / grand narratives, nor on the universals of ethnicity, but it arises from the interaction of people in language and from a sense of the determinate body (the Workman hips and other *Selected Organs*), which when articulated can locate human beings as a species.

In Book 3, the tatter-heap of memories of the saints is a geography that "i cannot recall." Instead "i want to write a history of this present moment," which involves moving among other people, "friends // friends // friends // this is how the false 'i' ends" for writing the present means writing "we," "that necessity for a community of feeling the saints never knew / kept wandering places by themselves / the stupid fucking fools." But if this community of feeling is what the speaker wants to

move toward, it is not a simple action to do so. Constantly waylaid by
"visions and oracles" of the saints "we do forget we" and set out again
with the saints over water. But when the charts fail and the certainties
fade, "we cry for you now / not for oracles / for friends / receding
shorelines / carry us into each other's bodies." Section 5 of Book 3 in
which this commentary occurs opens out the discussion about "i" "we"
and "me" as the main pronouns, into a series of observations about
language that are mediated by the metaphorical field of geography /
space and history / time. Of poets with whom connections are being
made, the speaker says "i call these poets friends / tho i cannot attend
to them daily / there is a we / different the same / links us in the law
language comprehends / i have to trust to carry me thru into
somewhere."

This "we" is not the fixed ideological "we" of a history that "lacks
connections," not the "collective place poverty and pressure brings
you to," not the "we which is not we but slabs of meat / stacked up to
feed the mouths of commerce." This "we" is a different history "which
does not end"; "we is a human community / bounded more by space
than time / we push against it as need presses" and language like
geography links "the whole body." But the "i" is not yet there, does not
yet have "a we i have sensed the fringes of / a new voice to speak
with," does not have "a sense of continuity ... family," does not have "a
sense of history / a real sense of time." When "i" remembers it finds
"memories of a we that never worked / existed in a timelessness which
is not memory / only a standing still as years go past." What it needs
instead is to reclaim "the myths that give no history / a geography of
time" for myth is space, a sense of place in dreamtime.

The attempt at community is diverted and distracted not only by
private visions but also by the kind of public that is immediately
apparent in the stable representations of state ideology, the "non / man
who / believes ONLY in his own self interest," so "the idea of privacy
grows as the space shrinks." Both are isolated from each other,
existing alone beside each other and needing that mutual exclusion to
exist. The "current of a we which is history" cannot be found, it can
only be spoken out of. It is a narrative we make with the possibilities
of language but it is not a narrative we can know in advance, for
stories are as radically different as the places and times they are
written out of: like "gilgamesh & beowulf / wrestling for days / enkidu

& grendel / the one ends in friendship / the other in war / it is the difference 2000 years breeds in stories."

Finally, for this reason that people live inside langauge, the saints cannot be forgotten; they are part of the geography of the body, "the land you claimed carries your memory / every bush haunted by what went before / history is with us in viscera & bone / holy places filled with stones & trees / we let the landscape write us" and write the community. Even more explicitly: "a notion sainthood still could be / but for love of something / one or some human gesture / creed / the writing is / as 'we' can come to be." Significance is something that is vital and possible, but cannot be designated, has to come from language's potential being used by and for the community in the needs of a present: "as much as hold together we can call we / moves into future memory." Situating the self with words is about connecting the individual with the social, connecting memory with history.

Memory and History: Need for community
I am aware that in telling a story about memory from Nichol's *Martyrology* in the way that is here occuring, the work of his *language* is disappearing although the quotations carry some of this load. The strategy emerges partly from the demands of a chapter that is focusing on a topic: personal and public memory and its relation to self within until recently colonized nations, and partly because the generic links with science fiction so carefully wrought in Books 1 and 2 are ideologically dominant narrative techniques. If Books 1 and 2 chart the story of cloudland, and of the saints' emigration or "fall" to earth, Book 3 consciously artificializes the device and uses it as a fictional token ambivalently fixing and unfixing memory. That ambivalence or release of the significance begins to seep more and more insistently through the linguistic strategies of Book 3 so that, at the point that the "i" narrator turns to speak "we" and "me," Nichol arrives at the "CODA: Mid-Initial Sequence" in which he situates his play with words, phonemes, morphemes, syllables, graphic wit, his processes of language: the catalogue of devices that provide the ground upon which the reader enters or does not enter the community of language that he offers. Book 4 can then begin here and offer possibilities. But again, he is not playing the game of Hegel's search for innate representative sounds, but loosening up the fabric of articulation and weaving it into a multitude of possibilities from which readers can build significance.

Books 1 and 2 mimic through genre the enclosed structure of fantasy needed to effect private control over language: They play with the arbitrariness of words that permits total control over their significance; and they recount the failure of that control and the confusion it generates. The reverse, the subjection of the individual by the state through the ideological control of representation in language, is something only to be answered by a community of feeling that can learn to make present significance and closeness for a group, to move from identity to entity.[25] Book 3 offers a parallel debate between fixed chronology and time as process, between fixed place and geography as changing space, between the isolated "i" and the "me" involved in "we" of community: each second term requiring an engagement with language that uses its resources to respond to present needs. Book 4 transposes language firmly into the processual structures of memory and history and discovers politics, society and community.

The "grid" of language is "no longer apparent / buried in the history of the race" as the speaker of Book 4 brings together the continuing commentaries on ordinary life with the words on language and the now empty cloudland. Delicately the reader is led out from the daily/mundane into the difficulty of speaking it, writing it down "to re member / re articulate / eyes / mouth / instability of limbs / in the dream time / connectives vanish." The writer "makes a rhetoric of daily speech" to "weave the world / out of the or/binary / the note spun / out of the dinary into the few"; and uses story, consonants as nouns, vowels as verbs, writing following sound, the jogging of memory with syntax and semantics to re-build connectives for dream in "rimes [that] exist beyond the text / contextual / textural," to spell out the changes in the present and reveal the actual that is always veiling and re-veiling itself. The rhetoric makes a plan or a placement, "not in the sense of plot/ pre-conceived / but there / readable / if am able to / see man / writable / purpose'. Indeed, cloudland is precisely referred to as a veiling of the real.

In life where there are always contradictions "literature is no guarantee of a common good," so "you start with what's local." Here Nichol tries to locate the voice in "a tangled dreaming / an immigrant nation of / uncertain history." What is immediate is "no sense at all really / simply this canadian foot / following a tentative line" that's social and political. But having just rejected the ever-shifting streets of a dislocated cloudland of isolated language, the multiplicity of saints' voices and the continual arbitrariness of their control, he warns that purpose or location itself "can become conceit," the political can become no longer significant but expedient, ambivalence be no longer revealing but veiling, needing legal experts to interpret it. What the speaker specifically says is "purpose can become conceit, shift beneath the feet, the line of speech that's called political, the signified slides below the signifier, gets lost in what's // expedient." This concern with surfaces and sliding signifiers becomes one of the focuses for Book 5 as Nichol deals with the postmodern dilemma of ensuring that the local becomes neither isolated nor overwhelmed by the structures of ideology. To face this problem Nichol tackles head-on the medium of writing and then its relation to memory and history.

If this appears a too-familiar rehearsal of the philosophical discussions of the 1980s about simulacra, graphics, postmodernism and deconstruction, we should remember that Nichol is tackling these issues in the 70s and continually stepping back from the discourse of rationalism that these discussions usually fall into for want of appropriate articulation. The rhetoric/poetic he develops in its place uses particular devices of language that foreground our expectations of graphic communication. However, unlike the generic which has become so culturally specific, so commodified that bookshops and libraries often organize their shelves by genre, linguistic device has not yet become so self-consciously recognized. It may be *because* the written genre needs the organization of capitalism to disseminate, that it becomes so easily commodified. And it may be that because the devices of written language developed by Nichol are so detailed, so frequently associated with the oral, and so often dependent on shifting the alphabet from a phonetic to a pictorial or even syllabic writing system, that they are particularly resistant to commodification in the present ideological structures of education and publishing in the western capitalist world.

What Nichol's devices achieve is certainly an unsettling of how that ideology is mediated. The recent discussions of postmodernist representations of ideology have got stuck on way that representations cannot be fixed.[26] Nichol, in common with many other writers/artists, knows this as a condition of communication (Books 1, 2 and 3) and is more concerned with how that ambivalence of communication works (Books 4 onward), and how it can work to help us articulate self. In his writing we suddenly find a representative given or device where we had never expected it, in for example the reversal of 'b' to 'd' or in pun, palindrome, anagram, and so on.[27] Or, for example, the large structure of Book 5 is a series of numbered chains to which the writer alerts the reader at several points in the text by way of small superscripted numbers. Nichol notes to the reader[28] that "you can continue thru the chain of ideas you're already following, or you can choose, at different points, to diverge." This shift of the narrative convention develops into the 6 Books of *Book 6* and the 'loose leaf' format of *Gifts*, that question the structure of the book as a predictable and commercial object. Readers' responses to these devices are often nervous and anxious as if we are not sure whether this is futile playing of games with an innate language and structure, or fundamentally questioning and releasing response: the anxiety is an indication of the challenge that such writing offers us.

One of the primary problems for postmodernism is how to deal with significance if there is no fixed source or origin. The reason that the problem arises in the first place is due to the way that the ideology of the nation state behaves as if there were a fixed source, a set of *a priori* assumptions that are self-evident and the case. Hence, when words are suddenly released from fixed signifieds this is perceived as a loss or a problem and understood as superficiality or simulalcra. Chain 2 of Book 5 speaks of those writers who "can still talk it whole // emotion ideation a unity" yet "there is a hole there / behind the w / the emptiness shows thru / these configurations spellings / evoke the feelings we cannot pretend are strangers." For this writer 'feelings' or 'aesthetics' or 'the body,' is the field of the given in a sense elaborated upon in *Gifts...*, and different from 'the case.' Language can for the self be either a "conjunction tween a past world & the next" or "anti-past / a-historical / i tied to my own life of / fictions." Self can be significance coming through the words or a fixed fiction of created significance, but the writing starts always with the "I remember when..." of memory.

Chain 3 of Book 5 observes the way that narrative is conventionally created in european languages simply by reading left to right. The letters, words and life are "a sign / beneath which signifieds slide" evoking contradictions. Even his name is "adrift between the signifier & the signified / sliding thru the years / myself as definition changing," a constellation of contradictions held only by the present's moment. So where does significance come to rest even if only temporarily? The discussions of Book 5 study the way that writing finds/constructs significance by interaction with the body, which interaction starts in dream. But rather than leaving dream's work unarticulated, Nichol analyses as closely as he can its work through memory into writing, "the signs /   hazardous connections to their signifieds / are severed / re-connected by the dream's logic" [Ch. 1]. And these arbitrary signs accumulated from lived events need memory to be articulated or absorbed. Dream residues arise and are structured "out of that regioned memory we know third hand / reflected back in waking / structures of the everyday" [Ch. 3]; we do not understand how memory strategies work but they seem to provide sudden frames of reference to return feeling to the body. The process of memory is almost to contextualise dream and in doing so both contain and constrain the sharpness of the past. Memory not only restructures "worlds of dreams & felt feelings" [Ch. 1] into a "world of whispered presences" that receive validation from present needs—like the sudden remembering that a friend is dead—but also archeo-orders the feelings "to the past again," constructs the necessary forgettings.

Writing becomes a "gesture // memory trace," that is a trace of choices not taken. When we re-read we can either attempt to make sense of and repeat earlier rimes, or we can let the words speak again through themselves by breaking up the graphic representations and letting in air, literally breathing air into the language [Ch. 4]. The former is like repeating the cliché from an image bank where the poem is "recycled / enters the world of print and passes from us / megalithic structures we call poems" [Ch. 3]. It is defined largely by the "sway print holds over you" [Ch. 5], insisting on a fixed spelling and punctuation that lets the pen contain the "felt words of feeling," penning it in, into ideology whose "referential glare" is beauty. The glare needs to be stripped away, to be dispersed [Ch. 5], ridden of "conceits of knowing" that breed ignorance.

Running as a thin but clear note under the comments on these different writings and readings is a concern with the complicated working of the ordinary and the local that is intimately tied to "ignorance." There is the ignorance of those caught in the ruins of North America and distrusting all its systems, ignoring the ordinary. To ignore is to distort "what is obvious"; it leads to "monumentalization / whatever the political belief / the ordinary man or woman is forgotten / because they are not known / sentimentalized or swept aside / no one takes the time to talk to them" [Ch. 8] and the local is overwhelmed and dismissed. But there is also the ignorance of the ordinary. In Chain 1, Nichol speaks of two communities: the one of daily life where we participate in a superficial selving responding to history's demands often precisely because of the "full weight of civic sprawl," "we dull our senses/overcome by the immensity of it all"; and the other community of writers/selves writing not the history of "white man's record" where "we name as fits our purpose / shape language to our own ends / all the lies, dishonour, death & treason such a use portends," but "a writing of a listening," writing "as i hear," "the race trace of memory," a "conversation."

Chain 6 returns to a drama of cloudland, which is again "dismembering the heart's history." But Books 1 and 2 dismembered as a melancholic record of the failure of control over language that permits isolation of the private and the local; the dis-membering that happens in Book 5 is a taking away of the cultural presuppositions, the referential glare, and it leaves the character/ letters dispersed to be taken up into different conversations and dialogues. Dialogue becomes the necessity: "you start with that person in front of you / dialogue / acknowledgement of being / the 'real' you get into poetry is/the 'real' of speech / the fact you try to reach / pleasure some other body from your own." Poetry "describes more perfectly than any other / that heightened sensibility talk should be / an act of family." It is family, "a weight thru history," that starts the dialogue, gathering together to give stories, to trust to the lines. The "real" speech also reaffirms "relationships between the self & others": "realating of realationship's shape / between the letter & the letter / word & worlds of / friends & where the words begin and end / feelings ..." [Ch.7]. This dialogue holds the constructions of self in memory; its language enacts reality "always closing down / opening again / somewhere else," not a fixed place or time but made communally.

Chain 3 offers an example of this in its recounting of Donna's death. The casual shock of the sudden unexpected phrase "my sister Donna died / six weeks old / as i almost died / six months old" immediately raises the potential in memory for narcissism: that history can be common to all but memory is developed by each individual so that this kind of memory becomes the private reconstruction of history for a particular person who uses memory to heroize the self. But the following several leaves lead the speaker and reader through memory,

memories of places, family life, more places he has lived in, places of
the dead, to other words and memories of Donna—finding "only her
shoes," and echoes of her name in his sister and brother Deanna and
Don: "Donna echoed twice / her death / sounds in our family's daily
speech." Again taking us through memories released by the reserves
of language, including the three poems to her "caught up in the sob
informs my breath line / lin / li / l & i remain / one and one,' into
language itself, its grammar, poetics, fiction, "new / clear fissions" that
achieve "momentarily reality." The memories of the unknown Donna
have become the speaker's self; he says "sometimes i wonder if
Donna's speaking thru me" and says this is why he tried to relearn
language through play, to find "my 'own' path" and now "i only know
i try to follow thru / truths an attention to language yields." Donna's
death, the congruence of this with his own near death, is something
more difficult to deal with than the first casual mention indicated.
Searching the words of his memories for her, he searches for himself,
breaking open conventions of language and fiction to find the basis of
"family daze," but having done that, having structured a self by taking
us through his actions and movement in language, he moves on.

Memory/History: Remaining attentive to present need
The flux of words around "family" comes to dominate the structure of
The Martryology Book 6 Books. The 6 Books of *Book 6* shift from
thoroughly modulated essays about history, memory, writing and the
self, to tense and fragile excursions into family, memory, body and
language and the closeness needed for work on new common grounds
that will enable social action that responds to the needs of the present.
Book 1 is a formal presentation of the difficulties that arise because
we can never know the truth about the past. How can we derive
significance from anywhere if there is not that certainty? The essay
suggests a mythical truth for the ideological relationship between
Europe, specifically Britain, and Canada. In a sense the myth/leg-
end/rumour/truth of the giant Buamundus is a common ground for
looking at precisely what Canadians think their history is, given the
rapid succession of immigrant histories that have colonized its
Aboriginal peoples and its geography. And Nichol offers a variety of
possible images including those of Captain America, the capitalist
hero, and Frankenstein, the stalking monster of imperialist colonialism. What is more interesting is the way the writing provides a series
of takes on how language is used to deal with that variety. There are

the details and flashbacks on events, theories mapping possible resolutions, biographical notes with claim to some generic authority of authenticity; there is the unknown, mediated by poetry; there are scenarios and more scenarios, additions to deal with facts, science and history which attempt to predict "the end," myths and legends: All components of a possible reality that permit words to work from the moment and amidst uncertainty.

Almost as if having presented this as the case, Book 2 looks in detail at the grouping of history, memory, writing and self that Nichol has been refining over the 20 years of the earlier parts of *The Martyrology*. The "Hours" of Book 2 introduce all the psychiatric states of postmodernism: cynicism, paranoia, "the old narcissus bit" and sets them against "i *feel* that": feeling that wanders through the "wordrobe" of memory to find where the self/ves are for the moment. A poem becomes a history of a writing at the same time as a re-membering of a life, not with "loss" but with contradiction and crisis at its centre focused by memory into a "lands' cape we / disembark on." Hour 5 has an image that will expand, one which pulls people by the linear track of a train through the space and time of memory. In an elaboration of "racial memory" which is fundamentally linguistic although often confused in people's minds with heaven and reincarnation, the poet takes us elsewhere with three-line variations on clichés. The examples "people need space to grow in," "lonely without you," "they want to be buried together," "that's the situation in a nutshell" and more, take the conventional and release it into the associative with syntactical, morphemic, lexical and semantic structures: "loose a fir / gain a pine," "sitting in the station / stationary in the sitting room / that's the situation / the sitcom ...."

If this is how memory is *felt* to work, Hours 6 and 7 yield a study of how the body's dreams necessitate memory. Dream pushes the sleeper out into "the waking world" where the elements of dream images rustle on the line of "the living & the dreaming," brought into "the memory & the memoried," into "awake & breathing," Heightened by fever in this account, the dreamtime is on a borderline between animal and body, as if dream and memory are how the body gathers together, how the body orders. Our consciousness of this is momentary only, as in Hour 7, a flicker of self, an "impossible memory trace" of the choice the body makes in the hour before we dream. But then how do we connect the memory trace with writing's trace of memory, "trying to connect it all / impossible brief perspective of the present" (Hour 10). History is a possibility, but it hovers ambivalently on the borderline between obscuring systems of ideology and potentials for social memory.

The only way to ensure a social memory is "opening the present," entering the "we" of community, which the poet does by opening the sound, rhyme and rhythm of language and which his daily life does with the pregnancy of Ellie and hope of birth, followed swiftly by the grief on the death of their stillborn baby in Hour 12 which drives him back into isolation. The vibrant opening of language in the hours before 12 bring together life and language in the "choices // the myriad voices of the worlds / the selves / shifting as the letters shift"; and the death reminds the poet, through the slow dissolve of memory, how there is no possession of either life or language. Life is "not so much as belief but/ as continuity," "not so much a continuity but a passage" between the two unknowns of birth and death. The negation death brings seems to deprive the writer of the desire to continue to find the moment's history, the real, and the poetry becomes overwhelmed in Hour 16 by "the great void of human history," or history as ideology. The intimate patterning of language and life begins to work once more when daughter Sarah is born, the sequence finishing with Hour 19 and the "heartbeat" for and of Ellie, "1 & i."

The connection between the body memory of self and the social memory is vital, and finds its most persuasive ground in Nichol's writing about the implications of birth and death and the structures of family that then come about. Hours 20 to 22 elaborate on the family story, the bio/geography of self and country, through grandma/grammar. If "i-i-i-i" is a picket-fence line of the individual self through history, then the process of re-membering the "flicker" of grandma constructs a "we," a social connection of geologos/local. At the same time, the vast unknown of death seems to leave the writer's punning as "a door in / the floor i / fall thru / surface after surface" without stop. The falling via pun is an actuality of death, for pun as the text elaborates a little later, usually leads the writer to some ground upon which can be built a different significance, yet here there is no appropriate ground except the act of poetry itself which is the only connection between self and the social. In the concluding Hour 28 we are reminded that so many words are about monumental history, about inhumanity, about conscience, but so few words about what significance there is in being human and how to construct that significance: the real region of religion (Book 1 of Book 6).

"Continental Trance," inserted here as Book 3 of *Book 6 Books,* is a more distanced and less risk-taking text than "Hours" and more conventional in its language, but one of its movements is toward shifting the con/sequences of linear narrative. The poem goes back over the geographical ground of the past commenting on writing, memory and history, and pointing to the body, the self and the community. The train journey initiates a "linear narrative of random sequential   / accidents of geography, history & circumstance / the given." Instead of a plotted story, the story forms from the coincidences of the journey, the givens of life. Or as is later said "given, of course, the conscious choice of voice / the train of that you choose." Once on the journey the trick is to recognise not symbol or simile but "the moment when the feelings focus"; the thrill of nearing significance (and control over words) and "the rimes that disappear as you draw closer to their sense," a revelation vanishing with the sickness of consciousness eluding one, the flicker of self not quite articulate and the sign of inappropriate control. In the end the poem is not an identifiable "i," not a biography but "geography's the clue / locale & history of the clear *you,*" "a community of speakers / history of a race."

In sharp contrast to the temporal linearity of a journey, Book 4 "In Choate Road" examines from the stationary the pun as a memory process of language. Words lead and are led into memory: for example, II 2 (see text opposite). Here playing with a number of words over the 8 parts of section II, the writer says he's "looking for the place where the puns flesh out / the body of speech is re-vealed, the veil / drops away" into dance, where the grammar hammers the breath. There is constant punning on the word "memory" itself, as if to break the letters apart lets him through the superficial into the water, with a need to know the depth: "i am engulfed, flooded with / même mer, e' says, or / the same more e' / experienced be- / fore." Water ensures that he can never make the "local" his own; he's always aware of its flux and the impossibility of possessing it, all the more needful of working out appropriate ways for building significance.

beginning with lead & wood	in which the 'lead & wood'
mark the course of this writ- **ing's later**	of the child's pencil begin
ink as the words begin to flow	to write the course of later words in 'ink' which
late rink lights coming on	generates 'rink'. The
shouts of the kids on the frozen **water &**	'course' begins to 'flow',
later th'aw	but is captured first in the
flooding spring	memory of 'frozen water'
hot streatches of summer	only later 'flooding' into hot
falls	summer that falls: All
ice/water	movement ordered by 'th'aw'
ice/water	that springs the water from
ice	the ice.

When he steps out upon the surface (III 8) he finds himself "heirs to the veaucabulairies" that "enact tradition / monstrously / familiair / familheir / tri bull / labyrinthinemine / a tour of / gnossos / logos / osos." Yet "minos most of our memory / we function out of loss." To function in the moment of contradiction, we need memory and we need to be able to release it from convention: can't write "unless i've got a pun."

Nichol is concerned with syntax, lexis, and the morphemic and phonemic, particularly because we are so conventionally possessive about them; in terms of recent studies in significance they are the least analyzed and the most conventional; they are what we most often take for granted as innate. Similarly, if pun is both a memory and a history of language so blood is a memory and history of the body. When the writer returns in Book 5 to the "Plunkett Hotel" where his grandparents worked, he says both "blood is the line you write thru history" and "i is trying to come home / i piles i's bags on the bedside table / i lives there." But a building with no people is a word with no context, a person with no community: just a frame. There is "only the memory of conversations" held with his grandma which are not much now "to feed a story." Instead, the idea of family extends, "the me runs everywhere / like a theme / moving reservoirs of cells & genes / [...] we trace our dreamtime in blood / [...] tribal, restless, constant only in the moving on / over the continents / thru what we call our history / tho it is more mystery than fact, / more verb than noun, / more image, finally, than story." What the stay in the Plunkett Hotel does is remind us that "i's in motion / crossing the flickering division lines of history / [...] moved by love." Any self there is comes from memory responding to the immediate through language which involves it into the social, the larger family of human beings as a species.

The penultimate section "The Grace of the Moment" moves toward words for an even more difficult articulation than for memory, that of "now," the present moment in which social memory works to articulate together the personal and the public/political. The poetry speaks of the way that the present pulls, carries the past into the unmapped futures; of the problem of an immediate flashing back on the moment because we cannot observe it the first time; the immense fragility of this thing called life that we try to apprehend, carried by blood and body, "brief bright ribbon we wrap the present in / this human grace." The writing is reflective, and about the grace of the moment, rather than working in that moment as do the final leaves of "After Bird." To write about what significance there is to life is to seem to be thinking about the past, while actually we are re-membering, Now. Our bodies are re-doing, flowing back over the past in the present. We know it's "now" but not when we do it, only when we recognize its appropriate ability to anticipate future process. When we recognize that in the moment—that's grace. The problem, as Nichol says citing Wittgenstein, Stein and McLuhan in their concerns with language, is to make the connection.

The Martyrology is an autobiography in the sense that Nichol brings together into the various books the places where he searches for an appropriate ground. The premise of the whole story is that what we take for granted is only arbitrary. If we do not question it, it controls us. But as the saints found out control by the individual instead is delusory, leading to melancholia and cynicism as it disintegrates. Control over language, in this sense, can only work within generically specified forms that ask for a conventional pattern of grammar, poetic and rhetoric, and since Nichol is dealing here with graphic, publishable media for language, a substantial set of assumptions that need to be questioned are those surrounding the book as a material object. But then he is left with the difficult assumptions of language itself, which he wants to question so that he can value, re-member the necessary significances from which they came, and assess their appropriateness to his present need. This of course is done with genre by other writers, but Nichol is concerned with the linguistic detail that supports generic representation, and which we more often take to be innate.

The questions are to do with constructing the ground upon which an individual can choose and act, which have to involve how that individual connects to their wider society. If we reject control from dominating structures, and we reject the individual's reduplication of that domination, how do we find significance both as individuals and in a group. Nichol focuses on the work of history as group memory,[29] and self as individual memory, looking first at how language can both criticize and encourage fixed versions of history and self, yet more and more at how language can locate through play the places/grounds where significance emerges from an apparent connection between memory and articulation (writing or speech, more properly graphic or sound), between the body and its momentary need: what Nichol calls a "given." How this works is something that *Book 6 Books* and *Gifts* consider and expand upon in their commentary on identity/entity, family as hierarchy and family as blood process, truth and myth, and the multitude of poetic strategies for play with language.

Gifts: The Martyrology Book(s) 7 &, edited carefully after Nichol's death by Irene Niechoda, opens with "read, dear" which she has placed for understandable reasons at the start of the sequences.[30] "read, dear" could be a summary of the commentaries Nichol made on memory and its working into language and writing. In it he notes "assumptions masking as givens / the way belief sits outside the rational," for the taken for granted can so easily seem like the suddenly given appropriate moment of "grace." The series of "Assumptions" in *Gifts* refer continually to this confusion or elision between the taken for granted assumption and the appropriate or given, and the way that both their elision and their distinction are mediated by memory and articulated in language. The writer in 1986 goes back over a poem written in 1963 wondering "that sentence. / a language of assumptions or / givens [...] / asserting the world was doing *this,* / easy assumption of synecdoche / when what i mean is, *really.*" Assumptions can tie you to nouns, to assertions of state, and pull you away from the processes of language. The writer cannot give a "given"; they give themselves when readers and words and writers find an appropriate significance. But once recognized they form a ground for action. The "Assumptions" are subtitled "A Counting Book," accounting for self necessarily inadequate but at least voiced.

With *Monotones* finally here in *The Martyrology* as early examples of finding ground, and with *Scraptures* and various 'saints' pieces and others, almost a box of attempts or essays into language and meaning, there is the sequence "St. Anzas: basis/bases (*Martyrology* Bk (10)$_8$". St. Anzas I to X, with tact honesty and care, explore ways in which meaning/significance is made. Each takes a need to speak and plays with language, the conventional and the broken, in an attempt to articulate that need. Stanza V looks specifically at the way language choices, like mathematical bases, provide a "deliberate construction of / chance, a range meant / voices to choose from, / assumptions," and at what may happen when the bases (linguistic, mathematical, ...) change yielding "a sense, an essence / like no sense you ever knew / [...] you gave in to & followed." Stanza VI tries the "rules by which the light flows thru" language; Stanza VII tries out the relationship between assumption and belief and extends this in IX to question the connection between the poet and God. But there is no "fax machine" link between the two, but "divine presence a pressure." God is then an "unknown" "presence and absence" "unspeakable" and writing a "gest-ture" (St. Anza X).

In this sequence Nichol is dealing with a cluster of issues that currently besets all postcolonial and cross cultural thinking: The tolerance of difference allows for many voices as long as they keep separate, but as long as they keep separate there will be fear with its attendant contestatory discourse and focus on self and other. To move beyond this position, which has been characterized as the "multicult-ural," there is a need to work actively with the multiplicity of different voices to develop some closeness of common ground. This is not simply to provide a set of assumptions that different people can "live with" and resent in different ways, but an attempt to hammer out at least some vocabulary that these different people recognize as appropriate to the way they want to live. The writing here suggests that we hammer these out best with words. Finding that appropriateness is so difficult and rare that it often conveys a sense of the inexplicable, and Nichol lodges this firmly with a sense of the religious underlining his belief in a commonly held deep structure of humanity with the metaphor of "base/basis."

Nichol's *Gifts* was assembled as he was dying, a death foregrounded by the series of "body paranoia" and "bp:if" on single sheets of pages "to be interleaved" from a pocket on the back cover of the book. The writing carries a weight of emotion for a contemporary Western reader, partly in the cultural context provided for Nichol's work by the words of thanks to him and his editing that occur in so many books by recent Canadian writers, partly because of the way we treat death, and particularly if we, as he with Donna, work through the words reading out a new set of common grounds for ourselves. Nichol talks about the process of reading, of following the trace of a life lived and avoiding infatuation with words that cloud the mind, as some part of:

what family is, other minds enter, other lives you pledge a constancy to / [...] / living among family you are changed, it is the way your vocabulary increases, you occupy certain nouns, are caught up in the activity of certain verbs, adverbs, adjectives, syntax too. tone. / the language comes alive as you come alive and the real mysteries remain. ("You Too, Nicky" VII)

This closeness needs a "loyalty" to reading the words, sticking with them "not blindly, but allowing them, always, to evolve under the scrutiny that time permits." But the radical experiments with language that Nichol conducted have seemed to many readers impassable/massive/impossible. Although they work without exception within a humanist framework, they toss aside the stable and fixed representative structure of the ideology of the nation state and can appear to alienate. However, Nichol's attempt to articulate the ways that memory can respond to present needs by creating a different set of common grounds effects an intimacy and trust that neither consoles nor threatens. His poems are not objects handed over, but ways of making significances.

Conspiracy/Utopia: Needs and Desires
The contradiction between the dislocation and relocation of the *production* of ideology that Nichol works within is also one attempted

by Robert Kroetsch. Kroetsch's writing specifically places the contradiction into the field of power. Playing robustly with the figures of Western mythology and the strategies of graphic presentation—notes, documents, catalogues, as well as the fictional genres—the writer cuts through the techniques for consumption of family narrative we have been taught by psychoanalytic criticism and casts a series of graphic and linguistic modulation through the representations. Known more widely for his novels such as *The Studhorse Man,* or *Badlands* or *Alibi* among others, Kroetsch in his poetry often explores the concrete graphic object as a narrative of potential meaning. In *Seed Catalogue* (1977) the words of the catalogue set off memory stories, and the two sit beside each other like incongruous twins of intimacy and descriptive detail. Chunks are literally/graphically taken out of letters in *The Sad Phoenician* (1979), not to release their own significance but to indicate the way that the alphabet allows a written language of "sound," of "commotion," that is poetry. Not the writing of the priest, but a condition of "civil unrest," the poet "as lover."

The poem "The Frankfurt *Hauptbahnhof*" writes precisely about the issues of identity, self, memory, history and fame, in terms of "notation"; how to articulate the present need. Schematically, the poem writes a story about the poet going to Trier to lecture; "courtesy of External Affairs" of the Canadian government the writer goes out to sell himself "swinging / at the old / suckerball ..." of fame and recognition again. Along the way the poet expects to investigate his grandmother's town of origin, hoping to find the "Kirche" where she went to pray (200). Instead he finds history, Marx and Constantine the Great, whose reputations have eradicated any memory of a grandmother from time. Both this loss and this preservation are to do with notation, not only in the written word, for the grandmother is famous in Minnesota "for having shied a stick of wood" at her husband (204). The poem becomes a set of critical queries into the activity of notation and is responded to both by the crows swooping up and down in the Vienna sky and by the parallels with the recognition of self remembering when the poet meets his double in the Frankfurt station. The first query into "what is   notation" is answered by "Barrie" (bpNichol) who says "prediction / a saying (assaying) of / what will be said" (198). The crows yield "notation > divination > augury" (202), and notation becomes "a set / of instructions for / reading (in) the / future" (204). What the ruins of past notations speak is to do with "the reader in the text." In a literary critical summary which could be a coded version of Nichol's loyalty, trust, family and grace, Kroetsch's poem says:

> The narrator, always, fears his/her own tyranny. The notation in the poem occasions the dialogic response that is the reader's articulation of his/her presence (the ecstatic now of recognition? the larger, if not always enduring, experience of transformational vision?) (205)

Yet Kroetsch's version of notation and recognition hovers near stasis: "Notation is the double of the poem. Or: we are the poem, and cannot hear except by indirection. We can only guess the poem by encountering (by being surprised by) its double" (206). The series of potential responses to notation indicates the writer's worry about stasis and interrupts it with "or: notation is flying," and finally, "the notation keeps it moving" (208).

All public memory is carried by the ruins of notation that enable future readers a moment of recognition;[32] but precisely what is recognized is ambivalently carried by the personal memory of the writer lost in the station suddenly being told where to go by someone he doesn't know but thinks he recognizes. As his memory restructures this experience, the man who speaks to him is presented as a younger version of himself, someone who speaks with his voice exactly but one who wears a hat: "I never wear a hat." In re-structuring his double he defines himself by difference, provides a notation for himself; but it is an "I" that cannot be heard except "by indirection," and an "I" that is kept moving by the differences between himself and the double, in a notation inhabited by the reader. In one sense the reader is put in charge of the speaker's self; the reader can exercise his/her own tyranny. And in another sense the reader allows the notation to become part of their life, only arriving at any sense of self if it becomes appropriate.

The writer provides a repertoire of syntactical variations and lexical fields that call on literary theory, travelogue and tale-telling, as well as broken line and a range of grammatically correct but discursively tense sentences. This collection of strategies needs considerable textual attention to read as inadequate and 'moving on.' A similar kind of wordplay can be found in the much-anthologized 'Sketches of a Lemon' that circles linguistically around potential significances for "lemon." As intriguing and involving as the series of jokes, metaphors, narrations, graphics, etc. can be, the necessary denial of conventional reading strategies is alienating for many readers. Kroetsch is far more broadly enabling in his larger works that can lead the reader into some of the signifying power and loss of literary and linguistic strategies as they obsessively repeat the techniques and devices. But the longer the work, the more convincingly taught the strategies are, the greater the risk of isolating the reader in another club culture, yet another closed system of writing that mimics ideology.

All Kroetsch's novels are concerned with destabilizing mythological and ideological frameworks, although the various characters within them are often caricatures of their effects. Like the isolated female characters in Ondaatje's novels, the women in Kroetsch's work are often the "mysterious others" of the narrative, although usually also part of some kind of dislocated family structure. Kroetsch's early Oedipal figures that stumble-stride across the plains enveloped in the madness of national passions are not on a Freudian quest for self, but a hunt for the 'other,' a recognition of family in a shared significance that they suspect or fear is absent.[33] At the centre of this fear is the post-modern/colonial anxiety about power, that Kroetsch maps increasingly onto the power structures of gender relations. *Alibi* (1983) explicitly puts one man into the position of acting out another man's desires for control, which is the classic strategy for nation-state power structures. Kroetsch offers in *Alibi* an allegory of the individual voice working within and coping with a powerful gendered ideology which simultaneously mimics his own needs and appears to define them.

The novel provides the doubled name of William William Dorfen for its central character and this potentially split life as both 'free' individual and conspiracy-determined clone: conspiracy being to empowered groups, here wealthy white males, analogous to what utopia is to the disempowered. On constant quests for the perfect collection, Dorf appears to scan the world for groups of objects quite at whim, yet his employer Jack Deemer always knows where he is. Indeed most of the other people in the novel know where he is, although he never knows where they are or where he himself is going. Much of the writing in the "journal" that the novel purports to be or be taken from (Dorf does and does not write it, he does and does not keep the journal), is like "The Frankfurter *Hauptbahnhof*,'" a retrospective re-membering of moments in which Dorf has acted and hence determined a sequence of events, but acted without apparent reason. The re-membering usually leaves the reader with a sense that some sequence of events has been "noted" but has slipped through the fingers, not been "notated"; in Nichol's vocabulary, it has been "recollected" but precisely not "re-membered." Lack of memory work that re-members the appropriate ground seems to be the condition for Kroetsch's postmodernism.

Dorf gradually begins to articulate the "plot that connives the world into visible being" (195). Deemer's money has bought and manipulated a series of collections, but Dorf comes to the realization that it's not the money but Dorf's own "talk" that makes the collection, "The collection itself only confirms the discontinuity of this scattered world; it's my talk that puts it together. I rave the world into coherence for Deemer" (195). Authoritarian power needs economic and ideological control over others, but it counts on them mimicking back the version of the world that it needs. This power demands control over knowledge; it collects facts and objects to categorize them. At the same time the activity of collecting and categorizing, that Dorf does initially for beauty, becomes a device to hide real economic power behind.

Alibi is a text-book construction of postmodern concerns, and carefully provides the necessary strategies for foregrounding those concerns by repetitive disruptions and patternings of the narrative structure, character, and graphical indicators in print and chapter headings, that the reader has a chance to learn and to enjoy as the writing moves on. However, the topics of sexuality and gender that permeate every aspect of the narrative turns the writing into a curious and provocative version of a feminist text. In saying this it must be emphasized that a lot of Kroetsch's writing is wildly out of touch with women, to the point of being crudely vicious. A writer steeped in irony, he seems not to understand that many disempowered people cannot afford it.[34] Irony no matter how challenging demands a tacit acceptance of certain assumptions, and many of the assumptions about sexuality and femininity in his work are simply too brutal to hold, even tacitly as a road to critical reading. But in *Alibi* Kroetsch has written a narrative about what man can do to avoid irony.

If Deemer is a caricature of masculinist desires for acquisition, possession and consumption, the cynic who plays at power knowing that individual power is a game, Dorf becomes the man within a masculine world who doesn't want to be there. He becomes one of the self-alienated powerful looking for ways of shedding power, shedding ironies about the disempowered, trying not to reduplicate the manipulation and force. The women in this novel are not mysterious 'others' but offered simply without context and therefore necessarily unpredictable. The problematic events of the story could be read as a checklist of Freudian indicators for male sexuality, yet Dorf seeks not to reject sexuality but to find another sexuality. Parallel to many early feminist texts he reaches his final orgasm tactfully well before the end of the book, under the direction of a hermaphrodite. But while this is normally an assuming of involvement by women, for Dorf the orgasm is something that is done *to* him, not done with him, which is the point of shedding power. The motif of Dorf's search for Deemer's perfect spa, that drives the narrative, is overtly referred to as a search for youth, health or life, but perhaps because there is an overt strand of individual participation in its construction, it is the search for sexuality, a sexuality that is not possessive, does not destroy or main that is most helpful. Like a woman in a world of a masculinist fantasy, this man cannot have an alternative sexuality.

Kroetsch's novel gains much resonance if the reader takes the gender relations as an allegory of national ideologies and their power to circumscribe and define our world. Like Atwood, Kroetsch is completely at home with the notion of authoritarian power, understanding the workings of the 'god game' of fantasy construction as she understands the 'doublethink' of ideology.[35] His overtly male view parallels her overtly female stance, and both shun romance. Yet he would attempt to build another sexuality while she forgoes it. He would discard memory or at least focus on forgetting, forgoing any more collections, and she would build everything on appropriate remembering / reappropriating memory. Perhaps that difference is a part of their gendered histories, and way that each gender participates differently in power.

Alibi is an account that discards the romance of 'chaos' and the utopia of 'the other' by denying memory and avoiding pursuit of any new sexuality.[36] Similarly the rearrangements of language that query the working of significance, avoid the offer of new structures for significance or for common ground. Dorf is someone who dare not trust, just so, his journal evades any intimacy and documents instead the beginnings of isolation and narcissistic paranoia which mark out the individual in the postmodern world who works within an ideology s/he does not want to belong to. But just as the disempowered cannot afford to accept all ironies, the disempowered, rather than self-alienated who are frequently those with power, cannot afford to avoid memory or to avoid significance. Whether they be from race minorities, from excluded gender-positions or from the poor, those excluded from ideology don't want to efface a discredited sense of self/common ground, but to build communication. They cannot afford to avoid reduplication of power structures by isolating themselves from them, because those structures will willy nilly infuse their isolation and satisfy the conditions of their fear. Because Kroetsch places the contradiction so firmly within structures of power, his writing can dislocate but has difficulty relocating. The novel moves past alienation and teaches the reader how to query the making of significance, without encouraging them to build isolating structures of their own: If they do, then they participate in the same 'god game' that the novel exposes as being without significance yet loaded with economic power.

Memory, History, and Appropriateness
The work of Daphne Marlatt takes the risk of difference all the time, as well as the risk of closeness. Marlatt's poetry, like Nichol's and Kroetsch's, often alienates readers because it undermines the assumptions of representation. However, the strategies the writing offers in return are there to re-build both memory and history. One of Marlatt's widely read early works, *Steveston* (1974), with photographs by Robert Minden, is a structure that allows the reader to build a number of different histories: most urgently of Japanese immigrants to the West Coast of Canada and their treatment during and after World War II, as well as of the life-cycle of the salmon, of environmental issues, of local fishing and fishery practices, of the geography, and more residually of the Aboriginal peoples, and of women. Each topic, and there are many others, becomes a ground for each other, and which history the reader reads depends much upon their personal memory. The histories that are made are an account/ their own story of the reader's memory. The writer tells us in the final naming poem "Steveston, B.C.," that the writing is "the story of a town, these are the people, whose history locates inside of dream" (89). The body of the text is a dreamtime articulated, from which, or rather within which, the reader's own dreamtime can find articulations that negotiate personal and public memory.

Steveston explicitly asks the reader to "imagine" a town, and
implicitly asks for a reconstruction of a particular political history; but
increasingly, Marlatt's writing asks the reader to exercise personal
memory explicitly *for* political history: whether it be of a colonial past
and immigrant present, of a family, or of women. Unlike Nichol
whose politics are of humanist community, taking/making the best of
common grounds arrived at by associative release responding to
immediate need: moments of grace in which significance is
recognized, but like Atwood, Marlatt has no moments of recognized
"grace." It seems there is nothing given, only assumptions and salvage
from "the wreckage of language so freighted with phallocentric values
it must be subverted and re-shaped."[38] In one sense Nichol can count on
retrieving some alienation by the wide recognition among readers
of his humanist values. Marlatt risks doubly alienating the reader who
is not only asked to question articulation and re-presentation for
ideology, but is asked to build another structure.

In Marlatt's lesbian and feminist writing, the reader has to work out
a basis for what is "appropriate" to necessity that is different to the
pervasive humanist cast of Western society. In contrast to Nichol who
does not want toleration, assimilation and effacement, but many
different voices, Marlatt is working tenaciously for the possibility of
one of those voices. Different voices cannot be *given* space, they have
to make space find place, along with the current owners, which means
they have, however crudely, first to name themselves, articulate self
through memory and make public space by negotiating and fighting
for a history. As Atwood recognizes, contemporary feminisms can
trap people in their own ideologies precisely because the rhetorical
structure of the dominant ideology of the nation-state which they can
mimic is so quickly and effectively consoling—a dangerous gift for
those already excluded from so much. But ideology is also like fact;
there is usually an historical event to which it was appropriate, to the
needs of which it responded: Recovering those needs and assessing
their present appropriateness is a large part of making a place for the
self in social and political life. This difficult relocation after radical
dislocation of the common grounds for action is something at which
Marlatt is particularly skilled.

Among the more difficult assumptions to dislocate let alone relocate
is, as Kroetsch shows us, sexuality. Women's sexuality/ies, caught so
often in fairly arid versions of heterosexual repetition that deny it

articulation, has rarely been written about—at least not to the extent of writing concerned with men's understanding of what that sexuality may be. One of the effects of feminism in the West has been to encourage women of all classes and colour to try to articulate their sexuality. In *Touch to My Tongue* Marlatt carefully brings together a concern with the way poetry works on the edge between "the already spoken and the unspeakable" (48), between consciousness and dream, and the parallel position of women carried by a language that is structured syntactically and generically to outline a way of life that is not theirs yet which they "inhabit" or which inhabits them.

Touch to My Tongue overtly works with lexis and syntax in its writing of a woman's sexuality. Marlatt suggests that woman's body is "postlexical" in that "certain words" take us back to "originally-related meaning," a "living body of verbal relations" that the writer must put together and in doing so put together a world. Analogous to Nichol's graphic and alphabetic association that releases words into punning free-fall until some appropriately significant sense is reached, the writer here uses etymology to release a history of words until a version appropriate to her woman's life is found. This is not based on anything so naive as a claim to "original meaning" and authority, but is a strategy for exploring how words carry us on and how far we go along with that or resist or change it. In the end we have to rebuild a world; we do not find it as a given. Since we cannot rebuild without a lexical base, then at least we may choose grounds that carry significance for women. Nevertheless, the resilience of the writing's lexical field is primarily located elsewhere, not in the etymological but in contemporary connotative fields in unusual juxtapositions such as "wild flesh opens wet" (23) with "nest, amative and nurturing," or in phonemic coherence playing against syllabic disruption for example "still the edge of summer gone in the grounding rain" (22).

It is in the syntax that the joy of this work comes through most immediately, particularly when it combines with sound. Nearly every phrase arrests conventional grammatical reading: A sample: "we went to what houses stars at the sea's edge," "a kiwi at four a.m. among the sheets green slice of cold going down easy on the tongue," or "it's all there, love, we part each other coming to, geyser, sparking pool, hidden in and under separate skin we make for each other through" (30). This is not to say that the phrases resist sense, but that the reader can make a number of senses out of them.

The readings translate into aspects of (women's) sexuality precisely at the point where the reader is released into a number of possibilities. Marlatt's writing does dislocate conventional grammar and semantics, but it does not leave the reader in a world of arbitrary pluralisms. The writing is self-consciously building a narrative about sexuality. It enacts etymological chains to infuse contemporary vocabulary with different connotations by stressing obscured sounds or clusters of letters: "bleak colour of your iris gone blue, that blue of a clear sky, *belo,* bright, Beltane, 'bright-/fire'" which moves into "*bleikr,* / shining white, radiant healing in bright colours, *blanda,* to mingle and blend: / the blaze of light we are, spiralling" (31), and brings "blue" and "blend" together with "bright" radiance at the same time as "spiral," that intimate mingling of separate strands, in a lexical cluster that referentially connects with meeting a lover.

The writing places in a sequence series of clauses and phrases that have no apparent grammatical or logical relation, yet they are carefully punctuated, entitled, blocks of words, chosen to follow one another. The copy-editor's curse of 'eye-skip' occurs frequently as the reader's eye seeks to order the sense and finds itself re-reading the same line or jumping ahead to find the track. Often this search is marked out by the interchange of voices between "i" and "you," the two lovers whose presence calls out a cultural expectation of narrative. Yet in a section such as "down the season's avenue" these voices are enfolded. Ostensibly telling about a plane landing and bringing two people together, the grammar undermines any logical definition for the one in the plane or the other on land: "we" approach the pivot of night and day; "you" climb what tree over the sea to gaze east"; "i" see "light lean along a curved plain": from a plane? gazing at the horizon for a plane?; then "i" "try the trees for company"; and when the plane comes in "you will be standing there": on the ground? at the door of the plane?; to the by now profoundly complicated logic of "i'm coming home": which folds the "i" and the "you" into each other.

Re-membering the Body

While I as a woman read *Touch to My Tongue* as a work of enabling example for female sexuality, it is interesting that many men who read it read it as enabling of their own sexuality. The writing does not address the narrow version of sexuality on offer from conventional gender relations, nor does it then move to melancholic contemplation or romantic designs of alternative essences/identities. What it does is deal with what it's got along the edge of the spoken/unspoken. It's working at the shoreline of the body and language, or becoming aware of the body, where memory works. This image is openly politicized in Marlatt's novel *Ana Historic* (1988), where she takes a substantial area of French and Québecoise feminist theory about "writing the body" as a social and political necessity for women if they are to move away from oppositional action and from the tearing splits of doublethink identity which inform much postmodern paranoia.

What *Ana Historic* tells is a story about the way that personal memory makes public memory, the way the building of self can shape and/or build history. Unlike any of the other writers discussed here, who find history variously as huge, external, dominating, split, overwhelming or embarrassing, Marlatt takes on history as a task, something to change the way we might change house or even our sexuality, or even because we might change these other things. And what is particularly interesting is the way that newly written versions of the past must always appear fictional, and always demand the imaginative reconstruction of memory.

The book offers a structured counterpoint between history and personal memory as Annie Richards/Torrent attempts to write an account of Ana Richards, a woman who came to Canada in the nineteenth century, and who appears in a few newspaper references and short journal. As Annie writes, her account is interrupted by memories of her mother Ina, by more recent memories of her broken marriage to "Richard" and by an on-going conversation with a friend called Zoe. The account of Ana Richards's life provides a topical ground for the issues that crowd into the present, and the resolutions of memory around Annie's mother and ex-husband relocate into the account and define a way of finding self that enables Annie to move into a relationship with Zoe.

The public memory of history is an account of the past to which a group of people have assented. In a world where the written word has increasingly become the store place for such accounts, writing becomes the key to new versions of the past. However, the written word as history is there to resist change and often for good reason: if we eradicated the history of slavery we would, among many other things, lose an example of the process of repression and resistance from which we can learn bases for action needed in our contemporary lives. We may, however, want to change the stance of the account. If a history is written that obscures or omits events in the past, such as the complete loss of domestic history, then again we have to change the stance of existing history. Written history can be changed by group writing, from collaborative community ventures, to the institutional accounts of science, to government programs such as the Canada Council which aims to write Canada into a broader cultural history. But the way in which we encourage individual writers, the whole profession of authorship, and the structure of the printing and publishing business means that writing by individuals is often the most effective way of changing historical accounts. Thus the interaction between individual personal memory and public memory becomes necessary.

Ana Historic opens with a series of interrupted accounts from personal memories of the narrator's childhood and relationship with her mother, to excerpts from reports on logging in the nineteenth century and newspaper articles from early British Columbian history, to fictional attempts to reconstruct Mrs Richards' life. History is cast as factual, useful, the story of "dominance mastery," "the real story the city fathers tell of the only important events in the world" (28). In contrast, as Munro reminds us, story is something mothers tell children until they grow up and learn about lies, stories are the "inauthentic" (30) versions of the past, so often a woman's past. This conglomeration of fiction, history, personal and public memory is then passed through a lens (37-42) in which the narrator/writer gives Mrs Richards her own name, so that she does not have only "the name of a dead man." The name is literally given in that the narrator Annie gives the character the name Ana, which is the same in sound but becomes different in the written version, for Ana will allow Annie to become a different person.

The transposition of Annie's name, through "Ina" the name of her mother, to "Ana," builds a set of links into history for the contemporary woman, at the same time as it discovers the past to be empty of that history and recognizes a need to fill it with story. The following segment of writing (43ff) is largely concerned with the relationship between history and story. The reader finds a few sentences presumably from Ana Richards' journal (about which the archivists are suspicious [30]) which contain crossings-out and erasures. The narrator asks "what is she editing out and for whom?" (46). To the question "why write at all?", she answers "because there is 'into --' what? frightening preposition. into the unspoken urge of a body insisting itself in the words" (46). Writing is a "disappearing act" for the self that allows "she, unspoken and real in the world" to run ahead and "embrace it. // she is writing her desire to be, in the present tense, retrieved from silence" (46-47).

Helping this nineteenth-century woman to be written is a way of retrieving her from silence. Yet the narrator overlays this story-making onto her memories of her mother Ina whom she tried, as a child encouraged to seek male approval from her father, to erase (50-51). Through Ana, the narrator "re-members" Ina, puts "things back together again, the things that have been split off, set aside" (51); and in this way also "re-members" herself, retrieves herself from silence. It is important that the narrator, trained by her husband Richard the conventional historian, writes Ana's history by gathering "facts," and that one of these "facts" is the account of personal memory written by Ana herself. Writing the self is writing history; and writing history is writing the self. For Marlatt personal and public memory are the same, and must be given equal value to avoid the "impasse: impossible to exit. dead end. when the walls close down. the public/private wall" (23) that isolates the individual, here her mother Ina, into privacy; and which also underwrites the delusory stability of contemporary western ideology.

Given that the most immediate way of writing Ana's history would simply reduplicate the structure of dominance that has kept it silent and, in placing it on the same basis as conventional history, would leave it failing by comparison, the segment "Ana's fascination" (75ff) moves on to explore women and language, opening with "the silence of trees / the silence of women // if they could speak / an unconditional language / what would they say" (75). Annie tells of her "patient assistance" to her husband's work and the difference in her own writing which he calls "scribbling." Rather than his history, she wants to write her own story, but "the truth is our stories are hidden from us by fear" (79), the mother's fear of what she might find if she tried to articulate "all the ways we don't fit into a man's world" (79): Particularly what body she might find if she ceased to "trade" in the economy of male sexuality and the hysteric, split, self-defeating version of her body that it offers. As Zoe says in answer to this part of the story "'you haven't even begun to think about what it would be if it could be what you want'" (90).

The analysis of what female sexuality lacks is acute, but is still caught inside the fear of what the narrator might find if she moved on: the lurking terrifying figure of something that is not Frankenstein, yet monstrous, inherited from Freud's fantasies.[39] Interrupting the story of Ana and re-membering of Ina, Annie tells the personal memories of her adolescent joy in another woman's body against the pressures of ideological gender definitions (90ff). These are mapped onto the "fork between two roads so long ago" that offered two different sexualities, and the conclusion of the segment leads her to the possibility that Ana and another woman, Birdie, could fascinate each other. This is something she "had not imagined—this // as history unwritten" (109). In response, Annie tries to return "to the solid / ground of fact" (111). She recounts probable conversations among the women Ana knew, centring on the birth of a boy child. Inexorably, within the historical context of colonialism, the metaphors of woman as "goods" or commodity, woman as "ship" to carry men's objects of desire, infuse the text. This allows the carefully written placing of her mother within an emerging postcolonial world, and of contemporary women as objects of trade in the male economy of sexuality, all to overlap each other in the central event of the birth. That the baby is male means that from the first he is different from all these women. At birth he is given into surroundings where he is "at home from the beginning" (127). Ana and Ina and Annie as immigrants and as women are not born into their home, nor into the country of their own bodies, but into someone else's. Just so, the postcolonial nation state is born into a global world.

Zoe repositions this birth as something important for Ana not because of the birth of the baby but because of the intimacy and labour of the woman: "out and in. out *and* in.' (125): The unwritten history of the gift of that labour of the body. The narrator has come to the "a-historic," the writing of the yet unwritten woman's body and the difficulty of that. Annie speaks of trying to give birth to her immediate reader who is Ina her mother, and at the same time she knows that Zoe thinks of her as "stuck in the unspoken, unen-acted—half born," stuck in "past history" (132). But past history "never is"—past, that is. The only way to deal with the history we have is to write another, and initially she tries to write it a-historically. What

Annie now writes for Ana is the possibility of a sexuality focused on another woman, and as if the character has walked past her, the narrator says "you've moved beyond what i can tell of you" (139). Annie then realizes that this is as if conventional history has "won," the ideological has succeeded in making it impossible for the writer's personal memory to imagine another way, and she asks if perhaps we can "live in history *and* imagination" (139): "but once history's onstage, histrionic as usual (all those wars, all those historic judgements), the a-historic hasn't a speaking part. What's imagination next to the weight of the (f)actual?" (139).

This impossibility of imagination about another sexuality is Annie's own impasse, her own private/public wall just like Ina's. It is in the concluding pages of the text, where Annie talks about Ina's electric shock therapy, that she follows the terrible destructiveness acted out on people who cannot with/under/stand the doublethink of identity. To 'cure' her mother of the paranoia brought on by the suffocating privacy of the isolated family, and the taken-for-granted unwritten story of that domestic labour that commodifies the person into a replaceable object, she is given electric shock therapy. The treatment "overloaded the circuits so you couldn't bear to remember. re-member," and "it wasn't just your memory they took. they took your imag- ination, your will to create things differently" (149). The narrator says that if she denies the anahistoric or the possibility of imagining differently for herself, then history *will* win. Unlike the a-historic, the anahistoric is risky, fearful and difficult, but the alternative is Ina, or Ana's marriage to Ben Springer, or Annie's own suffocating marriage to Richard.

While the stories of Ana and Ina end here, Annie's life continues and she goes to visit Zoe, whom she trusts and fears for the unknown of lesbian sexuality she may find. In the brief two or three pages at the end of the book, she finds a group of friends and at the same time a terror, not the Frankenstein fear of her youth, but "the trembling that takes you out of yourself" (152) in this other sexuality that is "the reach of your desire, reading us into the page ahead" (153). This different sexuality is not something that comes from the words, although the writing enables Annie to realize that it may be there as Ana "walks past" her. It is not a matter of releasing language into free fall and waiting for a moment of recognition or of grace. The different path is one made possible through interaction with other people which is not wholly or even primarily linguistic. The urgency of words comes from the need to articulate this other possible sexuality, partly for the pleasure that that gives in itself but mainly because articulating that sexuality, writing it, is the primary means for resisting both its obliteration and its abuse. More positively, not only is the articulation necessary to help other people who are trying to imagine/move toward another sexuality, but also simply by writing in contradiction to ideological stability the writing enacts the possibility of any alternative—sexual, national, racial, economic.

History can only be written out of what people can imagine. But imagination has to be hammered out of interaction with other people and the way that language can re-member that interaction. If your interaction with people cannot be or is not, articulated, then you are not re-membered by history, you have literally nobody/no body literally, you can be objectified and commodified. Writing the body is for Marlatt not a writing out of 'lack' or 'loss' that leads to aggressive or repressive strategies as Lacan, stuck with concepts of stable representations and fixed ideology, would have it. Writing the body is the individual re-membering a self into history and simultaneously writing a history. The absence of gendered labour, of domestic labour, of sexual labour from "history," allows that labour to be commodified. Re-membering becomes parallel with reproducing that labour as necessary action.

But this action of imagination, that changes self and history, needs a different kind of relationship between body, memory and writing, than "historical account" conventionally gives, because it asks the writer and the reader to walk on past where they now are, breathe into the page ahead. The feminine plural Ana-historic, is the way this particular book sets up that relationship. Parallel stories of women at different times are focused through the lens of what the writer can imagine now. Marlatt's ability to enable the reader to read on past the page is attested to in the "Salvage" section of *Salvage* (1991) which reworks/reclaims/re-members parts of *Steveston* (1973) through a feminist reading. *Steveston* is a work that two decades of readers have read back into the women's lives which it seems so clearly to indicate but not emphatically speak of. Reading "Salvage" is like recognizing a reading that the writer has only just written, a reading that comes before the writing although out of another writing that made it possible.

There is nothing esoteric in this. Marlatt is simply suggesting that fundamental change, no matter how necessary, is terrifying to the individual until it is realized in daily life, in language of day-to-day interaction that can be agreed upon and taken as common ground for discussion and action. No matter how much help the written, or any other medium, can give to an individual or a group, change away from ideology is fearsomely difficult because it seems to challenge the notion of any re-membered self or society. It seems to challenge it particularly because in the state ideologies of western nations, stable or even fixed identities for individual subjects and state nationalisms are an *a priori*, an assumption.—even though well hidden in hyperliberal bourgeois isolation.

That is, to state the obvious, where modernism and postmodernism derive their impetus: to challenge the commodification of the person. For postcolonial countries ever aware of the dead-end of opposition to powerful economic units, and often torn apart by the pressures of accepting and rejecting the dominant ideologies of the colonizer past or present, the possibility of walking on past that colonizing occurs when the representative stability of ideology becomes less important than people coming together in the labour of a group.

The Canadian writers here all explore memory and history, in an attempt to connect individuals with their societies and structure those societies into a geographically defined 'national' culture. These writers are committed to the importance of writing as a medium within which these connections and negotiations take place. They offer a variety of genre and language strategies not only to criticize, oppose, and challenge the stable set of representations on which ideology of the nation state depends, but to resist, change, restructure, and build new ground for the articulation of different voices that redefine the modes of personal and public/political action.

NOTES

Chapter One

1. The relevant papers here are: L. Weir, "The discourse of 'Civility': Strategies of containment in literary histories of English Canadian literature" (1988); R. Lecker, "The Canonization of Canadian literature; An inquiry into value" (1990); F. Davey, "Critical Response" (1990); T. Ware, "A Little Self-Consciousness is a Dangerous Thing: A response to Robert Lecker" (1991); and B. Godard, "Canadian? Literary? Theory?" (1992).
2. L. Hunter, "Ideology as the Rhetorical Ethos of the Nation State," paper given to the Canadian Society for the History of Rhetoric, Ottawa, 1993; Forthcoming *Rhetorica,* 1996.
3. There is a set of rhetorical analyses behind this claim, one of the most obvious of which derives from a study of how ruling polities are structured when they are made up of only a very small percentage of the populace.
4. A. Grafton and L. Jardine, *From Humanism to the Humanities* (London: Cambridge UP, 1986).
5. The double-edgedness of the sword can be sensed throughout the analysis of support offered by A. Dagg in *The 50% Solution: Why should women pay for men's culture.* Women may want support commensurate with their presence, but the finance may co-opt them into the system. But if they gain the luxury of refusing support, they only fund others who collaborate against them.
6. See for example L. Hutcheon, "History and / as Intertext," in ed. J. Moss, *Future Indicative* (1987).
7. W. Tallman, "Wonder Merchants" (1984).
8. The European canon of contemporary English-language Canadian literature tends more to the structural, but we need to ask whether we emphasize this approach simply because it is easier for us to evade the historical context. Not only does the different emphasis underline the different needs of reading communities—something that also applies to the variety of Canadian communities—but also it does mean that we can and do read Laurence and Munro for their rhetorical strategies not their issues,

an approach which is often neglected in Canadian criticism.

9. See the discussion of these issues with relevance to Québec in L. Bersianik, "Aristotle's Lantern," in ed. S. Kamboureli and S. Neuman, *A Mazing Space* (1986).

10. There were of course exceptions, such as the University of Montreal, but these were not many.

11. M. Arnold is instrumental to the canon of Engish literature because he organized the editing of the anthologies essential to the teaching profession after the Education Acts of 1867 and 1870, just as F. Leavis responds to nationalist desire in the 1930s by mapping out a Great Tradition for the purpose of validating the university study of English literature.

12. See for example J. Gray's account "Book Publishing," in ed. George Whalley, *Writing in Canada,* (Toronto: Macmillan, 1956), pp. 53-64; but see also P. Webb's tacit rejoinder to the reluctance of publishers to take risks in "The Poet and the Publisher," also in this collection, pp. 78-88.

13. This may possibly be due to the kind of people involved with the early discussions about support for Canadian literature. The constituency meeting in Kingston in 1955 listed in *Writing in Canada*, is almost entirely academic. And see F. Sutherland, "Frisking Laura Secord,"in ed. J. Metcalf, *The Bumper Book* (Toronto: ECW Press, 1986), p. 15.

14. *TISH* is one of the more well-known of the many university magazines. Several writers give accounts of the reading tours which were new to the 60s and may well have grown out of a perception of the popularity of the Beat poets" performances in the US. Jack McClelland was one of the initiators of this kind of publicity, touring Layton, Purdy and Cohen early in the 60s. McClelland says that he was interested in encouraging "promotion" tours where authors would be interviewed and sign books, but was "not very happy about ... the concept of the author reading from their book" because so few could do it successfully (private communication). He adds that *all* the writers "loved it."

16. See M. Tippett, *Making Culture* (Toronto: U of Toronto P, 1990).

17. For an account of the early years of the New Canadian Library see M. Ross interviewed by K. Chittick in "Studies in Canadian Literature," *Canadian Literature* 92, pp. 260-1. For comments on early critical work see ed. C. Klinck, *The Literary History of Canada,* which arrives in 1965.

18. I was reminded of this by F. Davey. Reference may be found in *The Canadian Encyclopedia* (1985) under Hall, Emmet.

19. M. Gnarowski drew this report to my attention: R. Mathews and C. Steele, ed., *The Struggle for Canadian Universities* (1969).

20. See for example G. Woodcock's comments in "Poetry" in ed. C. Klinck, *A*

Literary History of Canada III (1976), pp. 284-5.

21. Publishers needed at least four publications before being able to apply to the Canada Council.

22. The Symons Report *To Know Ourselves: The Report of the Commis-sion on Canadian Studies* (1975) coalesced many initiatives being taken in the field of Canadian Studies, and certainly gave impetus to the growing European interest.

23. See for eample the entries in J.J. Dessick, *Doctoral Research on Canada and Canadians* (1986), pp. 321-39.

24. An early and important statement on this, phrased as a "humanist" bias, is F. Davey's 1974 essay "Surviving the Paraphrase," *Surviving the Paraphrase* (Winnipeg: Turnstone Press, 1983).

25. See L. Weir "The Discourse of 'Civility'," as above.

26. See for example B. Godard's overview "Structuralism / Post-Structuralism," in ed. Moss, *Future Indicative* or ed. Neuman and Kamboureli, *A Mazing Space.*

27. The evidence is there to see in the recent publications from the Department of Multiculturalism and Citizenship on *Hispanic Writers, Urdu Literature, Italian-Canadian Writing, Canadian-Hungarian Literature,* and *Literary Writing by Blacks in Canada.*

28. *Challenged Book List* (Toronto: Book Development Council, 1989), III, 1-6, which even includes R. Briggs' *Father Christmas* for promoting a "negative image" of Santa Claus.

29. As for example with the censorship imposed on a text book anthology by the Denominational Education Council of Newfoundland in 1989. It could be argued that the censorship exercised primarily over offensive words, although unacceptable in principle, has in practice diverted attention away from larger issue-based censorship. The censorship in this case, however, was carrried out in a manner that could be said to have misrepresented the case to the writers concerned; and the Council has an unusually extreme, not to say eccentric, record: for example, at the request of one of the denominational groups which discourages dancing, a photograph of a musical band was deleted from a textbook on the grounds that it seemed to give support to dancing.

30. Val Ross, *The Globe and Mail*'s writer on publishing issues, discusses this in "Who's to wear the mantle of minority" (1993).

31. See for example L. Elliott, *Literary Writing by Blacks in Canada,* ed. M. Batts (Ottawa: Department of Multiculturalism, 1988), p. 5, and M. Philip, "Gut Issues in Babylon," *Fuse* XII, 5 (April / May, 1989), p. 21.

32. Several people at the 1989 conference "Discourse pre-1860" discussed these forms of literature; and examples from earlier periods, although not

from the present day, appear to be legitimate texts for study.

Chapter Two

1. For example, before talking to a Canadian small press publisher, I had never heard of anyone anywhere publishing a book simply to encourage the author to move on to some othe more constructive work.
2. *Broken Words: Why five million Canadians are illiterate* (Toronto: Southam Newspaper Group, 1988).
3. J. Horsman, *Something in my mind besides the everyday* (1990).
4. "Women and Literacy" issue, *Canadian Woman Studies / les cahiers de la femme* 9, 3-4 (Fall / Winter 1990).
5. For example, J. Sherman's *What,* which became funded by Explorations at issue 8.
6. F. Davey, "Writers and Publishers in English-Canadian Literature," *Reading Canadian Reading* (1988), p. 90.
7. N. Bissoondath, "A question of belonging," *Globe and Mail,* Jan. 28, 1993.
8. A brief look at the "Language Arts" section in the book catalogue for the Ontario Institute for Studies in Education indicates the range of some of this teaching.
9. For example, the Ontario provincial government funded a Writers-in-Residence program for provincial libraries, from 1985.
10. This quotation and much of the surrounding detail has been taken from correspondence with Bonnie Burnard, who works for the Saskatchewan Arts Board.
11. See. M. Spufford, *Small Books and Pleasant Histories: Popular Fiction and its Readership in Sixteenth Century England* (London: Cambridge UP, 1981), which refers to the sixteenth to seventeenth century period, or the classic if outdated study by R. Altick of nineteenth-century British texts, *The English Common Reader* (Chicago: U of Chicago P, 1957); the conference held at the University of Toronto in April 1990, "Discourse pre-1860," brought together some discussion of the history of Canadian texts; as have the conferences organized by the Research Institute for Comparative Literature at the University of Alberta.
12. The Bibliographical Society of Canada, including for example the work of Patricia Fleming, has been laying the foundations for scholarly work for some time, and has recently generated publications such as *The History of the Book in Canada: A Bibliography* (Halifax, 1993).
13. R. Darnton, following the French scholars LeFebre and Martin, offers an economic system of relationships for British printing in "What is the history of the book?," ed. K. Carpenter, *Books and Society in History*

(1983); and M. Dimic and G. Garstin, following I. Even-Zohar, offer the socio-historical polysystem theory to their Canadian colleagues in "Polysystem Theory," *Problems of Literary Reception,* ed. E. Blodgett and A. Purdy (Edmonton: Research Institute for Comparative Literature, 1988).

14. See for example E. Mandel, "The Ethnic Voice in Canadian Writing," *Figures in a Ground,* ed. D. Bessai and D. Jackel (Saskatoon: Western Producer Prairie Books, 1978); Robert Kroetsch's editorial participation in *Canadian Ethnic Studies*; E. Blodgett, *Configuration: Essays on the Canadian Literatures* (Toronto: ECW Press, 1982); *Contrasts: Comparative Essays on Italian Canadian Writing,* ed. J. Pivato (1985); and *Other Solitudes, Canadian Multicultural Fictions,* ed. L. Hutcheon and M. Richmond (1990).

15. The Department of Multiculturalism has published a number of "Preliminary Surveys" to a variety of immigrant literatures since the late 1980s, including Canadian-Hungarian, Canadian-Italian, and Canadian-Hispanic. Most of the early publications appear to have been edited by M. Batts.

16. F. Caccia outlines some of the various linguistic needs of a community in "The Italian writer and language," trans. M. Leprince, in ed. J. Pivato, *Contrasts: Comparative Essays on Italian Canadian Writing* (1985).

17. In a collection that frequently refers to patterns of urban habitation of immigrant groups, *Two Nations Many Voices,* ed, J. Elliott (Scarborough: Prentice-Hall, 1979), the article by A. Matejko, for example, "Multiculturalism: The Polish-Canadian Case," notes that among the most important reasons for preference for living in an area where most people were of the same ethnic group were "language difficulties," p. 243.

18. Such a need, which became clear to me from a number of personal interviews conducted during August 1989, is formally presented in, for example, J. Black and C. Leithner, "Immigrants and Political Involvement in Canada: The role of the ethnic media," *Canadian Ethnic Studies,* XX, 1 1988.

19. Personal communications from Professor J. Pivato, who was kind enough to spend considerable time with me during a research trip to Canada in 1989, outlining various areas of importance to the development of ethnic literatures in Canada from which some of the immediately following observations are drawn.

20. This of course is a common concern for all small presses, which seem to get into a vicious circle of being funded by the govenment to publish special interest books that major publishers will not pick up, thus establishing themselves as small presses by definition, from which writers

wish to move on.

21. This bibliography was contained in a private paper, but a look at the *Newsletter/Bulletin of the Association of Italian-Canadian Writers,* no. 10 (Sept. 1989), p. 3, provides similar information.

22. 1976 was the year during which Bill 101 making French the only official language of Québec was passed.

23. For example, it is notable that Gail Scott's *Heroine* (1987) acknowledges help from the federal government and from the Ontario Arts Council, as well as from La ministère des affaires culturelles in Québec. Indeed this is partly interesting because it is one of the few English-language books to note such provincial assistance.

24. From personal interview, it was clear that English-language writers in Montreal noted that even the English-language *Gazette* rarely reviewed their work.

25. Quoted from a typescript copy, but published as: L. Leith, "Québec Fiction in English during the 1980s: A Case Study in Marginality," *Québec Studies* 9 (Fall 1989).

26. The procedure is outlined in J. Feather, *The Provincial Book Trade in Eighteenth-Century England* (London: Cambridge UP, 1985), and has been borne out by a number of case studies including L. Hunter, "Publishing and Provincial Taste," in C. Wilson, ed., *Regional Food East and West of the Pennines* (Edinburgh: Edinburgh UP, 1990).

27. There is also a substantial population that is francophone. For an introductory guide to this field see R. Sutherland, "No longer a family affair—Ethnic writers of French Canada," given as a paper at the conference on Canadian Literature in Catania, Italy, 1987.

28. See "After Modernism," in this book.

29. See M. Nourbese Philip, "Gut Issues in Babylon: Racism & Anti-racism in the Arts," *Fuse* XII, 5 (April / May 1989), p. 13.

30. For example, of the few publications about an Aboriginal audience, stocked by the Canadian Periodicals Publishers Association, even fewer appeared to be for that audience.

31. The efforts of Eugene Steinhauer, a Cree, in this area eventually led to the establishment of the Alberta Native Communications Society in 1968, and by 1984 there were 13 native communications societies: see R. Rupert, "Native People, Communications," in *The Canadian Encyclopedia* (Edmonton: Hurtig, 1985), p. 1212.

32. This account is now often given in the prefaces to relevant collections of literature such as *Northern Voices: Inuit Writing in English,* ed. P. Petrone (Toronto: U of Toronto P, 1988), or the series on *Algonquian and Iroquoian Linguistics,* ed. J. Nichols (Winnipeg: Algonquian and

Iroquoian Linguistics).

33. See L. Keeshig-Tobias, "The Magic of Others," in ed. L. Scheier, S. Sheard, and E. Wachtel, *Language in Her Eye* (1990), pp. 173-77.

34. For an account of some similar cultural problems arising in New Zealand with reference to the predominantly oral Maori culture, see D. MacKenzie, "The Sociology of a Text: Orality, Literacy and Print in Early New Zealand," *The Library*, 6th Series, VI, no. 4 (December 1984). B. Godard covers some of this ground in "Voicing Difference: The literary production of native women," in ed. S. Neuman and S. Kamboureli, *A Mazing Space* (1986).

35. See for example accounts of L. Keeshig-Tobias's accusations of subtle racism in the film *Where the Spirit Lives,* made in 1969 by non-Aboriginal K. Leckie yet acted in and supported by many Aboriginal people.

36. Bronwyn Drainie, "And in this corner ... Canadian writers in fighting trim," *Globe and Mail,* Feb. 24, 1990; this article reports on the debates between Kinsella and Wiebe.

37. A matter all too well underlined by the extent to which it has taken over S. Rushdie's *Satanic Verses.*

38. From an interview with J. Emberley who researches Aboriginal writings, and attended the bookfair. She has since written about the incident in *Thresholds of Difference* (1993). Also, now documented in *Telling It,* see footnote 39.

39. This debate, which included Gzowski, Zemans, Bissoondath, Bliss, Keeshig-Tobias, Robertson, Smart, and Wiebe, is reproduced in *Textual Studies in Canada* 2, 1992, pp. 30-48.

40. Edited by Telling It Book Collective (1990).

41. For example, Lee Maracle's *I Am Woman* could not find a commercial publisher and was published by Write-On Press formed specifically for the occasion.

42. This is probably one of the main factors behind the focus on precisely these communities, of the conference on "Literatures of Lesser Diffusion" held by the History of Literature Institution group at the University of Alberta, Edmonton, in April 1987. A description of this conference may be found in *Update* 4 (August 1988).

43. For example see *(f)Lip: a newsletter of feminist innovative writing,* which was not specifically lesbian, but provided a space for women, lesbian and heterosexual, to explore language.

44. Among the better known bookstores are Toronto's and Vancouver's Women's Bookstore, L'Androgyne, Ariel, Little Sisters, Peregrine Books.

45. Press Gang in Vancouver and Ragweed in Prince Edward Island both encourage work from the lesbian community. Press Gang's publicity

leaflet specifically states that it is trying to "de-mystify the printing process"; printing has traditionally been a highly protected trade union activity: see C. Coburn, *Brothers: Male Dominance and Technological Change* (London: Pluto Press, 1983).

46. Most of the following details were taken from personal interview.

47. Ed. M. Silvera, *Fireworks: The Best of Fireweed* (1986).

48. M. Nourbese Philip, "The Disappearing Debate: Or how the discussion of racism has been taken over by the censorship issue," *This Magazine* 23, 2 (July-August 1989).

49. It is this reasoning that seems to lie behind the West Word and East Word workshops generated by the Women and Words / Les femmes et les mots conference held in Vancouver in July 1983; see *in the feminine* (1985). The different approaches taken by the various workshops that have since been held need serious research.

50. The pamphlet "Let's talk about women and literacy" from the Canadian Congress for Learning Opportunities for Women also cites the threat that "men in a learner's life" may feel when she begins to become literate as a major barrier to progress in this area.

51. The group has been quite successful in achieving its aims. Much of this information was gathered for me by Elizabeth Driver, who contributed to the newsletter.

52. These observations are made from issues purchased during the summer and fall of 1989.

53. "Women and Literacy" issue, *Canadian Woman Studies / les Cahiers de la femme* 9, 3-4 (Fall-Winter 1988); all quotations are taken from this issue and page numbers follow in brackets.

54. *The SwiftCurrent Anthology* (1988).

Chapter Three

1. L. Elliott, *Literary Writings by Blacks in Canada*, ed. M.S. Bates (1988), p. 4. See also L. Elliott, ed., *Other Voices: Writings by Blacks in Canada* (1985), which is a literary companion piece to the biobibliographic listing.

2. There is a considerable tradition of writing from the Afro-Canadian community, see for example "Voices out the Whirlwind: The Genesis of Afro-Nova Scotian Literature," by George Elliott Clarke, in *The Atlantic Provinces Book Review* (May 1990). Post-war, the better known voices have included writers such as Austin Clarke and Lillian Allen.

3. See Silvera Makeda, "Immigrant Domestic Workers," *Fireworks: The Best of Fireweed* (Press, 1986), p. 38.

4. See discussion in chapter one of the present book.

5. M. Nourbese Philip is particularly eloquent on this issue. See the "Where they're at" section of "Gut Issues in Babylon: Racism and Anti-Racism in the Arts," *Fuse* XII, 5 (April-May 1989).

6. "Women and Literacy" issue, *Canadian Woman Studies / cahiers de la femme* 9, 3-4 (Fall-Winter 1988).

7. See chapter six of the present book.

8. L. Elliott, as above (1988), p. 5.

9. I am particularly grateful for the help I received from M. Nourbese Philip and the comments offered by Claire Harris on an earlier version of this essay; and I regret that there has been no extended discussion between myself and Dionne Brand, whose visit to the Ilkley Literature Festival in 1993 passed too quickly. The need for friendship among commentators has been put eloquently in M. Lugones and E. Spelman "Have we got a theory for you! Feminist theory, cultural imperialism and the demand for 'The woman's voice'," *Women's Studies Intenational*, Vol 6, No 6 (1983), pp. 573-581.

10. *A Mazing Space,* ed. S. Neuman and S. Kamboureli (1986).

11. C. Harris, "A Matter of Fact," *Imagining Women* (1988).

12. This understanding of "symbol" is taken from George Whalley, *Poetic Process* (1952); Whalley taught at Queen's University in Kingston from the 1950s to the 80s. His influence on generations of Canadian writers is testified to by the very large humber of poems and prose pieces written about and for him.

13. C. Harris, *Fables From the Women's Quarters* (1984).

14. C. Harris, *Translation Into Fiction* (1986), and *Travelling to Find a Remedy* (1986).

15. C. Harris, *The Conception of Winter* (1982).

16. C. Harris, "Against the Poetry of Revenge," *Fireweed* 23 (Summer 1986), p. 16.

17. D. Brand, *Primitive Offensive* (1982).

18. Early poetry also includes *Fore Day Morning* (1976) and a book of children's poetry *Earth Magic* (1980).

19. D. Brand, *Winter Epigrams and Epigrams to Ernesto Cardinal in defence of Claudia* (1983).

20. D. Brand, *Chronicles of the Hostile Sun* (1984).

21. D. Brand, *Sans Souci* (1988).

22. As described in "Organizing Exclusion," *Fireworks,* p. 184.

23. D. Brand and Krisantha Sri Bhaggiyadatta, *Rivers Have Sources Trees Have Roots—Speaking of Racism* (1986).

24. Brand has been carrying out a doctoral thesis on Women's History.

25. See *The Globe and Mail,* September 26, 1989, p. A19, or the pamphlet "P.E.N. Canada Locks Out Writers of Colour," *Vision 21—Canadian Culture in the 21st Century,* 'Multicultural Women Writers of Canada.'

26. M. Nourbese Philip, "The White Soul of Canada," in *Spectacular Failures* (Spring 1991), pp. 63-77.

27. See "Gut Issues ...," as above.

28. *Fireweed* 23, as above, p. 105.

29. M. Nourbese Philip, *Harriet's Daughter* (1988).

30. See M. Philip, "Gut Issues...," as above, p. 13.

31. See M. Philip, "Gut Issues...," as above, and "The Disappearing Debate," *This Magazine* 23,2 (July-August 1989).

32. In *Fireweed* 23, pp. 106-11, and *She Tries Her Tongue, Her Silence Softly Breaks* (1989).

33. In *Fireweed* 23, pp. 112-13.

34. M. Philip, "Burn Sugar," *Imagining Women,* as above.

35. M. Philip, *She Tries Her Tongue, Her Silence Softly Breaks,* p. 15.

36. C. Harris, "Poets in Limbo," as above, p. 121.

Chapter Four

1. TISH was a group of writers, mainly poets, working together in British Columbia during the 1960s. See *Beyond TISH,* ed. D. Barbour (1991).

2. See L. Hutcheon, *The Canadian Postmodern* (Toronto: Oxford UP1988).

3. This has been one of the primary arguments behind the privileging of the oral over the written, from Plato onwards; see L. Hunter "A Rhetoric of Mass Communication" (1990).

4. See L. Hunter. "Remember Frankenstein: Rhetoric and Artificial Intelligence" (1991).

5. B. Godard, "Structuralism/Post-structuralism: Language, Reality, and Canadian Literature" (1987).

6. L. Hunter, "Remember Frankenstein."

7. F. Davey, *Open Letter,* Series 1, 1 (1965), p. 18.

8. F. Davey, *Open Letter,* Series 1, 2 (1966), p. 7.

9. F. Davey, *Open Letter,* Series 1, 4 (1966), p. 24.

10. F. Davey, "More Heat on Daedalus," *Open Letter,* Series 1, 8 (1968), pp. 6-8.

11. L. Hunter, *Modern Allegory and Fantasy* (1989).

12. *Reading Canadian Reading,* p. 127, n. 1.

13. The former article appears in *Reading Canadian Reading* and the latter in *Open Letter,* Series 7, 1 (Spring 1988).

14. See L. Jardine, *Erasmus, Man of Letters: The construction of charisma in*

print (1993).

15. G. Bowering, *Errata* (1988), p. 5.

16. For example, see D. Barbour, *Open Letter,* Series 1, 8 (1968), p. 21.

17. A collection such as *Imaginary Hand* (1988) indicates the extent of this split.

18. G. Bowering, *Craft Slices* (1985), but also in *The Contemporary Canadian Poem Anthology* (Toronto: Coach House, 1984).

19. See the many commentaries in *Craft Slices* on this topic.

Chapter Five

1. In *Open Letter,* Series 8, 4, Summer 1992.

2. A recent summary is provided by A. Karasick, "Tract Marks," *Open Letter,* Series 8, 3, Spring 1992. Karasick tries to make a case for Marxian connections, but at least in the emphases she chooses I see more in common with American culturalism: i.e. cultural not economic production. The TRG papers have been brought together by Talonbooks in S. McCaffery, ed., *Rational Geomancy* (1993).

3. For a longer list see B. Godard, "Canadian? Literary? Theory?" (1992).

4.. E. Mouré, "Poetry, Memory and the Polis," p. 205.

5. G. Scott, "A Feminist at the Carnival" (1990), p. 250.

6. S. Kamboureli, Interview with R. Kroetsch, (1981).

7. Despite for example L. Bersianik, "Aristotle's Lantern," *A Mazing Space,* Kamboureli and Neuman (1986).

8. The tape of the editorial collective is held in the Special Collections section of the National Library of Canada. A much shortened version continuing some of this material is found in the editorial statement made in the first issue of *Tessera,* published as *A Room of One's Own* 8, 4, January 1984.

9. Although some writers clearly show this response operating and document their answer to it. See Libby Scheier in "Chopped Liver," in ed. L. Scheier, S. Sheard, and E. Wachtel, *Language in Her Eye* (1990).

10. Especially essays such as Cixous" "Sorties" and "The Laugh of the Medusa," and Kristeva's "Woman's Time."

11. N. Brossard, *These Our Mothers* (1977).

12. Indeed Brossard was invited to tour the UK courtesy of Cedric May of the University of Birmingham, while I was working at the University of Liverpool in 1978-79.

13. Such as "*Coming to Writing*" or *Vivre l'Orange* by Cixous, and *Speculum of the Other Woman* by Irigaray.

14. This was the argument of Bronwen Wallace as well as Dorothy Livesay

in her comments at the 1984 Longliner's conference on the Canadian long poem (*Open Letter,* Series 6, 2-3: 223-6).

15. L. Lemire Tostevin, *Gyno Text* (1983).

16. B. Warland, *Proper deafinitions, collected theorograms* (1990).

17. See for example M. Perloff and G. Hartley.

18. B. Warland, "the breasts refuse: suffixscript," in Scheier et al (1990).

19. See D. Marlatt in ed. Telling It Collective, *Telling It: women and language across cultures* (1990), p. 12.

20. L. Hunter, *Rhetorical Stance in Modern Literature* (1984), chapter two.

21. As above, chapter three.

22. See the bibliography for much-referred to primary texts, and for widely disseminated secondary commentaries.

23. L. Hunter, *Modern Allegory and Fantasy* (1989).

24. T. Modelski, *Feminism without Women* (1991), p. 162.

25. See M. Whitford, *Luce Irigaray: Philosophy in the Feminine* (1991).

26. T. Modleski, *Feminism without Women,* p. 163.

27. Many commentators have discussed this element; Marchessault uses it to focus her argument about the oppositional in "Is the Dead Author...," as above.

28. See L. Hunter "Artificial Intelligence and Representation," (1993).

29. See bibliography for several commentators on psychoanalysis and feminism.

30. N. Brossard, "Intercepting what's Real," *The Aerial Letter* (1985).

31. N. Brossard, *Picture Theory* (1982).

32. L. Wittgenstein is particularly helpful on this in *Philosophical Investigations* (1953).

33. A. Tanesini, "Whose Language?" (1993).

34. L. Hunter, "Artificial Intelligence and Representation," (1993). See also the work on tacit knowledge by A. Janik and the Swedish Centre for Working Life Studies; or the vocabulary of care, in for example D. Smith, *The Everyday World as Problematic: A Feminist Sociology* (Milton Keynes: Open University Press, 1987).

35. A. Tanesini, "Whose Language?"

36. *Open Letter,* Series 8, 4, Summer 1992.

Chapter Six

1. See E. LaRocque, "Preface," in ed. J. Perreault and S. Vance, *Writing the Circle: Native Women of Western Canada* (1990).

2. Thomas is quoted by D. Marlatt, "Introduction," in ed. The Telling It Book Collective, *Telling It: Women and Language Across Cultures, the*

transformation of a conference (1990), p. 13.

3. I was alerted to this while listening to Liz Stanley speak at a conference on Women and Autobiography, at the University of York, in 1990. Her paper "The knowing because experiencing subject' *Women's Studies International Forum, 16*, 1, 205-115, develops the ideas further.

4. Indeed many women new to writing, whether newly literate or not, turn to autobiography. See M. Humm, "Subjects in English: Auto-biography, women and education" (1989).

5. N. Brossard, "Tender Skin My Mind," trans. Dympna Borowska, in ed. Women and Words Collective, *In the Feminine: Women and words/ Les femmes et les mots* (1983), p. 180; see also the articles in ed. M. Belenky, B. Clinchy, N. Goldberger, J. Tarule, *Women's Ways of Knowing: the Development of Self, Voice*, and Mind (1986), many of which refer to the long history for metaphors of voice and silence in women's writing, such as Tillie Olsen's *Silences* (1965).

6. Liz Stanley speaks eloquently on this relationship between individual self and the collectivity in "Biography as microscope or kaleidoscope? The case of Hannah Cullwick's relationship with Arthur Munby," in ed. D. Farran, S. Scott, and L. Stanley, *Writing Feminist Biography* (1986).

7. Bettina Aptheker, *Tapestries of Life: women's work, women's consciousness, and the meaning of daily experience* (1989), pp. 16-17.

8. There is a growing body of critical work on these other forms of autobiography. For works specifically relating to women's autobiography, see ed. E. Jelinek, *Women's Autobiography: Essays in Criticism* (London: Indiana UP, 1980); ed. S. Benstock, *The Private Self: Theory and Practice of Women's Autobiographical Writings* (1988); L. Stanley, *The autobiographical I: the Theory and practice of feminist auto/biography* (1992), and ed. S. Neuman, *Autobiography and Questions of Gender* (1992).

9. See L. Hunter, "Writing, Literature and Ideology: Institutions and the making of a Canadian canon," in ed. P. Easingwood, K. Gross, W. Klooss, *Probing Canadian Culture* (Augsburg: AV Verlag, 1991); see also L. Hunter, "After Modernism: The writings of Dionne Brand, Claire Harris, Marlene Philip," in *University of Toronto Quarterly*, Winter 1993; and L. Hunter, "Alternative Publishing in Canada," in *Difference and Community* (Rodopki 1996).

10. As J. Horsman points out in *Something on my mind besides the everyday, women and literacy* (1990), there are many other structures of communication mediated outside of the literate, but Canadian culture on the whole validates social acceptability through literacy.

11. See P. Steel *The Autobiographical Passion: Studies in the Self on*

Show (1989); Liz Stanley spoke directly on this topic at the conference on autobiography held in York, January 1991.

12. For example, see many "public man" autobiographies that specifically write out intimacy, like that of Winston Churchill.

13. Alongside the flowering of Aboriginal writing in North America is an attendant critical commentary. See for example G. Bataille, "Transformation of Tradition: Autobiographical Works by American Indian Women" (1983); B. Godard, "Talking about ourselves: Native women's narratives," (1985), and "Voicing Difference: the literary production of native women," in ed. S. Neuman and S. Kamboureli, *A Mazing Space: Writing Canadian Women Writing* (1986); A. Krupat, *The Voice in the Margin: Native American Literature and the Canon* (1989); and W. H. New, "Editorial: Learning to Listen," (1990). A helpful text, although one among many others, for its outline of the issues surrounding the media of oral and written accounts of Aboriginal texts is in ed. J. Sherzer and A.C. Woodbury, *Native American Discourse: Poetics and Rhetoric* (1987).

14. These texts have had no critical attention from British critics.

15. G. Nowell-Smith (1977); and C. Gledhill "The Melodramatic Field: An investigation" in ed. C. Gledhill *Home is Where the Heart is: Studies in Melodrama and the Woman's Film* (1987).

16. For just one recent discussion of shame, in the context of guilt, see J. Carroll, *Guilt: The grey eminence behind character, history and culture* (1985).

17. See F. Nietzsche, *The Genealogy of Morals: A polemic* (London: Foulis, 1913), particularly "What is the meaning of ascetic ideals?'. I owe the lead to J.O. Thompson on this one.

18. Sky Lee, "Telling It: Women and Anger Across Cultures," in Telling It Book Colective, p. 185.

19. Indeed the physical unease arising from embarrassment is part of an important yet undiscussed area for literary studies, of psycho-physiological response. See C. Ricks, *Keats and Embarrassment* (1974), for comments on the nineteenth-century alliance between embarrassment and the body.

20. M. Campbell, *Halfbreed* (1983) originally published by McClelland and Stewart, 1973.

21. In "Maria Campbell, Interview," in D. Hillis, ed., *Plainspeaking: Interviews with Saskatchewan Writers,* (Regina: Cocteau Books, 1988), p. 46.

22. In "Maria Campbell, Interview," as above.

23. This account is noted by B. Godard in "Voicing difference," *A Mazing*

Space, ed. S. Kamboureli and S. Neuman (1986), p. 89, where Godard quotes Campbell from a tape of the Women and Words conference in Vancouver, 1983.

24. B. Culleton, *In Search of April Raintree* (1987), originally published 1983.

25. In "Beatrice Culleton," ed. A. Garrod, *Speaking for Myself: Canadian Writers in Interview* (St. John's Breakwater, 1986), p. 89.

26. "Beatrice Culleton," as above, p. 90.

27. In "Maria Campbell, Interview," as above, p. 56.

28. "Ethnicity and Identity: The question of one's literary passport," in ed. J. Balan, *Identifications: Ethnicity and the writer in Canada* (Edmonton: The Institute of Ukrainian Studies, 1982, p. 86.

29. J. Armstrong, *Slash* (1988), originally published 1985.

30. At the point of submission of this script, and too late to engage with properly, J. Emberley's *Thresholds of Difference* (1993) goes some way to providing a vocabulary for working on this difficulty.

31. The debate is theorietically carried out between the Baudrillardians and the neo-Frankfurt School writers.

32. Many Canadian critics have remarked on the "absent father" in older Canadian literature; the "separation" topos is generated by different economic and social patterns.

33. For example, see T. Morrison, *Beloved,* or M. Angelou, *I Know Why the Caged Bird Sings.*

34. R. O'Rourke with J. Mace, *Versions and Variety* (1992).

35. For example, Carolyn Steedman makes use of fairy tale in her skilful bio/autobiography *Landscape for a Good Woman: A story of two lives* (London: Virago, 1986).

36. E. Danica, *Don't: A Woman's Word* (1990, first published 1988).

37. A rather different approach to a similar issue is taken by L. Alcoff and L. Gray, "Survivor Discourse: Transgression or recuperation?" (1993). See also L. Warley, "Inhabiting Contradiction: The female subject in *Don't: A Woman's Word*" (1992).

38. Another account of the worry that a reader's position toward this text evokes may be found in J. Williamson, "'I Peel Myself out of My Own Skin': Reading *Don't: A Woman's Word,*" in ed. Marlene Kadar, *Essays on Life Writing: From Genre to Critical Practice* (1992).

39. See the introduction to *Don't* by Peter Gzowski for an account of the support that the writer received from the media subsequent to the publication of the book.

40. J. Dumas, *Madeleine and the Angel* (1989).

41. "Women and Literacy," *Canadian Women's Studies/Cahiers de la*

Femme, Fall / Winter 1988, pp. 57-60.

42. R. Dorion, *My Name is Rose* (1987).

43. M. di Michele, *Luminous Emergencies* (1990), pp. 3-8.

Chapter Seven

1. See among others G. Spivak, *In Other Worlds* (1987), and E. Said, *Orientalism* (1978).

2. F. Fanon is a central focus for the psychoanalytic emphasis of this kind of analysis, in for example *Black Skin, White Masks* (New York: Grove Press, 1967/1955); it has been elaborated and extended in the work of H. Bhabha, in for example "The other question...," *Screen*, 24, 6 (1983), in "Interrogating Identity," and in contributions to *Nation and Narration* (London: Routledge, 1990) edited by Bhabha. See also, H. Gates ed., *"Race," writing, and difference* (London: U of Chicago P, 1986); and R. Young, *White Mythologies* (London: Routledge, 1991).

3. See J. Dunning *et al,* "The Theory of International Production: Some Historical Antecedents," in ed. Hertner and Jones, *Multinationals: Theory and History* (Aldershot: Gower, 1987). This has recently and strikingly been seen to be the case by the NGOs in South Africa and Canada.

4. This has been a central concern for rhetoric where techniques are inexorably contextualized; this particular division has dominated western interpretations of power since Plato. See for example L. Hunter, "McLuhan's *From Cliché to Archetype.*"

5. For rather different accounts of this shift, see E. Gellner "Nationalism and the two forms of cohesion in complex societies," in *Proceedings of the British Academy LXVIII* (London: U of Chicago P, 1982), and J. Kristeva, "Woman's Time," trans. A. Jardine and H. Blake, in eds N. Keohane, M. Rosaldo and B. Gelpin, *Feminist Theory: A Critique of Ideology* (Brighton: Harvester, 1982/1976).

6. See S. Walters, "Community Organisations and NGOs in South Africa," paper given at the conference "Women in Literacy and Development," University of Warwick, 1993

7. R. Rorty has been one of the anxious worriers about this, see his *Contingency, Irony, and Solidarity* (1989); see also commentary on the anxiety by Z. Bauman, *Modernity and Ambivalence* (London: Polity, 1990).

8. On games resulting from the postmodern, see L. Hunter, *Rhetorical Stance in Modern Literature* (1984), and "Remember Frankenstein," *Rhetorica IX* 4 (Autumn, 1991); for a clear account of where postmodernism fails see L. Weir, "Normalizing the Subject" (1991).

9. For commentaries against and for this position see D. Beetham, *The Legitimation of Power* (1991), G. Gadamer, *Reason in the age of science*, trans. F. G. Lawrence (1976), and R. Rorty, *Objectivity, Relativism, and Truth*, Philosophical Papers vol 1 (1991).

10. This problematic lies at the heart of the attempts at theory from J. Baudrillard, who writes as though the artificiality of ideology is only recently recognized. This of course is a result of being caught inside an ideology that claims natural and referential representation.

11. P. Rowe and V. Schelling speak of the writing G. G. Marquez and many others doing this for Latin American countries; in Canada the foremost early example is Leonard Cohen's *Beautiful Losers* (1966), the ideological content of which remains of immediate importance to the 1990s.

12. Every culture and every age has its own version of memory; some of these are presented in the intriguing book by S. Rose, *The Making of Memory* (1992). S. Freud has of course dominated many western twentieth century metaphors, and his writing is full of work on memory, amnesia and dream; see among others *The Psychopathology of Everyday Life*, trans. A. Tyson, Gen ed. J. Strachey (1960), *The Ego and the Id*, trans. J. Riviere, rev. and ed. J. Strachey (1962), and *Civilization and its Discontents*, trans. J. Riviere (1955). For recent example of how cognitive psychology and other fields have been trying to develop new metaphors, see J. Greene, *Memory, Thinking and Language* (1987) or M. Reiser, *Memory in Mind and Brain* (1990).

13. P. Connerton, in *How Societies Remember* (1989), uses this analysis from Freud as a basis for his development of social memory.

14. See the popular book by F. Jameson, *The Political Unconscious* (London: Routledge, 1981) for a description of how this may work.

15. It has been suggested that societies achieve cohesiveness partly by way of their ability to habitualize, to forget the interpretative basis for agreement and turn it into bodily commemoration. But it is necessary to make a distinction between the bodily practice of tacit knowledge, and habit. P. Connerton, as above, p. 102.

16. For a discussion of this see L. Hunter, "Artificial Intelligence and Representation" (1993).

17. See L. Hunter, *Modern Allegory and Fantasy* (1989) for a compilation of readings of recent discussions on fantasy and narcissism.

18. Loss of memory was a central anxiety for commentators on the new medium of writing and later of print; for a background on this concern, see L. Hunter, "A Rhetoric of Mass Communication," in ed. R. L. Enos, *Orality and Written Communication* (Sage, 1990).

19. The primary text for this commentary is M. McLuhan, *The Gutenberg Galaxy* (1961). More recent writers extending his work include E. Eisenstein, *Five Hundred Years of Printing* (Cambridge: Cambridge U Press, 1978); B. Anderson, *Imagined Communities* (London: Verso, 1983); and S. During, "Postmodernism or post-colonialism today," *Textual Practice* 1:1 (1987), pp. 32-47.

20. "Writing the body" has been a focus for much feminist theory; for a clear if challenging account see the essays in H. Cixous, "*Coming to Writing*" *and other essays*, ed. D. Jenson, intro S. Suleiman, trans. S. Cornell (Cambridge Mass: Harvard UP, 1988). See also N. Brossard, *French Kiss* trans. P. Claxton (1986) and *The Aerial Letter* trans. M. Wildeman (1988).

Chapter Eight

1. These are often articulated in a manner close to that of J. Habermas, for example *The Philosophical Discourse of Modernity* (1987).

2. Most diligently pursued by Althusser, and known most popularly through his influential essay "Ideology and Ideological State Apparatuses" (1970); for a helpful and intelligent reading of this contentious paper see D. Macdonell, *Theories of Discourse* (1986).

3. T. Eagleton describes capitalist forgetting in terms almost identical to Freud's repetition-compulsion, in "Nationalism: Irony and Commitment," in *Nationalism, Colonialism and Literature,* intro. S. Deane (1990).

4. For detailed case study of this movement, see W. Rowe and V. Schelling, *Memory and Modernity* (1991).

5. There are many texts to which one could turn, but see for example the commentaries on women and language in J. Lacan, *Ecrits,* trans. A. Sheridan (1977).

6. P. Rowe and V. Schelling in *Memory and Modernity* speak about the popular accessibility in the Latin American context, as a necessary political move.

7. This effect often incenses critics to the point where they condemn Atwood's writing as anti-feminist propaganda; see for example the discussion of this issue in J. LeBihan's "Margaret Atwood's Feminist(?) Futures(?)," in ed. C. Howells and L. Hunter, *Narrative Strategies in Canadian Literature* (1991.

8. L. Leith comments on the phenomenon of genre writing among English-language writers in Québec in "Québec Fiction in English during the 1980s," *Québec Studies* 9 (Fall 1989).

9. The roll-call of names here could be huge, suffice it to mention G.K. Chesterton, Alain Robbe-Grillet, and George Bowering.

10. This procedure is described in George Orwell's *Nineteen Eighty-Four,* and is documented widely in terms of Nazi Germany in the 1930s and 40s as well as in Latin America in P. Rowse and V. Schelling, cited above.

11. For an elaboration on "whole-books" see A. Gurr, "Short Fictions and Whole-Books," in ed. C. Howells and L. Hunter (1991).

12. See for example R. Rorty, as above (1991). p. 25.

13. E. Gellner speaks convincingly about this cultural construction; although taken to task by J. Kellas, in *The Politics of Nationalism and Ethnicity* (1991) which favours a socio-biological interpretation, this argument proceeds by completely ignoring issues of rhetoric and representation.

Chapter Nine

1. Feminist theorists working from a background of race and gender, in particular, have contributed a substantial vocabulary for this difference-closeness discussion; see bell hooks, "Sisterhood," *Feminist Review* 24 (1986) and Bettina Aptheker, *Tapestries of Life: women's work, women's consciousness, and the meanings of daily experience* (1989).

2. This difficulty of structural distinction is also found in the overlap between studies of fantasy and allegory; see L. Hunter, *Modern Fantasy and Allegory.*

3. R. Rorty takes this as a positive feature, describing the world as a group of clubs around a bazaar; see Rorty, *Objectivity, Relativity, and Truth,* p. 209, and *Essays on Heidegger and Others*; and J. Kellas takes it for granted that club culture is a positive metaphor for nationalism, *The Politics of Nationalism and Ethnicity* (1991).

4. A Giddens, *A Contemporary Critique of Historical Materialism* (1981), p. 5.

5. For an analysis of the argumentative structure technology can pemit to discourse, see L. Hunter, "Remember Frankenstein: Rhetoric and artificial intelligence."

6. See in particular P. Rowe and V. Schelling, *Memory and Modernity.*

7. This literature derives from a focus on the rhetoric of the Nazi party during the 1930s and 40s, and fed into studies on advertising and general propaganda in the early developments of Communications Studies: the two being linked by the use of mass media technology to extend the narrative persuasions of nationalism into the authoritarian persuasions of totalitarianism.

8. This principle is the basis for the classical argument that education in rhetoric is necessary to avoid violence. See L. Hunter, *Rhetorical Stance in Modern Literature.*

9. Both B. Anderson and E. Gellner describe this move, albeit from different angles, in, respectively *Imagined Communities* and *Nations and Nationalism.*

10. The forgetting, or amnesia, necessary to successful nationalism is discussed by nearly all the recent commentators on the topic from Gellner (1982, 1983) and Anderson (1983), to T. Eagleton (1990a), to Kellas (1991). George Orwell theorized the strategy quite precsiely in *Nineteen Eighty-Four* (1948).

11. George Bowering's *Burning Water* (1980) is an excellent example of the concurrence of poststructural writing with postcolonial concerns. In many ways *The Empire Writes Back,* ed. B. Ashcroft, G. Griffiths, and H. Tiffin (London: Routledge, 1989), could be said to focus precisely on this dilemma.

12. Homi Bhaba, among others, has elaborated Fanon's theoretical concerns with identity and psychoanalysis and colonialism, in for example *Nation and Narration.*

13. G. Gadamer, *Reason in the Age of Science* (1981), lays out this position, and it has been the basis for a substantial debate in the 1980s among political theorists. R. Rorty denies that it is a problem; and Frank Davey, along with others such as J. Habermas, has come to articulate its drawbacks: see *Post-national Arguments* (1994), part of which was given as a paper, "The Canadas of Anglophone-Canadian Fiction 1967-1990," at the University of Leeds conference, *Difference and Community,* April 1992.

14. See also *Past the Last Post,* ed. I. Adam and H. Tiffin (Calgary: U of Calgary P).

15. See A. Aijaz, *In Theory* (1992) for a revisioning of 'third-world' as a category. For an interesting positioning of 'third-world' within feminism, see ed. C.T. Mohanty, A. Russo, and L. Torres, *Third World Women and the Politics of Feminism* (1991).

16. See, for example, G. Spivak, *In Other Worlds* (1987), and *The Post-colonial Critic: Interviews* (1990).

17. N. Ricci discusses this problem in "Questioning Ethnicity," *Alphabet City: Nations and Nationalism* 2 (Toronto 1992); see also Z. Bauman, *Modernity and Ambivalence* (Polity, 1990).

18. L. Cohen, *Beautiful Losers* (1966) is the classic Canadian text on this dilemma.

19. See. F. Jameson's shift from utopia in *The Political Unconscious* (1981)

to conspiracy in *Postmodernism, Or, The Cultural Logic of Late Capitalism* (1991); see also T. Eagleton on good and bad utopias in "Nationalism, Irony and Commitment" (1990).

20. The essays in Roy Miki's collection of commentaries on Nichol's work, *Tracing the Paths* (1988) illustrate a continual movement toward story and topos despite the ostensible focus on the way that Nichol's writing resists story.

21. For one account see R. Miki's "Reading ≠ Writing the Martyrology," in Miki, ed., *Tracing the Paths* (1988).

22. See the editor I. Niechoda's comments on the concluding leaves of *Gifts.*

23. For an analysis of club culture and the use of its rhetoric in Nazi Germany, see J. Huizinga, *Homo Ludens* (1944).

24. R. Rorty, "On Ethnocentrism: A Reply to Clifford Geertz," in *Objectivity, Relativism, and Truth* (1991), p. 209.

25. This movement, as many commentators have noted, is taken from a reading of Gertrude Stein.

26. For example, J. Baudrillard seems to have decided to ignore that the entire tradition of poetics since the Renaissance has been precisely the place where people discuss the difficulties and limitations of representative systems.

27. For an extensive list of Nichol's devices, see Miki, ed., *Tracing the Paths* (1988), particularly jw Curry, "passion for the Passional: a bibliography of *The Martyrology.*"

28. He explains this on the very last leaves of the book, which could imply that he thought readers would be well-enough acquainted with book conventions that they would look there for help, or that he assumed that since readers would read the book more than once they'd be bound to come across the note at some point. I have met students who, because they only read once, have felt enormously cheated by the note being put at the back.

29. P. Connerton, in *How Societies Remember* (1989), pursues a similar argument about social memory and the body. However Connerton argues that societies use the body to habituate themselves to certain grounds that they do not actively want to remember and negotiate, whereas Nichol is focusing on precisely the opposite: how societies can renegotiate their validity through individuals attending to their body behaviour and drawing these assumptions back from the habitual.

30. Although it has associations with Red Deer College in Alberta, which provides writer's space.

31. Wilson Harris, Third Ravenscroft Lecture, University of Leeds, February

1992.

32. See W. Benjamin, *The Origins of German Tragic Drama,* trans. J. Osborne (London, 1977), p. 178. This concept of language as "ruins" is further discussed in L. Hunter, *Modern Allegory and Fantasy* (1988).

33. This fertile structure for family relations is discussed by Terence Cave in *Recognitions* (London: Oxford, 1988).

34. This is a problem for a number of postmodern commentators such as R. Rorty, who do not understand that irony is yet another club—or they do understand this, but fail to comprehend the inequities of power inherent in club culture; for another, tougher analysis see C. Norris, *What's Wrong with Postmodernism* (London: Harvester, 1988).

35. See both R. Kroetsch, *Labyrinths of Voice,* ed. S. Neuman and R. Wilson (1982) and *The Lovely Treachery of Words* (1989).

36. *The Puppeteer* (1992) however does rather different things with approaches to sexuality. See L. Hunter, "Robert Kroetsch's *The Puppeteer:* Being wedded to the text," *Open Letter,* Series 9, 5-6 (1996).

37. The circle of melancholy, paranoia, cynicism, an narcissism that mark out postmodernism's self-reflection are illustrated in F. Jameson's *Postmodernism* (1991).

38. D. Marlatt, *Salvage* (1992), p. 9.

39. This has been a preoccupation of feminist theorists for much of the 1960s-80s, but some writers now seem to be finding alternatives. See earlier chapter on "sexual alternatives."

BIBLIOGRAPHY

Aijaz, Ahmad (1992). *In Theory: Classes, Nations, Literatures.* London: Verso.

Alcoff, L. and L. Gray (1993). "Survivor Discourse: Transgression or Recuperation?" in *Signs: Journal of Women in Culture and Society 18*, 2 (Winter).

Altick, R. (1957). *The English Common Reader.* Chicago: U Chicago P.

Anderson, Benedict (1983). *Imagined Communities: Reflections on the Origin and Spread of Nationalism.* London: Verso, 1991.

Andrews, B. (1979). "Writing Social Work and Political Practice," *LANGUAGE 2*, 9/10 (October).

Aptheker, B. (1989). *Tapestries of Life: women's work, women's consciousness, and the meaning of daily experience.* Amherst: U Massachusetts P.

Armstrong, J. (1985). *Slash.* Penticton: Theytus, 1988.

Association of Italian-Canadian Writers, *Newsletter/Bulletin of the Association of Italian-Canadian Writers.*

Atwood, M. (1966). *The Circle Game.* Toronto: Anansi.

_____ (1985). *The Handmaid's Tale.* London: Jonathan Cape, 1986.

_____ (1988). *Cat's Eye.* London: Virago, 1990.

Barbour, D., ed. (1991). *Beyond TISH.* Edmonton: NeWest and Vancouver: West Coast Line.

Bataille, G. (1983). "Transformation of Tradition: Autobiographical Works by American Indian Women," in P. Gunn Allen, ed., *Studies in American Indian Literature: Critical Essays and Course Designs.* New York: Modern Languages Association.

Bayard, C. (1989). *The New Poetics in Canada and Quebec: from concretism to post-modernism.* London: Toronto UP.

Beetham, David (1991). *The Legitimation of Power.* London, Macmillan.

Belenky, M. and B. Clinchy, N. Goldberger, J. Tarule, ed. (1986). *Women's Ways of Knowing: the Development of Self, Voice and Mind.* New York: Basic Books.

Belsey, C. and J. Moore, ed. (1989). *The Feminist Reader: Essays in gender and the politics of literary criticism.* London: Macmillan.

Bersianik, L. (1986) "Aristotle's Lantern," in S. Neuman and S. Kamboureli.

Benstock, S. ed. (1988). *The Private Self: Theory and Practice of Women's Autobiographical Writings.* London: U North Carolina P.

Bhabha, Homi (1983). "The other question...," in *Screen* 24, 6: 18-36.

_____ "Interrogating Identity," *Identity Documents* 6: 5-11.

_____ (1990). *Nation and Narration.* London: Routledge.

Bibliographical Society of Canada (1993). *The History of the Book in Canada: A Bibliography.* Halifax.

Bissoondath, N. (1993). "A question of belonging," *Globe and Mail*, Thurs. Jan. 28.

Bissoondath, N. et al (1992). *Textual Studies in Canada* 2: 30-48.

Black, J. and C. Leithner (1988). "Immigrants and Political Involvement in Canada: The role of the ethnic media," *Canadian Ethnic Studies, XX,* 1.

Blumberg, M. (1992). "Rereading Gail Scott's *Heroine*," *Open Letter*, Series 8, 2 (Winter): 57-69.

Book Development Council (1989). *Challenged Book List.* Toronto: Book Development Council, III: 1-6.

Bowering, G. (1974). *At War with the US.* Vancouver: Talonbooks.

_____ (1977). *A Short Sad book.* Vancouver: Talonbooks.

_____ (1980). *Burning Water.* Don Mills, Musson.

_____ (1984). *Kerrisdale Elegies* Toronto: Coach House P.

_____ (1985). *Craft Slices.* Toronto: Oberon.

_____ (1987). *Caprice.* Penguin, Viking.

_____ (1988). *Errata.* Red Deer: Red Deer College P.

_____ (1988). *Imaginary Hand.* Edmonton: NeWest.

Brand, D. (1982). *Primitive Offensive.* Toronto: Williams-Wallace.

_____ (1983). *Winter Epigrams and Epigrams to Ernesto Cardenal in defence of Claudia.* Toronto: Williams-Wallace.

_____ (1984). *Chronicles of the Hostile Sun.* Toronto: Williams-Wallace.

_____ (1986). "Organizing exclusion," in S. Makeda.

_____ (1988). *Sans Souci.* Stratford: Williams-Wallace.

Brand D. and Krisantha Sri Bhaggiyadatta (1986). *Rivers Have Sources Trees Have Roots—Speaking of Racism.* Toronto: Cross Cultural Communications Centre.

Brossard, N. (1974). *Daydream Mechanics*, trans. L. Shouldice. Toronto: Coach House, 1980.

_____ (1977). *These our Mothers*, trans. B. Godard. Toronto: Coach House, 1983.

_____ (1980a). *Lovhers*, trans. B. Godard. Montreal: Guernica, 1986.

_____ (1980b). *Surfaces of Sense*, trans. F. Strachan. Toronto: Coach House, 1989.

_____ (1982). *Picture Theory*, trans. B. Godard. Montreal: Guernica, 1991.

_____ "Tender Skin My Mind," trans. Dypna Borowska, in *In the Feminine.*

_____ (1985). *The Aerial Letter*, trans. M. Wildeman. Toronto: The Women's Press, 1988.

_____ (1974). *French Kiss*, trans. P. Claxton. Toronto: Coach House, 1986.

_____ (1987) *Mauve Desert*, trans. S. de Lotbinière-Harwood. Toronto: Coach House, 1990.

Butling, Pauline (1988). "bpNichol's Gestures in Book 6 Books" in Miki (1988).

Caccia, F. (1985). "The Italian writer and language," trans. M. Leprine, in J. Pivato.

Campbell, M. (1973). *Halfbreed.* Halifax: Goodread Biographies, 1983.

_____ (1982). "Ethnicity and Identity: The question of one's literary passport," in ed. J. Balan, *Identifications: Ethnicity and the Writer in Canada.* Edmonton: The Canadian Institute of Ukrainian Studies.

_____ (1988). "Maria Campbell, Interview," *Plainspeaking: Interviews with Saskatchewan writers*, ed. Doris Hillis. Regina: Cocteau Books.

The Canadian Encyclopedia (1985). Edmonton: Hurtig.

Canadian Woman Studies/les cahiers de la femme (1988), "Women & Literacy" issue, 9, 3&4 (Fall/Winter).

Carroll, J. (1985). *Guilt: The grey eminence behind character, history and culture.* London: Routledge.

Casson, Mark (1986). "General Theories of Multinational Enterprise," in Hertner and Jones.

Cheyette, B. (1993). *The Image of the Jew in Modern Literature* Cambridge UP.

Cixous, H. (1979). *L'Heure de Clarice Lispector Precede de Vivre l'Orange.* Paris: des femmes.

_____ (1988). *"Coming to writing" and other essays*, ed. D. Jenson, intro S. Suleiman, trans. S. Cornell. Cambridge Mass: Harvard UP.

_____ (1991). *"Coming to writing" and other essays*, ed. D. Jenson Cambridge: Harvard UP.

Cixous, H. and C. Clement (1986). *The Newly Born Woman*, trans. B. Wing. Manchester: U Manchester P.

Clayton, M. (1989). *The Story of Anthology.* Oxford: Ph.D. thesis.

Coburn, C. (1983). *Brothers: Male Dominance and Technological Change.* London: Pluto Press.

Connerton, P. (1989). *How Societies Remember.* Cambridge: Cambridge UP.

Culleton, B. (1987). *In Search of April Raintree.* Winnipeg: Pemmican.

_____ (1986). "Beatrice Culleton," ed. A. Garrod, *Speaking for Myself: Canadian Writers in Interview.* St. John's: Breakwater.

Curry, jw. (1988). "passion for the Passional: a bibliography of *The Martyrology*," in Miki (1988).

Dagg, A. (1986). *The 50% Solution: Why should women pay for men's culture.* Waterloo: Otter Press.

Danica, E. (1988). *Don't: A Woman's Word.* Toronto: McClelland & Stewart, 1990.

Darnton, R. (1983). "What is the history of the book?," ed. K. Carpenter, *Books and Society in History.*

Davey, F. (1972). *King of Swords.* Vancouver: Talonbooks.

_____ (1973). *The Clallam.* Vancouver: Talonbooks.

_____ (1974). *From There to Here.* Erin, Ont: P Porcepic.

_____ (1976). "Surviving the Paraphrase," *Surviving the Paraphrase* Winnipeg: Turnstone Press, 1984.

_____ (1984). *Edward and Patricia* (Toronto: Coach House P)

_____ (1987). *The Louis Riel Organ and Piano Company.* Winnipeg: Turnstone.

_____ (1988). *Post Card Translations.* Toronto: Underwhich Editions.

_____ (1988b). *Reading Canadian Reading.* Winnipeg: Turnstone.

_____ (1988c). "Writers and Publishers in English-Canadian literature," in Davey 1988b.

_____ (1990). "Critical Response I," *Critical Inquiry, 16* (Spring): 672-681.

_____ (1991). *Popular Narratives.* Vancouver: Talonbooks.

_____ (1993). *Post-national Arguments: The politics of the Anglo-phone-Canadian novel since 1967.* Toronto: U of Toronto P.

_____ (1994). *Canadian Literary Power.* Edmonton: NeWest.

De Lauretis, T. (1987). *Technologies of Gender.* London: Macmillan.

Dessick. J. (1986). *Doctoral Research on Canada and Canadians* Ottawa: National Library of Canada.

Dimic, M. and G. Garstin (1988). "Polysystem Theory," in *Problems of Literary Reception,* ed. E. Blodgett and A. Purdy. Edmonton: Research Institute for Comparative Literature.

di Michele, M. (1990). *Luminous Emergencies.* Toronto: McClelland & Stewart.

Drainie, B. (1990). "And in this corner ... Canadian writers in fighting trim," *Globe and Mail,* Saturday, February 24.

Doiron, R. (1987). *My Name is Rose.* Toronto: East End Literacy Press.

Dumas, J. (1989). *Madeleine and the Angel.* Saskatoon: Fifth House.

Eagleton, Terry, F. Jameson and E. Said (1990). *Nationalism, Colonialism and Literature,* intro S. Deane. Minneapolis: U Minnesota P.

Eagleton, Terry (1990). "Nationalism: irony and commitment," in T. Eagleton et al 1990.

Elliott, J. (1979). *Two Nations Many Voices.* Scarborough: Prentice-Hall.

Elliott, L. ed. (1985). *Other Voices: Writings by Blacks in Canada.* Toronto: Williams-Wallace.

_____ (1988). *Literary Writings by Blacks in Canada,* ed. M. Batts. Ottawa: Department of Multiculturalism.

Elliott Clarke, G. (1990). "Voices out of the Whirlwind: The Genesis of Afro-Nova Scotian Literature," in *The Atlantic Provinces Book Review* (May).

Emberley, J. (1993). *Thresholds of Difference.* Toronto: U Toronto P.

Fanon, F. (1955). *Black Skin, White Masks.* New York: Grove Press, 1967.

Farran, D., S. Scott, and L. Stanley ed. (1986). *Writing Feminist Biography.* Manchester: U Manchester P.

Feather, J. (1985). *The Provincial Book Trade in Eighteenth-Century England.* London: Cambridge UP.

Felman, S. (1987). *Jacques Lacan and the Adventure of Insight.* London: Harvard UP.

Flower MacCannell, J. (1986). *Figuring Lacan: Criticism and the Cultural Unconscious.* London: Croom Helm.

Foucault, M. (1970). *The Order of Things.* London: Tavistock.

_____ (1972). *The Archaeology of Knowledge.* New York: Harper & Row.

_____ (1976). *Language, Counter-Memory, Practice,* ed. D. Bouchard. Ithaca: Cornell UP, 1979.

Freud, S. (1902). *The Psychopathology of Everyday Life*, trans. A. Tyson, gen ed. J. Strachey. London: Ernest Benn, 1960.

_____ (1919). "Das Unheimliche," *The Standard edition of the complete psychological works of Sigmund Freud*, trans. J. Strachey. Vol XVII London: The Hogarth Press, 1955.

_____ (1920). *Beyond the pleasure principle*, trans. J. Strachey. London, 1961.

_____ (1927). *The Ego and the Id*, trans. J. Riviere, rev. and ed. J. Strachey. London: The Hogarth Press and the Institute of Psycho-analysis, 1962.

_____ (1930). *Civilization and its Discontents*, trans. J. Riviere. London: The Hogarth Press and the Institute of Psycho-analysis, 1955.

Gadamer, G. (1976). *Reason in the age of science*, trans. F. G. Lawrence London: MIT Press, 1981.

Gallop, J. (1982). *Feminism and psychoanalysis: The Daughter's Seduction.* London: Macmillan.

Gates, H., ed. (1986). *"Race," Writing, and Difference.* London: U of Chicago P.

Gellner, E. (1982). "Nationalism and the two forms of cohesion in complex societies," in *Proceedings of the British Academy* LXVII. London: Oxford UP, 1983.

_____ (1983). *Nations and Nationalism.* Oxford: Blackwell.

Giddens, A. (1981). *A Contemporary Critique of Historical Materialism.* Aldershot: Gower Publishing Co.

Gledhill, C. ed. (1987). *Home is Where the Heart is: Studies in Melodrama and the Woman's Film.* British Film Institute.

Godard, B. (1985). "Talking about ourselves: Native women's narratives," *CRIAW paper* 11. Ottawa: CRIAW.

____ (1986). "Voicing difference: The literary production of native women," in Neuman and Kamboureli.

____ (1987). "Structuralism/Post-Structuralism: Language, Reality and Canadian Literature," in Moss.

____ (1992). "Canadian? Literary? Theory?," *Open Letter*, Series 8, 3 (Spring): 5-27.

Gray, J. (1956). "Book Publishing," in Whalley, *Writing in Canada.* Toronto: Macmillan.

Green, G. and C. Kahn, ed. (1985). *Making a Difference: Feminist literary criticism.* London: Methuen.

Greene, J. (1987). *Memory, Thinking and Language.* London: Methuen.

Grosz, E. (1990). *Jacques Lacan: A feminist introduction.* London: Routledge.

Gurr, A. (1991). "Short Fictions and Whole-Books," in Howells and Hunter 1991.

Habermas, J. (1987). *The Philosophical Discourse of Modernity.* Polity.

Harris, C. (1984). *Fables From the Women's Quarters.* Toronto: Williams-Wallace.

____ (1986). *Translation into Fiction.* Fredericton: Fiddlehead & Goose Lane.

____ (1986b). "Against the Poetry of Revenge," *Fireweed*, 23 (Summer).

____ (1986c). *Travelling to Find a Remedy.* Fredericton: Fiddlehead & Goose Lane.

____ (1988). "A Matter of Fact," *Imagining Women.* Toronto: The Women's Press.

____ (1988b). *The Conception of Winter.* Stratford: Williams-Wallace.

____ (1992). *Drawing down a Daughter.* Fredericton: Goose Lane Editions.

Hartley, G. (1989). *Textual Politics and the Language poets.* Bloomington: Indiana UP.

Hertner, P. and G. Jones, ed. (1986). *Multinationals: Theory and History.* Aldershot: Gower.

Horsman, J. (1990). *Something in my Mind Besides the Everyday.* Toronto: The Women's Press.

Howells, C. A. (1987). *Private and Fictional Words.* London: Methuen.

Howells, C. and L. Hunter, ed. (1991). *Narrative Strategies in Canadian Literature.* Milton Keynes: Open University Press.

Humm, M. (1989). "Subjects in English: Autobiography, women and education," in H. Wilcox and A. Thompson, ed, *Teaching Women: Feminism and English Studies.* Manchester: U Manchester P.

Hunter, L. (1984). *Rhetorical Stance, Allegories of Love and Death.* London: Macmillan.

_____ (1984b). *George Orwell: The Search for a Voice.* Milton Keynes: Open University Press.

_____ (1989). *Modern Allegory and Fantasy.* London: Macmillan.

_____ (1990). "A Rhetoric of Mass Communication," in R. L. Enos, ed., *Orality and Written Communication, Written Communication Annual.* Sage Publications.

_____ (1991). "Remember Frankenstein: Rhetoric and artificial intelligence," *Rhetorica*, IX 4 (Autumn).

_____ (1991b). "McLuhan's *From Cliche to Archetype*," in L. Hunter, ed., *Toward a Definition of Topos.* London: Macmillan.

_____ (1993). "Artificial Intelligence and Representation: Rhetorical structures of legitimation," *AI and Society*, (Winter).

_____ (1993). "Ideology as the rhetorical ethos of the nation state," paper given to the Canadian Society for the History of Rhetoric, Ottawa. Forthcoming *Rhetorica,* 1996.

_____ (1994). "Social Contexts for Methodology," in M. Beetham et al. ed., *Humanities Methodology for Hypermedia.* London: Oxford UP.

Hutcheon, L. (1987). "History and/as Intertexts," in Moss.

_____ (1988). *The Canadian Postmodern.* Toronto: Oxford UP.

Hutcheon, L. and M. Richmond (1990). *Other Solitudes, Canadian Multicultural Fictions.* Toronto: Oxford UP.

in the feminine. Women and Words ed. coll. (1983). Edmonton: Longspoon.

Irigaray, L. (1985). *Speculum of the Other Woman*, trans. G. Gill. Ithaca: Cornell UP.

_____ (1991). *The Irigaray Reader*, ed. M. Whitford. Oxford: Basil Blackwell.

Jameson, F. (1981). *The Political Unconscious.* London: Routledge.

_____ (1986). "Foreword," in Lyotard (1986).

_____ (1990). "Modernism and Imperialism," in Eagleton et al 1990.

_____ (1991). *Postmodernism, or, the Cultural Logic of Late Capitalism.* London: Verso.

Johnson, B. (1982). "The frame of reference: Poe, Lacan, Derrida," in S. Felman, ed., *Literature and Psychoanalysis: The Question of Reading: Otherwise.* Baltimore: The John Hopkins UP.

Jardine, L. and A. Grafton (1986). *From Humanism to the Humanities.* London: Cambridge.

_____ (1993). *Erasmus: Man of Letters: The construction of charisma in print.* London: Cambridge.

Jelinek, E., ed. (1980). *Women's Autobiography: Essays in Criticism.* London: Indiana UP.

Jones, A. (1985). "Inscribing femininity: French theories of the feminine," in Greene and Kahn.

Kadar, M. ed. (1992). *Essays on Life Writing: From Genre to Critical Practice.* London: U Toronto P.

Kamboureli, S. (1981). Interview with R. Kroetsch. *Open Letter*, Series 5, 8-9: 47-52.

_____ (1990). "Theory: Beauty or Beast? Resistance to theory in the feminine." *Open Letter*, Series 7, 8 (Summer): 5-26.

Keeshig-Tobias, L. (1990). "The Magic of others," in Scheier, Sheard and Wachtel.

Kellas, James (1991). *The Politics of Nationalism and Ethnicity.* London: Macmillan.

Klinck, C., ed. (1965). *The Literary History of Canada.* Toronto: U Toronto P, 1976.

Kristeva, J. (1976). "Woman's Time," trans. A. Jardine and H. Blake, in N. Keohane, M. Rosaldo and B. Gelpin, ed., *Feminist Theory: A Critique of Ideology.* Brighton: Harvester, 1982.

Kristeva, J. (1981). "Women's time" trans. A. Jardine and H. Blake, *Signs*, 7.

Kroetsch, R. (1970). *The Studhorse Man.* Toronto: Simon and Schuster.

_____ (1975). *Badlands.* Trendsetter Edition.

_____ (1982). *Labyrinths of Voice,* ed. S. Neuman and R. Wilson. Edmonton: Newest.

_____ (1983). *Alibi.* Toronto: Stoddart, repr. General Publishing, 1984.

_____ *The Lovely Treachery of Words: Essays Selected and New.* Toronto: Oxford UP.

_____ (1989). *Completed Field Notes, The Long Poems of Robert Kroetsch.* Toronto: McClelland and Stewart.

_____ (1992). *The Puppeteer.* Toronto: Random House.

Krupat, A. (1989). *The Voice in the Margin: Native American Literature and the Canon.* Oxford: U California P.

Lacan, J. (1966). *Ecrits: A Selection,* trans. A. Sheridan. London: Routledge, 1977.

LaRocque, E. (1990). "Preface," in Perreault and Vance.

Lecker, R. (1990). "The Canonization of Canadian literature: an inquiry into value," *Critical Inquiry, 16* (Spring): 656-671.

Leith, L. (1989). "Quebec Fiction in English during the 1980s: A Case Study in Marginality," *Quebec Studies, 9* (Fall).

Lemire Tostevin, L. (1983). *Gyno Text* (Toronto: Underwhich)

_____ (1988). *'sophie.* Toronto: Coach House.

_____ (1990). Interview with C. Dewdney. *Open Letter,* Series 7, 7: 84-95.

Lionnet, F. (1989). *Autobiographical Voices: Race, Gender, Self-Portraiture.* London: Cornell UP.

Lugones, M. and E. Spelman (1983). "Have we got a theory for you! Feminist theory, cultural imperialism and the demand for 'The Woman's voice,'" *Women's Studies International,* vol. 6, 6.

Lyotard, J. (1986). *The Postmodern Condition,* trans. G. Bennington and B. Massumi. Manchester: U Manchester P.

McCaffery, Steve (1988). "In Tens/tion: Dialoguing with bp," in Miki (1988).

McCaffery, Steve, ed. (1992). *Rational Geomancy: The Kids of the Book Machine: The Collected Research Reports of the Toronto Research Group 1973-1982.* Vancouver: Talonbooks.

Macdonell, D. (1986). *Theories of Discourse.* Oxford: Basil Blackwell.

MacKenzie, D. (1984). "The Sociology of a Text: Orality, Literacy and Print in Early New Zealand," *The Library,* 6th Series, VI, 4 (December).

Mandel, E. (1978). "The Ethnic Voice in Canadian Writing," *Figures in a Ground*, ed. D. Bessai and D. Jackel. Saskatoon: Western Producer Prairie Books.

Marlatt, D. (1974) *Steveston*. Vancouver: Talonbooks.

_____ (1984). *Touch to my Tongue*, and C. Sourkes. Edmonton: Longspoon.

_____ (1988). *Ana Historic*. Toronto: Coach House Press.

_____ (1991). *Salvage*. Red Deer: Red Deer College Press.

Miki, Roy, ed. (1988). *Tracing the Paths: Reading ≠ Writing The Martyrology*. Vancouver: Talonbooks.

_____ (1988b). "Reading ≠ Writing *The Martyrology*: An Introduction," in Miki (1988).

Modleski, T. (1991). *Feminism without Women: Culture and Criticism in a 'Postfeminist' Age*. New York: Routledge.

Mohanty, C.T., A. Russo, and L. Torres, ed. (1991). *Third World Women and the Politics of Feminism*. Bloomington: Indiana UP.

Moi, T. (1985). *Sexual/Textual Politics: Feminist Literary Theory*. London: Methuen.

Moss, J., ed. (1987). *Future Indicative*. Ottawa: U Ottawa P.

Mouré, E. (1983). *Wanted Alive*. Toronto: House of Anansi.

_____ (1985). *Domestic Fuel*. Toronto: House of Anansi.

_____ (1988). *Furious*. Toronto: House of Anansi.

_____ (1989). *WSW (West South West)*. Montreal: Véhicule.

_____ (1990). "Poetry, memory and the polis," in Scheier et al.

_____ (1992). *Sheepish Beauty, Civilian Love*. Montreal: Véhicule.

Munro, A. (1968). *Dance of the Happy Shades*. Toronto: McClelland & Stewart.

_____ (1985). *The Progress of Love*. London: Chatto and Windus, 1987.

Neuman, S. ed. (1992). *Autobiography and Questions of Gender*. International Specialised Book Services: F.Cass.

Neuman, S. and S. Kamboureli, ed., (1986). *A Mazing Space: Writing Canadian Women Writing*. Edmonton: Longspoon/NeWest.

New, W.H. (1990). "Editorial: Learning to Listen," *Canadian Literature*, nos. 124-5: 4-8.

Nichol, bp (1972). *The Martyrology, Books 1 and 2*. Toronto: Coach House; revised edition 1977.

_____ (1976). *The Martyrology, Books 3 and 4*. Toronto: Coach House.

_____ (1982). *The Martyrology, Book 5*. Toronto: Coach House.

_____ (1987). *The Martyrology, Book 6 Books*. Toronto: Coach House.

_____ (1988). *Selected Organs: Parts of an Autobiography*. Windsor Ont: Black Moss Press.

_____ (1990). *Gifts: The Martyrology Book[s] 7 &*. Toronto: Coach House.

Nichols, J., ed. (1984...). *Algonquian and Iroquoian Linguistics*. Winnipeg: Algonquian and Iroquoian Linguistics.

Nourbese Philip, M. (1988). *Harriet's Daughter*. London: Heinemann.

_____ (1989). "Gut Issues in Babylon," *Fuse, XII*, 5, (April/May).

_____ (1989b). "The Disappearing Debate: Or how the discussion of racism has been taken over by the censorship issue," *This Magazine*, 23, 2 (July/August).

_____ (1989c). *She Tries Her Tongue, Her Silence Softly Breaks*. Charlottetown: Ragweed.

_____ (1989d). "Burn Sugar," in *Imagining Women*.

_____ 1991). "The White Soul of Canada," in *Spectacular Failures* (Spring).

_____ (1991b). *Looking for Livingstone: An odyssey of silence*. Stratford: Mercury.

Ondaatje, M. (1970). *The Collected Works of Billy the Kid*. Toronto: Anansi.

_____ (1976). *Coming Through Slaughter*. Toronto: Anansi.

_____ (1982). *Running in the Family*. Toronto: McClelland & Stewart.

_____ (1987). *In the Skin of a Lion*. Toronto: McClelland & Stewart.

_____ (1992). *The English Patient*. London: Picador.

Open Letter (1965-93).

O'Rourke, R. with J. Mace (1992). *Versions and Variety*. London: Goldsmith's.

Parry, B. (1987). "Problems in Current Theories of Colonial Discourse," *Oxford Literary Review* 9, 1-2.

Perloff, M. (1990). *Poetic License: Essays on Modernist and Post-modernist lyric*. Evanston: Northwestern UP.

Perreault, J. and S. Vance, ed. (1990). *Writing the Circle: Native Women of Western Canada*. Edmonton: NeWest.

Petrone, P. ed. (1988). *Northern Voices: Inuit Writing in English*. Toronto: U Toronto P.

Pivato, J. (1985). *Contrasts: Comparative essays on Italian Canadian Writing*. Montreal: Guernica Editions.

Reiser, M. (1990). *Memory in Mind and Brain: What Dream Imagery Reveals.* Basic Books.

Ricks, C. (1974). *Keats and Embarrassment.* Oxford: Clarendon P.

Rooke, C. (1988). "Getting into Heaven," *Malahat Review,* 85 (Summer).

Rorty, R. (1989). *Contingency, Irony, and Solidarity.* Cambridge: Cambridge UP.

_____ (1991). *Objectivity, Relativism, and Truth,* Philosophical Papers vol. 1. Cambridge: Cambridge UP.

_____. *Essays on Heidegger and Others,* Philosophical Papers vol. 2. Cambridge: Cambridge UP.

Rose, J. (1986). *Sexuality in the Field of Vision.* London.

Rose, S. (1992). *The Making of Memory, from molecule to mind.* London: Bantam Press.

Ross, M. (1984). Interviewed by K. Chittick. *Studies in Canadian Literature 9,* 2: 260-1

Ross, V. (1993). "Who's to wear the mantle of minority," *Globe and Mail,* Saturday, June 12.

Rowe, W. and V. Schelling (1991). *Memory and Modernity: Popular Culture in Latin America.* London: Verso.

Said, E. (1978). *Orientalism.* London: Routledge.

_____ (1991). "Yeats and Decolonialisation," in Eagleton et al.

Scheier, L., S. Sheard and E. Wachtel, ed. (1990). *Language in her Eye* Toronto: Coach House.

Scheier, L. (1990). "Chopped liver," in Scheier et al.

Scobie, Stephen (1984). *bp Nichol: What History Teaches.* Vancouver: Talonbooks.

_____ (1988). "On Dangerous Ground: Two Essays on Six Books," in Miki (1988).

_____ (1989). *Signature Event Cantext.* Edmonton: NeWest Press.

Scott, G. (1987). *Heroine.* Toronto: Coach House.

_____ (1990). "A feminist at the carnival," in Scheier et al.

_____ (1993). *Main Brides, against ochre pediment and aztec sky.* Toronto: Coach House.

Second, Second Sister Collective (1989). *Imagining Women* Toronto: Women's Press.

Sellers, S. ed (1988). *Writing differences: Readings from the seminar of Helene Cixous.* Milton Keynes: Open University Press.

Sherzer, J. and A. Woodbury, ed. (1987). *Native American Discourse: Poetics and Rhetoric.* Cambridge: Cambridge UP.

Shiach, M. (1991). *Helene Cixous: A politics of writing.* London: Routledge.

Silvera, M. (1986). *Fireworks: The best of Fireweed.* Toronto: The Women's Press.

_____ (1986b). "Immigrant domestic workers," in M. Silvera.

Southam (1988). *Broken Words: Why five million Canadians are illiterate.* Toronto: Southam Newspaper Group.

Spivak, G. (1987). *In Other Worlds.* London: Methuen.

_____ (1990). *The Post-colonial Critic: Interviews, Strategies, Dialogues,* ed. Sarah Harasym. London: Routledge.

Spufford, M. (1981). *Small Books and Pleasant Histories: Popular Fiction and its Readership in Seventeenth Century England.* London: Cambridge UP.

Stanley, L. (1992). *The Autobiographical I: the Theory and practice of feminist auto/biography.* Manchester: U Manchester P.

_____ (1992b). "The knowing because experiencing subject," *Women's Studies International Forum, 16,* 1.

Steel, P. (1989). *The Autobiographical Passion: Studies in the Self on Show.* Melbourne: Melbourne UP.

Sutherland, F. (1986). "Frisking Laura Secord," *The Bumper Book,* ed. J. Metcalf. Toronto: ECW P.

Swiftcurrent (1988). *The SwiftCurrent Anthology.* Toronto: Coach House.

Tallman, W. (1984). "Wonder Merchants," *Boundary 2* III i (Fall).

Tanesini, A. (1993). "Whose Language?," unpublished ms.

Telling It Book Collective (1990). *Telling it: Women and language across cultures.* Vancouver: Press Gang.

Tessera (ed. coll.) (1984). Vol. 1, in *A Room of one's Own 8,* 4 (January).

_____ (1982?). Cassette tape of editorial meeting, held in the archives of the National Library of Canada.

Wachtel, E. (1988). "Putting up fences in the garden," *Tessera* 5 (September).

Ware, T. (1991). "A Little self-consciousness is a dangerous thing: A response to Robert Lecker," *English Studies in Canada XVII,* 4 (December): 481-93.

Warland, B. (1990). *Proper Deafenition: Collected Theorograms.* Vancouver: Press Gang.

Warley, L. (1992). "Inhabiting Contradiction: The female subject in *Don't: A Woman's Word*," *Open Letter*, Series 8, 2 (Winter): 70-80.

Webb, P. (1956). "The Poet and the Publisher," in J. Gray.

Weir, L. (1988). "The Discourse of 'Civility': Strategies of Containment in Literary Histories of English Canadian literature," in E. Blodgett and A. Purdy, ed., *Problems of literary reception/problemes de reception litteraire* (U of Alberta).

_____ (1991). "Normalizing the Subject: Linda Hutcheon and the English-Canadian postmodern," in ed. R. Lecker, *Canadian Canons: Essays in Literary Value.* Toronto: U of Toronto P.

Whalley, G. (1952). *Poetic Process.* Greenwood.

Whitford, M. (1991). *Luce Irigaray: Philosophy in the feminine.* New York: Routledge.

Williamson, J. (1992). "'I Peel myself out of My Own Skin': Reading *Don't : A Woman's Word*," in M. Kadar.

Wittgenstein, L. (1953). *Philosophical Investigations,* trans. G. Anscombe. Oxford: Basil Blackwell, 1967.

Woodcock, G. (1976). "Poetry," in C. Klinck.

Yale French Studies (1972). *French Freud: Structural studies in psychoanalysis.* No 48.

Young, R. (1991). *White Mythologies.* London: Routledge.

INDEX